100 Activprimary™
WHITEBOARD LESSONS

TERMS AND CONDITIONS

IMPORTANT – PERMITTED USE AND WARNINGS - READ CAREFULLY BEFORE USING

Minimum specification:
- PC with a CD-ROM drive and at least 128 MB RAM
- Pentium III 800 MHz processor
- Microsoft Windows 2000 or higher
- Microsoft Office 2000 or higher
- Interactive whiteboard
- Activprimary software
- Facilities for printing and sound (optional)

YEAR 6

Scottish Primary 7

CREDITS

Authors
Eileen Jones (English); Linda Best (mathematics terms 1 and 2, and science); Anthony David (mathematics term 3); Rhona Dick (history); Alan Rodgers and Angella Streluck (geography); Martin Flute (other foundation subjects)

Project Editor
Wendy Tse

Editor
Sally Grey

Assistant Editor
Niamh O'Carroll

Illustrators
Jim Peacock (flipchart illustrations), Garry Davies (flipchart and book illustrations), Theresa Tibbetts (additional flipchart illustrations)

Series Designer
Joy Monkhouse

Designers
Rebecca Male, Allison Parry, Andrea Lewis, Melissa Leeke and Erik Ivens

CD-ROM developed in association with
Q & D Multimedia

Flipcharts created in association with
Promethean Technologies Group Ltd

ACKNOWLEDGEMENTS

Activprimary™ is a trademark of Promethean Technologies Group Ltd.

Microsoft Office, Word, Excel and PowerPoint are either registered trademarks or trademarks of Microsoft Corporation in the United States and/or other countries.

With grateful thanks for advice, help and expertise to Margaret Allen (Business Development Manager), Peter Lambert (Business Development Manager), Michele Horsburgh (Voting Systems Business Manager) and Sarah Aspden (Digital Producer) at Promethean Technologies Group Ltd.

All Flash activities designed and developed by Q & D Multimedia.

Interactive Teaching Programs (developed by the Primary National Strategy) © Crown copyright.

Extracts from The National Literacy Strategy and The National Numeracy Strategy © Crown copyright. Reproduced under the terms of HMSO Guidance Note 8.

Material from the National Curriculum © The Queen's Printer and Controller of HMSO. Reproduced under the terms of HMSO Guidance Note 8.

Extracts from the QCA Schemes of Work © Qualifications and Curriculum Authority.

Every effort has been made to trace copyright holders for the works reproduced in this book, and the publishers apologise for any inadvertent omissions.

Adobe, the Adobe logo, and Reader are either registered trademarks or trademarks of Adobe Systems Incorporated in the United States and/or other countries.

Includes Adobe® Reader

Made with Macromedia is a trademark of Macromedia, Inc. Director ® Copyright © 1984-2000 Macromedia, Inc.

MADE WITH macromedia®

Published by Scholastic Ltd
Villiers House
Clarendon Avenue
Leamington Spa
Warwickshire CV32 5PR

www.scholastic.co.uk

Designed using Adobe InDesign.

Printed by Bell and Bain Ltd, Glasgow

1 2 3 4 5 6 7 8 9   6 7 8 9 0 1 2 3 4

Text © 2006 Eileen Jones (English); Linda Best (mathematics terms 1 and 2, and science); Anthony David (mathematics term 3); Rhona Dick (history); Alan Rodgers and Angella Streluck (geography); Martin Flute (other foundation subjects)

© 2006 Scholastic Ltd

British Library Cataloguing-in-Publication Data
A catalogue record for this book is available from the British Library.

ISBN 0-439-96577-2
ISBN 978-0439-96577-4

The rights of the authors of this work have been asserted by them in accordance with the Copyright, Designs and Patents Act 1988.

CONTENTS

100 ACTIVPRIMARY™ WHITEBOARD LESSONS

'There is a whiteboard revolution in UK schools.'
(Primary National Strategy)

Interactive whiteboards are fast becoming the must-have resource in today's classroom as they allow teachers to facilitate children's learning in ways that were inconceivable a few years ago. The appropriate use of interactive whiteboards, whether used daily in the classroom or once a week in the ICT suite, will encourage active participation in lessons and should increase learners' determination to succeed. Interactive whiteboards make it easier for teachers to bring subjects across the curriculum to life in new and exciting ways.

What can an interactive whiteboard offer?

For the **teacher**, an interactive whiteboard offers the same facilities as an ordinary whiteboard, such as drawing, writing and erasing. However, the interactive whiteboard also offers many other possibilities to:

- save any work created during a lesson
- prepare as many pages as necessary
- display any page within the flipchart to review teaching and learning
- add scanned examples of the children's work to a flipchart
- change colours of objects and backgrounds instantly
- use simple templates and grids
- link flipcharts to spreadsheets, websites and presentations.

Using an interactive whiteboard in the simple ways outlined above can enrich teaching and learning in a classroom, but that is only the beginning of the whiteboard's potential to educate and inspire.

For the **learner**, the interactive whiteboard provides the opportunity to share learning experiences as lessons can be delivered with sound, still and moving images, and websites. Interactive whiteboards can be used to cater for the needs of all learning styles:

- kinaesthetic learners benefit from being able to physically manipulate images
- visual learners benefit from being able to watch videos, look at photographs and see images being manipulated
- auditory learners benefit from being able to access audio resources such as voice recordings and sound effects.

With a little preparation all of these resource types could be integrated in one lesson, a feat that would have been almost impossible before the advent of the interactive whiteboard!

Access to an interactive whiteboard

In schools where learners have limited access to an interactive whiteboard the teacher must carefully plan lessons in which the children will derive most benefit from using it. As teachers become familiar with the whiteboard they will learn when to use it and, importantly, when not to use it!

Where permanent access to an interactive whiteboard is available, it is important that the teacher plans the use of the board effectively. It should be used only in ways that will enhance or extend teaching and learning. Children still need to gain practical first-hand experience of many things. Some experiences cannot be recreated on an interactive whiteboard but others cannot be had without it.

100 Activprimary™ Whiteboard Lessons offers both teachers and learners the most accessible and creative uses of this most valuable resource.

Safety note: Avoid looking directly at the projector beam as it is potentially damaging to eyes, and never leave the children unsupervised when using the interactive whiteboard.

Introduction

About the series

100 Activprimary™ Whiteboard Lessons is designed to reflect best practice in using interactive whiteboards. It is also designed to support all teachers in using this valuable tool by providing lessons and other resources that can be used on a whiteboard with little or no preparation. These inspirational lessons cover all National Curriculum subjects. They are perfect for all levels of experience and are an essential for any users of Promethean's Activprimary™ software.

About the book

This book is divided into four chapters. Each chapter contains lessons and photocopiable activity sheets covering:

- English
- Mathematics
- Science
- Foundation subjects.

At the beginning of each chapter a **planning grid** identifies the title, the objectives covered and any relevant cross-curricular links in each lesson. Objectives are taken from relevant National Strategies, National Curriculum Programmes of Study (PoS), or the QCA Schemes of Work. All of the lessons should therefore fit into your existing medium-term plans. The planning grids have been provided in Microsoft Word format on the CD-ROM for this purpose.

Lesson plans

The lessons have a consistent structure with a starter activity, activities for shared and independent work and a plenary to round up the teaching and learning and identify any assessment opportunities. Crucially, each lesson plan identifies resources required (including photocopiable activity sheets 🄿 and flipcharts that are provided on the CD-ROM ⊙). Also highlighted are the Activprimary™ tools that could be used in the lesson.

Photocopiable activity sheets at the end of each chapter support the lessons. These sheets provide opportunities for group or individual work to be completed away from the board, but link to the context of the whiteboard lesson. They also provide opportunities for whole-class plenary sessions in which children discuss and present their work.

Two general record sheets are provided on pages 170 and 171. These are intended to support the teacher in recording ways in which the interactive whiteboard is used, and where and how interactive resources can be integrated into a lesson.

What's on the CD-ROM?

The accompanying CD-ROM provides an extensive bank of Activprimary™ flipcharts. The flipcharts support, and are supported by, the lessons in this book. As well as texts and images, a selection of flipcharts include the following types of files:

- Embedded Microsoft Office files: These include Microsoft Word, Excel and PowerPoint documents. The embedded files are launched from the flipchart and will open in their native Microsoft application.

- Embedded interactive files: These include specially commissioned interactive files as well as Interactive Teaching Programs (ITPs) from the Primary National Strategy.

    Printable PDF versions of the photocopiable activity and record sheets, as well as the answers to the mathematics, are also provided on the CD-ROM.

 5

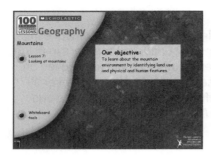

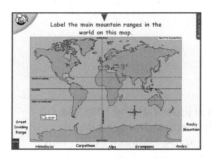

The flipcharts
All of the flipcharts have a consistent structure as follows:

Title and objectives page
Use this page to highlight the focus of the lesson. You might also wish to refer to this page at certain times throughout the lesson or at the end of the lesson to assess whether the learning objective was achieved.

Starter activity
This sets the context to the lesson and usually provides some key questions or learning points that will be addressed through the main activities.

Main activities
These activities offer independent, collaborative group or whole-class work. The activities use the full range of Activprimary™ tools and include some opportunities for voting. Although Activote devices are useful, these pages can be used without them. Alternative methods of voting include:

- taking a tally of answers on individual whiteboards
- hand counts
- using coloured cards for true/false or yes/no questions, for example, blue for *yes* and red for *no*.

What to do boxes are also included in many of the prepared flipcharts. These appear as tabs in the top right-hand corner of the screen. To access these notes, simply pull out the tabs to reveal planning information, additional support and key learning points.

Plenary
A whole-class activity or summary page is designed to review work done both at the board and away from the board. In many lessons, children are encouraged to present their work.

Whiteboard tools page
The whiteboard tools page gives a reminder of the tools used in the lesson and provides instructions on how they are used.

HOW TO USE THE CD-ROM

Setting up your screen for optimal use
It is best to view the Activprimary™ flipcharts provided on the CD-ROM at a screen display of 1024 × 768 pixels. To alter the screen display, select Settings, then Control Panel from the Start menu. Next, double-click the Display icon and click on the Settings tab. Adjust the Screen area scroll bar to 1024 × 768 pixels. Click OK.

If you prefer to use a screen display setting of 800 × 600 pixels, ensure that your Activprimary™ Page Scale is set to Best Fit. To alter the Page Scale, launch Activprimary™ and click on the Teacher tools menu button. Next, click on the Menu button and then Page Scale. Finally, select the Best Fit button. If you use this screen display setting, text in the prepared flipchart files may appear larger when you edit on screen.

Viewing the printable resources

Adobe® Reader® is required to view the printable resources. If you do not have it installed already, a version is provided on the CD-ROM. To install this, right-click on the Start menu on your desktop and choose Explore. Click on the + sign to the left of the CD drive entitled *100WBLY6* and open the folder called Adobe Reader. Run the program contained in this folder to install Adobe® Reader®.

If you experience any difficulties viewing the PDF files, try changing your Adobe® Reader® preferences. Select Edit, then Preferences, within Adobe® Reader®. You will then be able to change your viewing options. For further information about Adobe® Reader® visit the Adobe® website at **www.adobe.com**.

Getting started

It is advisable to launch Activprimary and to switch to Desktop mode before running the *100 Activprimary™ Whiteboard Lessons* CD-ROM program. The CD-ROM program should run automatically when you insert the CD-ROM into your CD drive. If it does not, use My Computer to browse to the contents of the CD-ROM and click on the *100 Activprimary™ Whiteboard Lessons* icon.

When the program starts, you are invited to register the product either online or using a PDF registration form. You also have the option to register later. If you click this option, you will be taken, via the Credits screen, to the Main menu.

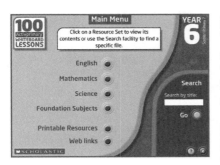

Main menu

The Main menu divides the flipcharts by subject: English, mathematics, science and foundation subjects. Clicking on the appropriate blue button for any of these options will take you to a separate Subject menu (see below for further information). The activity sheets are provided in separate menus. To access these resources, click Printable resources.

Individual flipcharts or pages can be located using the search facility by keying in words (or part words) from the resource titles in the Search box. Press Go to begin the search. This will bring up a list of the titles that match your search.

The Web Links button takes you to a list of useful web addresses. A help button ❓ is included on all menu screens. The Help notes on the CD-ROM provide a range of general background information and technical support for all users.

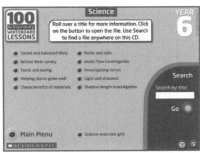

Subject menu

Each Subject menu provides all of the prepared flipcharts for each chapter of the book. Roll over each flipchart title to reveal a brief description of the contents in a text box at the top of the menu screen; clicking on the blue button will open the flipchart. Click on Main menu to return to the Main menu screen.

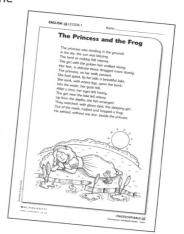

Printable resources

The printable PDF activity sheets are also divided by chapter. Click on the subject to find all the activity sheets related to that subject/chapter. The answers to Chapter 2, mathematics, are also provided.

To alternate between the menus on the CD-ROM and other open applications, hold down the Alt key and press the Tab key to switch to the desired application.

English

The lessons in the English chapter are arranged chronologically to match the medium-term planning in the National Literacy Strategy. There is a balance of word-, sentence- and text-level activities, which also interact with each other. For example, in the sentence-level work, that term's fiction and non-fiction writing are frequently used as a vehicle for putting the grammar into practice.

These English lessons are a stimulating resource to which the interactive whiteboard offers pace and visual excitement. Words can be made to appear or disappear; text can be manipulated; the children can see sentences being constructed and watch paragraphs and stories emerging.

Be generous with the wonderful powers of the whiteboard and involve the children as much as possible in operating the board's tools. This will bring special benefits to children with dominant visual and kinaesthetic styles of learning. The interactive whiteboard is a stimulating resource for the teaching of English. Its role should always be to support the interaction between you, the children and literacy.

Lesson title	Objectives	What children should know	Cross-curricular links
Term 1			
Lesson 1: Word classes 💿 🅿	**S1**: To revise from Y5: the different word classes.	• Words have different roles in sentences.	**Science** QCA Unit 6A 'Interdependence and adaptation'
Lesson 2: Word building 💿 🅿	**W5**: To use word roots, prefixes and suffixes as a support for spelling.	• A word may be constructed of different parts.	**History** QCA Unit 15 'How do we use ancient Greek ideas today?'
Lesson 3: Human poems 💿	**T10**: To write own poems experimenting with active verbs and personification; produce revised poems for reading aloud individually.	• Editing and refining are important parts of written composition.	**Speaking and listening** Objective 58: Attracting and holding listeners' attention through what is said and how it is delivered.
Lesson 4: Journalism 💿 🅿	**T16**: To use the styles and conventions of journalism to report on real or imagined events. **T18**: To use IT to plan, revise, edit writing to improve accuracy and conciseness and to bring it to publication standard.	• Familiarity with newspaper text.	**Geography** QCA Unit 23 'Investigating coasts'
Lesson 5: Verb changes 💿	**S2**: To revise earlier work on verbs and to understand the terms *active* and *passive*; being able to transform a sentence from active to passive, and vice versa. **T16**: To use the styles and conventions of journalism to report on real or imagined events.	• Verb forms vary.	**Speaking and listening** Objective 60: To understand and use a variety of ways to criticise constructively and respond to criticism.
Lesson 6: Connectives 💿 🅿	**S4**: To investigate connecting words. **W6**: To investigate meanings and spellings of connectives.	• The term *connective*.	**History** QCA Unit 11 'What was it like for children living in Victorian Britain?'
Lesson 7: Narrative planning 💿	**T7**: To plan quickly and effectively the plot, characters and structure of their own narrative writing.	• Narrative writing needs to be planned.	**History** QCA Unit 15 'How do we use ancient Greek ideas today?'
Lesson 8: Complex sentences 💿	**S5**: To form complex sentences.	• There are different sentence types.	**Speaking and listening** Objective 60: To understand and use a variety of ways to criticise constructively and respond to criticism.

Lesson title	Objectives	What children should know	Cross-curricular links
Lesson 9: Word count 💿	**T18**: To use IT to plan, revise, edit writing to improve accuracy and conciseness and to bring it to publication standard. **T8**: To summarise a passage, chapter or text in a specified number of words.	• A sentence can be shortened yet retain its meaning.	**Geography** QCA Unit 23 'Investigating coasts'
Lesson 10: Biographies 💿 🅿	**T14**: To develop the skills of biographical and autobiographical writing in role.	• Accuracy can be essential to a text.	**History** QCA Unit 11 'What was it like for children living in Victorian Britain?'
Lesson 11: Sophisticated punctuation marks 💿 🅿	**S6**: To secure knowledge and understanding of more sophisticated punctuation marks.	• Punctuation may vary.	**History** QCA Unit 19 'What were the effects of Tudor exploration?' QCA Unit 11 'What was it like for children living in Victorian Britain?'
Term 2			
Lesson 12: Poetry and words 💿 🅿	**T3**: To recognise how poets manipulate words. **T4**: To investigate humorous verse.	• Poets can use words in unusual ways.	**Speaking and listening** Objective 58: To use a range of oral techniques.
Lesson 13: Proverbs 💿	**W6**: Collect and explain the meanings and origins of proverbs.	• Some English expressions have roots in the past.	**History** PoS (5c) Communicate their knowledge and understanding of history in a variety of ways.
Lesson 14: The passive voice	**S1**: To investigate further the use of active and passive verbs. **T10**: To use different genres as models to write.	• Verbs can be active or passive.	**Science** QCA Unit 6E 'Forces in action'
Lesson 15: Formal and official language 💿	**S2**: To understand features of formal official language. **T20**: To discuss the way standard English varies in different contexts.	• Writing style must match the purpose of the text.	**Physical education** QCA Unit 26 'Net/wall games'
Lesson 16: Conditionals 💿 🅿	**S5**: Use reading to investigate conditionals.	• Words may express possibilities.	**Physical education** QCA Unit 26 'Net/wall games'
Lesson 17: Effective arguments 🅿	**T15**: To recognise how arguments are constructed to be effective.	• Language must fit its purpose.	**Citizenship** QCA Unit 9 'Respect for property' **Speaking and listening** Objective 59: To analyse and evaluate how speakers present points effectively through use of language and gesture.
Lesson 18: Spelling mnemonics	**W4**: Learn and invent spelling rules; invent and use mnemonics for irregular or difficult spellings.	• A spelling aide-mémoire is useful.	**ICT** QCA Unit 6A 'Multimedia presentation'
Lesson 19: Contracting sentences 💿	**S4**: To revise work on contracting sentences.	• You may want to reduce a text.	**History** QCA Unit 19 'What were the effects of Tudor exploration?'
Lesson 20: Paragraphs 💿 🅿	**T2**: To analyse how individual paragraphs are structured in writing.	• Texts are divided into paragraphs.	**Science** QCA Unit 6A 'Interdependence and adaptation'

Lesson title	Objectives	What children should know	Cross-curricular links
Term 3			
Lesson 21: Connecting paragraphs ● ℗	**T21**: To divide whole texts into paragraphs, paying attention to the sequence of paragraphs and to the links between one paragraph and the next.	• A text must be connected.	**History** QCA Unit 15 'How do we use ancient Greek ideas today?'
Lesson 22: Reading narratives ●	**S1**: To revise the language conventions and grammatical features of the different types of text. **T7**: To annotate passages in detail in response to specific questions.	• Quick reading can overlook detail.	**History** QCA Unit 15 'How do we use ancient Greek ideas today?'
Lesson 23: Writing narratives ●	**S1**: To revise the language conventions and grammatical features of the different types of text. **T7**: To annotate passages in detail in response to specific questions. **T21**: To divide whole texts into paragraphs, paying attention to the sequence of paragraphs and to the links between one paragraph and the next.	• Writing narrative in paragraphs. • Poetry may contain *hidden* meaning.	**Speaking and listening** Objective 67: To devise a performance considering how to adapt the performance for a specific audience.
Lesson 24: Non-fiction texts ● ℗	**S1**: To revise the language conventions and grammatical features of the different types of text. **T19**: To review a range of non-fiction text types and their characteristics, discussing when a writer might choose to write in a given style and form. **T22**: To select the appropriate style and form to suit a specific purpose and audience, drawing on knowledge of different non-fiction text types.	• There are different non-fiction text types.	There are no specific links for this lesson.
Lesson 25: Spelling rules ● ℗	**W4**: To revise and consolidate work from previous five terms.	• Spelling may conform to a rule.	**Speaking and listening** Objective 66: To identify the ways spoken language varies according to differences in context and purpose of use.
Lesson 26: Persuasive advertisements ●	**S1**: To revise the language conventions and grammatical features of the different types of text. **T19**: To review a range of non-fiction text types and their characteristics, discussing when a writer might choose to write in a given style and form. **T22**: To select the appropriate style and form to suit a specific purpose and audience, drawing on knowledge of different non-fiction text types.	• Writing must suit an audience.	**PSHE and citizenship** PoS (3a) To learn what makes a healthy lifestyle, including the benefits of healthy eating.
Lesson 27: Explanations ●	**T15**: To secure understanding of the features of explanatory texts from Year 5 Term 2.	• The term *explanation*.	**Science** QCA Unit 6F 'How we see things'
Lesson 28: Book cover blurb ●	**T10**: To write a brief synopsis of a text. **T11**: To write a brief helpful review tailored for real audiences.	• Experience of identifying key points.	**Speaking and listening** Objective 58: To use a range of oral techniques to present persuasive argument.
Lesson 29: Linked poems ●	**T13**: To write a sequence of poems linked by theme or form.	• Making connections between texts.	**Speaking and listening** Objective 60: To understand and use a variety of ways to criticise constructively and respond to criticism.
Lesson 30: Word fun ●	**W5**: To invent words using known roots, prefixes and suffixes.	• Familiarity with dictionaries.	**History** QCA Unit 15 'How do we use ancient Greek ideas today?'

Word classes

Learning objective:
NLS Term 1
● S1: To revise from Y5: the different word classes.

Resources
'Word classes' flipchart file; photocopiable page 41 'The Princess and the Frog'; individual whiteboards and pens.

Links to other subjects
Science
QCA Unit 6A 'Interdependence and adaptation'
● Ask the children to refer to the frog's habitat in their poems.

Whiteboard tools
Use the Floating keyboard in the Text editor tray to add text to the flipchart.

- Pen tool
- Highlighter tool
- Marquee select tool
- Text editor tool
- Eraser tool
- Floating keyboard
- Delete button

Starter
Go to page 2 of the 'Word classes' flipchart. Challenge the children to define *adverb* on individual whiteboards. Move or erase the red rectangle on the flipchart to reveal the definition: *An adverb is a word that answers a question about the verb.* Ask the children if their definitions are similar to this.

On page 3 of the flipchart, there are four circles labelled: *How? When? How often? Where?* In pairs, the children should alternate as speaker and questioner:
- The speaker says a short sentence without an adverb. (For example, *She spoke.*) The questioner uses one of the questions on the flipchart to encourage the speaker to add an adverb.
- The children list the adverbs and the questions they answer. Let them experiment before comparing results. Write some adverbs in the circles on the flipchart.

Whole-class shared work
- Explain that adverbs and adverbial phrases can have a wider role, depending on their position in the sentence, and the other words in the sentence.
- Display page 4. Explain that the children will be creating four sentences to fit four adverb roles. Tell them that each sentence will use the adverb *really*, but not always in the same position or doing the same job.
- Organise the children into groups of five. Reveal the first set of words by deleting the rectangle. Group members should each write one of the words on their individual whiteboard.
- Allow time for groups to arrange their boards in the correct order to make an adverb and verb sentence. Demonstrate on the interactive whiteboard by moving the words to the correct order.
- Repeat the group exercise with each subsequent rectangle.
- Work in the same way with page 5, revealing one set of words at a time and having each group standing, individual whiteboards held in front, in a living sentence. (Two of the sentences contain six words, rather than five.)
- On page 6, sentence number 4 is repeated. Identify the highlighted phrase as a prepositional phrase (erase the first rectangle to show this). Ask: *Which word is the preposition?* Erase the second rectangle to reveal the answer (*down*). Erase the third rectangle to explain that, as with adverbials, prepositional phrases can occur anywhere in a sentence.
- On page 7, use the Highlighter tool to point out the prepositional phrases in each line. Discuss whether any can change their place. Experiment together. Provide each child with a copy of photocopiable page 41 and ask them to annotate the poem with their conclusions, for example:
  - When prepositional phrases start sentences, commas are needed.
  - A preposition modifying a noun comes straight after the noun it modifies.

Independent work
- Go to page 8 for instructions for the Independent work.
- Support less confident children by supplying example phrases.
- As an extra challenge, ask the children to add a verse with varied adverbial use.

Plenary
- Type or write one of the verses produced by the children onto page 9. Identify and discuss prepositional phrases.

Word building

Learning objective
NLS Term 1
● W5: To use word roots, prefixes and suffixes as a support for spelling.

Resources
'Word building' flipchart file; photocopiable page 42 'Word clusters' for each child; individual whiteboards and pens.

Links to other subjects
History
QCA Unit 15 'How do we use ancient Greek ideas today?'
● Ask the children to research clusters of words linked to Greek roots.

Starter
Page 2 of the 'Word building' flipchart shows a circle with *aero* written in the middle. Ask the children to list, on individual whiteboards, words containing *aero*. (For example: *aeroplane; aerobics; aeronaut; aerosol*.) Invite them to give a partner clues to their words. Can the partner guess the word they have written? Write some of the children's examples in the circle.

Whole-class shared work
● Go to page 3 and give the children two minutes to list words with *super* in them. (For example: *superb; superficial; superhero; supermarket*.)
● Compare results, writing words in the circle.
● Ask the children to consider what the word *super* means. Delete the panel to reveal the answer (above). Explain that in this context *above* means *greater*. Which of the children's words belong in this circle? (Words with the same spelling and meaning.) Check if any now have to be deleted.
● Encourage the children to define the words, using the word *above*. Do the same with the *aero* (air) circle on the previous page.
● Repeat the activity with the word *prim* on page 4. (For example: *primary; primrose; primitive; primate*.)
● Go to page 5. Demonstrate how to use an etymological dictionary. Ask the children to research *tri*. They should find out what it means (three) and its history (Greek and Latin prefix). Delete the panels to reveal the answers. Challenge the children to write a derived *tri* word on their whiteboards. Ask them to show their answers and write some examples in the yellow triangle. Repeat the activity on page 6 for *re*.
● Go to page 7 and explain that the children must find the words to fit the meaning clues. There is a mixture of prefixes, suffixes and roots that can be combined to build the words.
● Allow the children thinking time for each clue and time to write words on their individual whiteboards. Discuss answers before dragging and dropping the labels into place to form the words.
● Underline or highlight the word parts in different colours. Encourage the children to explain what each part means? Compare answers, before deleting the red rectangle, then erasing the green ones beneath to reveal the meanings of the word parts.

Independent work
● Provide each child with a copy of photocopiable page 42 'Word clusters'. The children should complete the word clusters, writing a word on each petal which uses the root in the flower centre.
● The new words must contain both the root's meaning and letters.
● Support less confident children by allowing them to work in pairs.
● Challenge more confident children to use etymological dictionaries to research the history of each root. If there is time, give them new copies of the photocopiable sheet and encourage them to add more words.

Plenary
● Use pages 8 and 9 of the flipchart to discuss the exercise. Encourage the children to share their answers and annotate the petals with their words.

Whiteboard tools
Use the Floating keyboard in the Text editor tray to add text to the flipchart.

● Pen tool

● Highlighter tool

● Marquee select tool

● Text editor tool

● Floating keyboard

● Eraser tool

● Delete button

Human poems

Learning objective
NLS Term 1
● T10: To write own poems experimenting with active verbs and personification; produce revised poems for reading aloud individually.

Resources
'Human poems' flipchart file; individual whiteboards and pens; exercise books and pens; computers with word-processing application (if available).

Links to other subjects
Speaking and listening
Objective 58: Attracting and holding listeners' attention through what is said and how it is delivered.
● Use partner or small group occasions for the children to present their poems to an audience.

Whiteboard tools
Use the Floating keyboard in the Text editor tray to add text to the flipchart.

 Pen tool

✎ Marquee select tool

ⓣ Text editor tool

▤ Eraser tool

⊜ Floating keyboard

Starter
In pairs, ask the children to explain the terms *simile* and *metaphor* to each other. Ask them to write an example of each. Go to page 2 of the 'Human poems' flipchart, which shows a table divided into two: similes and metaphors. Challenge the children to decide on which side of the table their examples should be written.

Whole-class shared work
● Go to page 3 of the flipchart. Explain that similes and metaphors are devices for creating a strong image in the reader's mind. They are particularly effective in poems.
● Ask the children to define simile and metaphor before deleting or erasing the panels to reveal the definitions.
● Return to page 2 and ask: *Are any sentences in the wrong section?* Erase and rewrite as necessary.
● Display page 4 to remind the children of the purpose of a simile: to create a strong visual image. In order to do this the comparison must be unusual but still have an obvious link to the subject. Erase the panels to reveal examples.
● Move on to page 5 and make a list of classroom objects.
● Work together to create a few similes, reminding the children of their purpose as outlined on page 4.
● On page 6, investigate converting the similes into metaphors. Tell the children that they are going to turn the similes they created into metaphors, writing their ideas onto individual whiteboards. Reveal the example behind the pink rectangle.
● Write or type some of the children's conversions in the space provided.
● On page 7, focus on the example about the clock. Point out that the image makes the clock into a person. It is therefore a metaphor and an example of *personification*.
● Ask: *What does* personification *mean?* Delete the panel to reveal a definition and an example. Point out that personification lets the poet extend a metaphor beyond the initial image.
● Ask the children to extend the metaphor on page 8. Let them experiment on their whiteboards before revealing the example behind the panel.
● Click on the button to return to the children's examples of metaphors on page 6. Challenge them to extend these in the same way.

Independent work
● Go to page 9 and ask the children to write a poem about *The living classroom* using personification of the classroom's objects.
● Encourage the children to make some initial rough drafts. They could use a word-processing application, if computers are available, to make it easier for them to edit and improve their work.
● Write some useful phrases in the space provided to support less confident children.
● As an extra challenge, ask the children to use personification in a poem about weather.

Plenary
● Invite individuals to read their poems aloud, and ask the audience about the images that form in their minds.
● Write some of their suggestions on page 10.

Learning objectives
NLS Term 1
● T16: To use the styles and conventions of journalism to report on real or imagined events.
● T18: To use IT to plan, revise, edit writing to improve accuracy and conciseness and to bring it to publication standard.

Resources
'Journalism' flipchart file; photocopiable page 43 'Wolf News' for each child; computers for the children; individual whiteboards and pens; selection of newspapers.

Links to other subjects
Geography
QCA Unit 23 'Investigating coasts'
● Link newspaper writing to the topic of coasts and erosion.

Journalism

Starter
Open the 'Journalism' flipchart and go to page 2. What do the children expect a newspaper report to be like in appearance and style? Ask them to write notes on individual whiteboards and compare them with a partner. Share ideas as a class, annotating the flipchart with some suggestions. Look at some newspaper front pages together.

Whole-class shared work
● Display *Wolf News* on page 3 and give each child a copy of the article (photocopiable page 43).
● Working together, identify the journalistic features. Investigate the beginning of the text. Identify the headline; the column layout; the photograph and how it is written in paragraphs.
● Page 4 shows the first paragraph of the article. Encourage the children to read it closely, before discussing together how it presents the main facts.
● Five question words are displayed on the page: *Who? What? Where? When? Why?* Ask the children to consider how these questions are answered in this paragraph. Move the spyglass over the question words to reveal the answers. Emphasise that the children can remember these words by counting them off on the fingers of one hand.
● Establish that later paragraphs add detail in the news story. Return to *Wolf News* on page 3. Point out that quotes from witnesses of an event are typical of a newspaper article. Go to the writing frame on page 5 to continue the lesson.
● Write or type on the yellow rectangles on page 5 to create labels for relevant sections of the article. Agree on each label (the first one has been done for you).
● Use the labels to create a newspaper writing frame. Ensure the labels are in sequential order on the page.
● If possible, print copies of the writing frame 🖶 or leave it on the board for the children to see. Alternatively, save it in a shared computer folder for the children to access on their computers.
● Discuss ideas for another newspaper report, using the subject of coasts. For example: Beach disappears overnight; Wolf family in beach drama; Wolf family lose house.
● Demonstrate how you would make notes, with bullet points, on the writing frame.
● Give the children practice in making notes on their individual whiteboards. Remind them to consider the five question words on page 4. Share ideas.

Independent work
● Display page 6, which sets out the Independent work. Explain to the children that they are going to write their own newspaper report, but that they must first plan their report by writing notes.
● Clear any notes from the writing frame on page 5, leaving the labels. Encourage the children to use the frame to make notes for their report. Limit planning time to between five and ten minutes.
● Ask the children to begin a new page for their report if they are using computers.
● Support less confident children by helping them with their plans.
● As an extra challenge, encourage children to report on a real event.

Plenary
● Use the empty plan on page 7 for children to present their plans to one another. Point out and discuss journalistic features.

Whiteboard tools
Use the Print button from the Teacher tools menu to print relevant flipchart pages.

🖊 Pen tool

🖌 Highlighter tool

🔧 Marquee select tool

🖶 Print button

🛠 Teacher tools menu

Verb changes

Learning objectives
NLS Term 1
● S2: To revise earlier work on verbs and to understand the terms *active* and *passive*; being able to transform a sentence from active to passive, and vice versa.
● T16: To use the styles and conventions of journalism to report on real or imagined events.

Resources
'Verb changes' flipchart file; individual whiteboards and pens.

Links to other subjects
Speaking and listening
Objective 60: To understand and use a variety of ways to criticise constructively and respond to criticism.
● Use partners and small groups in which the children help one another to recognise the difference between the active and passive voices.

Whiteboard tools
Use the Floating keyboard in the Text editor tray to add text to the flipchart.

● Pen tool

● Marquee select tool

● Delete button

● Eraser tool

● Floating keyboard

Starter
Display page 2 of the 'Verb changes' flipchart. Ask the children to define *verb* on their whiteboards and compare their definition with a partner's. Reveal the definition beneath the blue panel on page 2. Ask the children to write a sentence containing a verb. Write a selection of these in the space provided on the flipchart.

Use page 3 to revise the terms *active* and *passive*. Encourage the children to suggest what the terms mean and write or type ideas on the flipchart. Explain that they are the two verb voices. Look at the sentence at the bottom of the page: *The picture was painted by Monet*. Can the children tell you whether the sentence is active or passive? Click on the words *active* or *passive* for sound effects which indicate whether they are correct.

Whole-class shared work
● Go to page 4. Explain that most sentences are in the active voice. Discuss the sentence: *The lady bought the car*. Check that the children recognise:
  ● the *verb* (bought)
  ● the subject or *agent* of the verb (lady)
  ● the object or *recipient* of the verb (car).
● Delete the labels to reveal the answers.
● Explain that sentences in the active voice always follow this pattern: *agent – verb – recipient*. Use the Marquee select tool to drag the labels to annotate the sentence.
● Go to page 5. Invite the children to write a new active sentence about the lady. Let them check a partner's sentence to see if the correct pattern has been followed. Ask the children to hold up their boards for you to make a quick check. Tell them to leave the sentences on their individual whiteboards, and add some of their examples to the flipchart.
● Display page 6. Explain that in the passive voice the sentence is turned around, with the subject and object changing places: the agent of the verb becomes the recipient. For example: *The car was bought by the lady*.
● Draw attention to the pattern for a passive sentence: *recipient – verb – agent*. Move the labels to annotate the sentence.
● Challenge the children to write the passive version of the active sentences on their individual whiteboards. Again, allow them to check a partner's work before holding up their whiteboards for you to see. Point out where changes in verb forms were needed. Add some examples to page 7.
● Play the miming game on page 8 together. Write or type some examples of active and passive sentences on the page.
● Extend the activity on page 9. Encourage the children to write an active and a passive sentence, on their whiteboards, to describe their actions. Add some examples to the corresponding boxes on the flipchart.

Independent work
● Move on to page 10. Ask the children to write a newspaper report on events involving the characters in the picture. Most sentences will be in the active voice, but there must be at least five in the passive voice.
● Support less able learners with some sentence openers.
● Click on the button on page 10 for an extra challenge for more able learners.

Plenary
● Annotate pages 11 to 13 with some of the children's sentences.
● Ensure that the children recognise the agent, verb and recipient in the sentences.

Learning objectives
NLS Term 1
● S4: To investigate connecting words.
● W6: To investigate meanings and spellings of connectives.

Resources
'Connectives' flipchart file; photocopiable page 44 'Victorian school life' for each child; individual whiteboards and pens.

Links to other subjects
History
QCA Unit 11 'What was it like for children living in Victorian Britain?'
● Link the Independent work to Victorian life.

Connectives

Starter
Open the 'Connectives' flipchart and go to page 2. Using individual whiteboards, ask the children to write three sentences about three different events that happened yesterday. Tell them to read their sentences to a partner and exchange whiteboards. Write some examples in the space provided on the flipchart.

Underneath the original work, ask the children to turn their partner's sentences into a paragraph. Encourage them to read the texts to each other.

Go to page 3. Click on the button to reveal the definition of a connective. Invite the children to read out their sentences before and after using connectives. List some examples in the circles on the page.

Whole-class shared work
● Go to page 4 to show *Wolf News*. Explain that each space should be filled by a connective.
● Work through the text, giving the children time to think of words. Annotate the spaces with their suggestions.
● Move the rectangles (and annotations) to reveal the author's choice. Discuss whether you prefer your ideas.
● Go to page 5 and ask the children to use dictionaries and thesauri to find the meanings and synonyms of the words displayed. Show and compare results, adding some examples to the page.
● The connectives from *Wolf News* are on page 6. Add any alternatives that the children thought of.
● Focus on the connectives *however* and *moreover*. Ask: *What do they have in common?* Delete the panel to reveal the two words broken down into their original parts.
● Ask: *What are such words called?* (Compound words.) Delete the orange rectangle to reveal the answer. Explain that compound words often originated as phrases.
● Move on to page 7. Work together to group the connectives into simple and compound words. Drag each connective into the correct circle.
● Point out that the meanings of unfamiliar compound-word connectives can usually be worked out by looking at their separate parts.
● Next, use page 8 to explain that connective position can vary, and page 9 to confirm why connectives are important.

Independent work
● Display page 10. Ask the children to use connectives to convert the facts about Victorian schools into a report. Provide each child with a copy of photocopiable page 44 'Victorian school life'.
● Support less confident children by pairing sentences.
● Challenge more confident children to list six more facts about Victorian childhood, and to create a linked text with connectives.

Plenary
● Type or write one of the children's reports on page 11. Encourage the children to identify the connectives. Address any misconceptions.

Whiteboard tools
🔲 Pen tool

🔲 Marquee select tool

🔲 Floating keyboard

🔲 Delete button

🔲 Highlighter tool

Narrative planning

Learning objective
NLS Term 1
● T7: To plan quickly and effectively the plot, characters and structure of their own narrative writing.

Resources
'Narrative planning' flipchart file; individual whiteboards and pens.

Links to other subjects
History
QCA Unit 15 'How do we use ancient Greek ideas today?'
● What has been passed down to us from the ancient Greeks? Use a story title related to Greek antiquities.

Starter
Display page 2 of the 'Narrative planning' flipchart. Ask the children to think about the last story they wrote. Provide individual whiteboards and ask them to make a quick plan of their story for a partner to write. Ask: *Can your partners follow the plans?* Share ideas about story planning. Encourage the children to consider whether their method was quick and efficient.

Whole-class shared work
● Go to page 3. Do the children recognise the layout? Delete the red panel to reveal it as a mind map: a quick way to plan narrative. The story title or subject is in the centre, and ideas are developed on branches from the central stem. (The ideas, concepts and terms such as *mind map* are taken from *Mind Maps for Kids* by Tony Buzan (HarperCollins).)
● Encourage the children to suggest using five single-word questions for each branch. Agree on the following:
  ● What?
  ● Who?
  ● Why?
  ● Where?
  ● When?
● Ask the children to write a word or phrase on their individual whiteboards for the first branch. Compare results before revealing the author's choice by removing or erasing the small rectangles. Repeat the process for the other four questions and their branches.
● Move on to page 4. Explain that shorter branches can be used to add detail to the ideas on the main branches. Investigate one short branch at a time, letting the children write a suggestion on their individual whiteboards before revealing the author's word by filling the rectangles with white ●.
● Examine how the mind map is working: main information is closest to the centre of the map, and additional detail is further out. Ask: *How is it clear which information is most important?* (Larger; branch size; proximity to central stem.)
● Explain that the mind map can keep expanding, with new shorter branches added as more detail is thought of. Continue to page 5, which displays the extra detail. Ask: *Why can a picture be useful?* (A picture records detail.)
● Emphasise the predominant use of single words. Look together at the completed mind map. Could the children write a story from this?
● Demonstrate using the plan, by reading some of the mind map aloud, expanding the single written words into oral sentences. Give the children similar practice.

Whiteboard tools
Use the Fill tool to reveal hidden text. Convert handwriting to text using the Recognition tool. Use the Lines tool to add more lines to the mind map in the Plenary.

● Pen tool

● Marquee select tool

● Eraser tool

● Fill tool

● Recognition tool

● Lines tool

Independent work
● Ask the children to plan a story with a title linked to history, such as: *The Grecian Urn; The Museum Treasure; A Victorian Doll.*
● Write some suggestions for story titles on page 6.
● Remind the children that letter size in a mind map indicates a word's relative importance and suggest that a picture can trigger new thoughts.
● Support less confident children by providing an empty mind map for them to fill in.
● As an extra challenge, ask children to create a new mind map for a story called *The Clue*.

Plenary
● Invite individuals to write their plans onto page 7 of the flipchart. Encourage the authors to *read* them to the class.

Complex sentences

Learning objective
NLS Term 1
● S5: To form complex sentences.

Resources
'Complex sentences' flipchart file; writing books and pens; individual whiteboards and pens.

Links to other subjects
Speaking and listening
Objective 60: To understand and use a variety of ways to criticise constructively and respond to criticism.
● Organise group discussions in which the children listen to each other's independent writing and comment constructively on the sentence types and the way clauses are joined.

Starter
Open the 'Complex sentences' flipchart and go to page 2. Explain to the children that you would like them to work on individual whiteboards to punctuate the text so that there are four sentences. Ask them to number the sentences 1–4.

Use the Edit text tool 🔵 to punctuate the text before clicking on the red box to see the correct version. Ask: *Which three sentences belong together?* (Numbers 1, 2 and 3.) *Why?* (They are complex sentences; sentence 4 is simple.) Fill the red panels with white to reveal the answers 🔵.

Whole-class shared work
● Go to page 4. Ask the children to explain the two sentence types. Pull the tabs to reveal the definitions.
● Focus on the complex sentences from the Starter. Investigate sentence 2 which is repeated here. Ask: *Which is the main clause? How is the main clause joined to the subordinate clause?* Highlight the main clause (*Elephant trumpeted greetings*) and the connective (*until*).
● Investigate complex sentences 1 and 3 on page 5. Highlight the words beginning the subordinate clauses. (*Sensing* and *Pleased*.) Can the children identify what type of words these are? Delete the panel to reveal that they are *non-finite verbs,* used to join subordinate and main clauses.
● Look at the extra sentence on page 5. Ask: *Is this simple or complex? How are the clauses joined?* Pull the tabs to reveal the answers. Explain that a semi-colon can act as a connective.
● Move on to page 6 to begin the multiple-choice game. Allow time for recording an answer on individual whiteboards or using Activote devices, if available. Click on the chosen answer to hear a sound effect which indicates whether it is correct.
● Continue the game on pages 7 to 17. Encourage the children to identify complex sentence features: (main clauses; subordinate clauses; varied connective positions; commas; non-finite verbs beginning a subordinate clause).
● Display page 18. Give the children oral practice in creating simple and complex sentences. Encourage them to work with partners to identify effective complex sentences, and simple sentences that might benefit from being linked to form complex sentences.
● Point out that effective writing usually has a mixture of simple and complex sentences. Discuss the merits of both sentence types and annotate the appropriate boxes with the children's ideas. Pull the tabs to reveal examples of the merits of each type of sentence.

Whiteboard tools
To change existing text, double-click on the text and select Edit text from the Object edit toolbox. Use the Fill tool to reveal hidden text. Convert handwriting to text using the Recognition tool.

🔵 Pen tool

🔵 Marquee select tool

🔵 Floating keyboard

🔵 Edit text tool

🔵 Fill tool

🔵 Recognition tool

🔵 Activote (optional)

Independent work
● Go to page 19. Ask the children to write more about Tiger, using a mixture of simple and complex sentences.
● Emphasise varying the way clauses are linked in the complex sentences.
● Support less able learners with suggested clauses, by writing examples on page 19.
● As an extra challenge, let children investigate pages of a novel and identify complex sentences using a range of punctuation (such as colons, brackets, dashes).

Plenary
● Choose one child to write some of their further sentences about Tiger on page 20.
● Encourage the children to identify sentence types and links between clauses.

Word count

Learning objectives
NLS Term 1
● T18: To use IT to plan, revise, edit writing to improve accuracy and conciseness and to bring it to publication standard.
● T8: To summarise a passage, chapter or text in a specified number of words.

Resources
'Word count' flipchart file; computers for the children; individual whiteboards and pens; computers (optional). (Microsoft Word is required to view the embedded text document in the flipchart.)

Links to other subjects
Geography
QCA Unit 23 'Investigating coasts'
● Link newspaper writing to the topic of coasts and erosion.

Starter
Display page 2 of the 'Word count' flipchart. Agree on a recent school event familiar to all the children (such as a class assembly). Allow the children four minutes to write, in sentences, a report on it. Let them compare results with a partner. Ask: *How much detail did you include? How many words did you write?* Read the children a newspaper article such as a sports report. Point out that considerable detail is often contained in relatively few words.

Whole-class shared work
● Page 3 shows a newspaper report from Lesson 6. Revise the features of a newspaper article. Point out the following:
  ● Headline: attracts attention, bold in content and visual style; short enough for a reader to absorb its information quickly.
  ● Subheading: adds a little more information; smaller print than the headline.
  ● First paragraph: contains main facts; later paragraphs add detail.
  ● Short paragraphs: help the reader to find information.
  ● Column layout: offers easy reading.
  ● Photograph: makes the article more interesting.
  ● Quotations from witnesses.
● Go to page 4. Explain that journalists write to a word count. How many words do the children think were used in *Wolf News*? Erase the panel to reveal the answer.
● Point out that, if original drafts were above the word count, the journalist would have had to cut some words leaving just the key facts. Ask: *How important are the opinions and statistics in the last paragraph?* Erase the panel to reveal the answer. (They are of minor importance.)
● Explain that rewording or restructuring can also save words.
● Move on to page 5. Ask for suggestions of ways to change the sentence at the top of the page so that it contains fewer words. Annotate the page with the children's ideas before filling the two panels with white 🖌 to reveal examples.

Independent work
● Display page 6 of the flipchart.
● If possible, save *Wolf News* to a shared computer folder so that the children can access it. Alternatively, click on the link on page 6 to open an editable version of the document which can be printed and distributed.
● Ask the children to reduce this report to the new word limit of 170 words.
● Working on a computer will make it easier for the children to edit.
● Support less confident children by providing a writing frame of paragraph beginnings.
● As an extra challenge, children could write a second version of the report, with a further reduced word count.

Plenary
● Let the children read their revised articles to the rest of the class. Discuss how the *journalists* have varied in what they have left out.
● Use page 7 to make notes.

Whiteboard tools

📝 Pen tool

🏹 Marquee select tool

🗑 Eraser tool

🖌 Fill tool

⌨ Floating keyboard

Biographies

Learning objective
NLS Term 1
● T14: To develop the skills of biographical and autobiographical writing in role.

Resources
'Biographies' flipchart file; individual whiteboards and pens; small pieces of paper, for example, sticky notes (six to eight per child); copy of photocopiable page 45 'Queen Victoria' for each child.

Links to other subjects
History
QCA Unit 11 'What was it like for children living in Victorian Britain?'
● Write a biography about an important Victorian.

Starter
Open the 'Biographies' flipchart and go to page 2. Give the children five minutes to provide, on individual whiteboards, their life story in note form. Use the Clock tool's Count down option ● to time them (see Whiteboard tools, below). When time is up, tell the children to exchange whiteboards with a partner. Ask: *Can your partner understand your autobiography?* Share views and write notes on the flipchart, pointing out examples of clear presentation.

Whole-class shared work
● Give the children photocopiable page 45 'Queen Victoria' to read in pairs.
● Ask them to identify and underline key facts in the text.
● Look at the text together on pages 3 and 4 of the flipchart. Discuss the children's results. Underline or highlight their suggested facts.
● Point out that as this is a non-fiction text, a biography, nearly everything is underlined.
● Explain that you want to write a shorter, more concise biography for inclusion in the *Who's Who?* section of a reference book.
● Look at the picture of Queen Victoria on page 5. Print copies for the children and give them between six and eight small pieces of paper (sticky notes would be ideal). Ask the children to use their underlining to identify the key facts about Victoria, record them in brief note form, and arrange them around the picture.
● Share results, discussing choices and pointing out that not every biographer includes identical information. Ask: *What do you think is the first key fact?*
● On page 6 the yellow squares represent the pieces of paper. Type brief notes (not sentences) onto them with the key facts you choose. Demonstrate the need to refer to the lengthy biography to check information, dates and names.
● Point out that a biography should follow chronological order. Look at the timeline at the bottom of the page. Ask: *Which key fact should be first?* Select arrows from the Lines tool tray ⬙ to link the notes to the appropriate places on the timeline.
● Suggest that the children alter any of the key facts that they have second thoughts about, but emphasise that choice of facts may vary.
● Encourage the children to draw a timeline on their individual whiteboards and arrange their key facts in chronological order.

Independent work
● Display page 7. Ask the children to use their whiteboard timeline as a writing plan.
● They must fill out their notes into a short biography of Victoria, using all their key facts.
● Emphasise the need for complete sentences, an interesting text, varied sentence openings, and appropriate connectives.
● Support less able learners with printed copies of your screen of key facts.
● As an extra challenge, ask more able learners to use a website to find key facts for a biography of another Victorian person.

Plenary
● Invite the children to share their biographies with the class. Discuss any differences in the facts they have chosen, and identify examples of effective sentences.
● Use page 8 to make notes.

Whiteboard tools
Use the Clock tool's Count down option to time the Starter activity. Set the timer to five minutes, the sound to *bong* and the action to *Do nothing*. Convert handwriting to text using the Recognition tool.

🖊 Pen tool

⛭ Highlighter tool

🢄 Marquee select tool

⌨ Floating keyboard

🕐 Count down tool

🔄 Recognition tool

⬙ Lines tool

🖨 Print button

Sophisticated punctuation marks

Learning objective
NLS Term 1
● S6: To secure knowledge and understanding of more sophisticated punctuation marks.

Resources ● P
'Sophisticated punctuation marks' flipchart file; copy of photocopiable page 46 'Ship's log' for each child; one copy of photocopiable page 45 'Queen Victoria' from Lesson 10; individual whiteboards and pens.

Links to other subjects
History
QCA Unit 19 'What were the effects of Tudor exploration?' QCA Unit 11 'What was it like for children living in Victorian Britain?'
● Use history texts for punctuation examples.

Starter
Open the 'Sophisticated punctuation marks' and go to page 2. Ask the children to rewrite the text using punctuation. Let them compare results with a partner. Discuss any differences in the punctuation marks they have used.

Punctuate the text on the flipchart, then pull down the screen to reveal the punctuated version.

Whole-class shared work
● Go to page 3 and ask the children to revise the meanings of the punctuation marks shown. Ask them to match the punctuation marks to the explanations shown on the page. They can do this by using the Marquee select tool to drag the panels, or by drawing lines.
● Go through the Starter text again (this time on page 4) and identify and explain the punctuation examples.
● Read the text on pages 5 and 6 of the flipchart (from Lesson 10 'Biographies'). Apply your explanations of the punctuation marks to the text.
● Investigate the sentences on page 7. The punctuation is highlighted. Read the first sentence and ask: *What do the colon and semi-colons do in this sentence?* Explain that the semi-colon here replaces a full stop.
● Read the second sentence and ask the remaining questions on the page. Point out that parenthetic commas could be substituted for the brackets.
● Click on the button to go back to the facts about Queen Victoria on page 5. Demonstrate, with annotation, the substitute commas working as a pair: *On the death of her uncle, William IV, Victoria became Queen.*

Independent work
● Display page 8. Provide each child with a copy of photocopiable page 46 'Ship's log' and ask them to punctuate the text.
● Support less confident children by reducing the number of sentences.
● As an extra challenge, encourage children to add text, using some of the punctuation marks studied.

Plenary
● Invite the children to share their work.
● Go to page 9 and show the punctuated version of 'Ship's log'. Discuss why those punctuation marks are appropriate.

Whiteboard tools
To alter existing text, double-click on the text and select Edit text from the Object edit toolbox.

 Pen tool

Marquee select tool

Edit text tool

Learning objectives
NLS Term 2
● T3: To recognise how poets manipulate words.
● T4: To investigate humorous verse.

Resources ◉ 🅿
'Poetry and words' flipchart file; individual whiteboards and pens; copies of photocopiable page 47 'Poem interpretation'.

Links to other subjects
Speaking and listening
Objective 58: To use a range of oral techniques.
● Organise discussion groups: partner, small group and whole class.

Whiteboard tools
If a microphone is available, use the Sound recorder to investigate sounds of words.

📱 Pen tool

🔦 Marquee select tool

⊜ Floating keyboard

🗄 Eraser tool

🗑 Delete button

◀)) Sound recorder (optional)

Poetry and words

Starter
Open the 'Poetry and words' flipchart and go to page 2. Ask the children what a *homophone* is. Agree that it is a word with the same pronunciation, but different meaning and spelling, as another word. As a class, think of homophones for each of the words on the page. (For example: *paws* and pause; *veil* and vale.)

Ask the children to write sentences using the words. Encourage them to think of sentences where listeners may think of both words. Listen to the sentences together and ask: *Can you always tell which word is being used?*

Whole-class shared work
● Display page 3 and tell the children that you will be reading 'Jabberwocky' by Lewis Carroll (pages 4 and 5). Ask the children to identify and write, on individual whiteboards, the nonsense words they hear. Invite them to write a definition for each word and then compare meanings with a partner. Write or type examples on page 6.
● Remove the panel to suggest that all the meanings are correct. Discuss this together before revealing the answer beneath the rectangle at the bottom of the page. (*The poet has used the sound and rhythm of the word to convey a mood but has left the audience free to make its own interpretation of the meaning.*)
● Go to page 7. Encourage the children to read the title and write, on individual whiteboards, a comment on what the poem could be about. Share ideas. Did the children notice the play on words?
● Suggest that they close their eyes as you say the title. Ask: *How would you expect to spell the main words? Why?*
● Reveal the first verse and ask the children to read it. Ask: *Do you like it?* Tell them to write *Yes* or *No* on individual whiteboards and hold the whiteboards up.
● Allow time for partner discussion before you ask the children to justify their answers.
● Encourage them to tell you whether they found the poem serious or humorous? Why or why not?
● Ask the children to identify examples of similar word play. Point out that sliding down a flume is usually associated with a water park, not sliding on a wet floor. Ask: *What is the double meaning of* Hit on? (Fell and realised.) *Which one did you think of first?*

Independent work
● Remove the green rectangle to show the second verse on page 7 and ask the children to read it.
● Encourage them to think about, analyse and interpret the words.
● Invite them to write about the verse, referring to the words.
● Support less confident children with the writing frame on photocopiable page 47.
● As an extra challenge, suggest children repeat the task with another poem by a significant poet of the past.

Plenary
● Hold a class discussion on *Wednesday*. Encourage the children to express their views.
● Write or type any key thoughts on page 8.
● If a microphone is available, use the Sound recorder ◀)) to investigate sounds of words, and to record readings of the poems in the flipchart.

Learning objective
NLS Term 2
● W6: Collect and explain the meanings and origins of proverbs.

Resources
'Proverbs' flipchart file; individual whiteboards and pens; paper, pencils and pens.

Links to other subjects
History
PoS (5c) Communicate their knowledge and understanding of history in a variety of ways.
● Point out the links that proverbs have with previous ages.

Proverbs

Starter
Go to page 2 of the 'Proverbs' flipchart and ask the children to make a sentence from each line on their individual whiteboards (they must use all the words). Compare results.

Use the Marquee select tool to rearrange the words on the interactive whiteboard. Ask: *What are the sentences called?* Delete the box to identify the sentences as proverbs.

Whole-class shared work
● Read the heading on page 3. Can the children tell you what a proverb is? Listen to their suggestions before deleting the panel to reveal the answer: *A short saying in general use. A proverb has origins in the past and may have changed a little over time; it states a belief about the world.*
● Look at the beginnings of the proverbs on the page and ask the children if they can complete them. Delete the boxes to reveal the answers.
● Move on to page 4. Investigate the literal meanings of these two proverbs. Delete the panels to reveal examples. Ask: *What pictures would you use to illustrate these proverbs?*
● Go to page 5. Give the children time to work out with their partner what these proverbs might mean in modern, general language. Remove the panels to reveal some examples.
● Ask the children to think of situations when they could say or write these proverbs. Share ideas, before revealing the examples at the bottom of the page.
● Look at the pictures and proverbs on page 6. Ask the children to work out which proverb fits which picture. They should write matching letters and numbers on individual whiteboards (such as 1-e). Move the proverbs to their matching picture or remove the green box to reveal the answers.
● Using page 7, explain that pictures have now been replaced by modern word descriptions. Repeat the task of matching letters and numbers. Move the proverbs to their corresponding situation or remove the box to reveal the answers.

Independent work
● Go to page 8. Ask the children to use their whiteboards, or paper, to draw two boxes for each proverb: one box should illustrate the proverb's literal meaning; the other box should describe briefly, in words, modern situations to suit it.
● Support less able learners with picture suggestions.
● As an extra challenge, encouage more able learners to find other proverbs.

Plenary
● Invite the children to share their answers. Write or type some examples on page 9.
● Address any misconceptions about meanings.

Whiteboard tools

🖊 Pen tool

🢔 Marquee select tool

⌨ Floating keyboard

🗑 Delete button

The passive voice

Learning objectives
NLS Term 2
● S1: To investigate further the use of active and passive verbs.
● T10: To use different genres as models to write.

Resources
Individual whiteboards and pens; exercise books and pens.

Links to other subjects
Science
QCA Unit 6E 'Forces in action'
● Ask the children to research science reference material. Ask: *What is the ratio of passive sentences to active sentences?*

Starter
Ask the children to write four sentences for a mystery story set in your school. Invite them to decide which part of each sentence they would like a reader to be most interested in. Encourage the children to read the sentences to a partner and discuss whether their partners focussed on the right parts of the sentences.

Whole-class shared work
● Revise (from Lesson 5) the terms: *active; passive; agent; recipient*.
● Type on a blank flipchart page: *General Grey removed the sword*.
● Check recognition of the *verb* (removed); the *agent* of the verb (General Grey); the *recipient* of the verb (sword). Establish that the sentence is in the *active* voice.
● Ask the children to change it to the passive voice on their whiteboards. Amend the flipchart: *The sword was removed by General Grey.*
● Read the passive sentence aloud. Discuss who or what is made more important: the sword or General Grey? Point out that views are probably mixed.
● Erase some words to leave this passive sentence: *The sword was removed*. Repeat the question. The answer is obviously *The sword* as the name of the agent is withheld.
● Discuss and list the reasons a writer may have for not naming an agent:
  ● The agent is unknown.
  ● The writer does not want the reader to know the agent's identity.
  ● The agent is unimportant in the story.
  ● The writer wants the reader to focus on the recipient, not the agent.
● Type some examples on the whiteboard:
  ● *The mirror had been broken.* (No one knows how, why or who broke it.)
  ● *Inspector Cluedup was poisoned.* (By whom/what?)
  ● *A letter was brought.* (It is unimportant who brought it.)
  ● *The major was laughed at.* (The major is important, not the person doing the laughing.)
● Point out that a passive sentence without the agent is invaluable in a *Whodunnit?* story.
● Search the Resource library ▭ for a large hotel and place it on a new flipchart page.
● Suggest that Inspector Cluedup was being entertained for Christmas at this hotel on Dartmoor. Sinister events were taking place. Write the story's opening on the whiteboard:
  ● *Inspector Cluedup was taken to his room. A mirror had been cracked...*
● Point out that your sentences are *passive* and omit *agents*.

Independent work
● Ask the children to continue the chapter in their exercise books. Sentences should be mainly passive, with agents left out.
● Support less confident children by supplying further sentence openers.
● As an extra challenge, children could write the final chapter, in which passive sentences reveal the agents.

Plenary
● Encourage the children to share their work. Together, write or type a selection of their passive sentences on the whiteboard.
● Ask: *Do these sentences make you want to find out who or what was doing these things?*

Whiteboard tools
Select a hotel from the Buildings folder in the Resource library. Convert handwriting to text using the Recognition tool.

🖊 Pen tool

⌨ Floating keyboard

🔧 Marquee select tool

✎ Recognition tool

🗄 Eraser tool

▭ Resource Library

Formal and official language

Learning objectives
NLS Term 2
● S2: To understand features of formal official language.
● T20: To discuss the way standard English varies in different contexts.

Resources
'Formal and official language' flipchart file; paper and pens; individual whiteboards and pens.

Links to other subjects
PE
QCA Unit 26 'Net/wall games'
● Encourage the children to use and adapt rules, strategies and tactics, using their basic knowledge of attack and defence.

Whiteboard tools
Use the Print button, found in the Teacher tools menu, to print any pages of the flipchart. Use the Fill tool to change the colour of shapes.

● Pen tool
● Highlighter tool
● Fill tool
● Marquee select tool
● Floating keyboard
● Teacher tools menu
● Print button
● Activote (optional)

Starter
Open the 'Formal and official language' flipchart and go to page 2. Allow five minutes for the children to write, on individual whiteboards, rules for formal letter-writing. Let them compare notes with a partner. Ask: *How many rules did you agree on?* You could hold an ad-hoc voting session, using Activote or alternative methods, to compare results. Add some examples to the flipchart.

Whole-class shared work
● Display page 3. Point out that some letters are very formal. Introduce the term *formal official language.* Ask the children what they think it means. To see some examples, fill the orange box with white.
● Fill the blue box with white to reveal further explanations about using standard English, making meanings clear, and avoiding ambiguity.
● Point out that in avoiding ambiguity, formal official language can become difficult to understand, because it is unfamiliar.
● Look at the examples on page 4 together. Invite suggestions for other examples and type them in the space provided.
● Describe the scene on page 5. Matt is marking out the area where Kylie must be positioned during their basketball practice.
● Move on to page 6. Ask the children to read and discuss the letter with a partner. Use further questioning to investigate the names. Make sure that the children realise that it is written to Matt, written by a solicitor and written on Kylie's behalf.
● Ask about the content: *What does Kylie want?* (The circle to be removed.) *What is she threatening?* (To take her basketball net away.)
● Experiment with the children, translating sentences into the language in which they would usually write.
● Investigate typical style features. Highlight examples of the passive voice (*is attached*); impersonal tone (*We are reliably informed*); formal politeness (*would be grateful*).
● Identify examples of formal official language. Copy useful words and phrases, adding them to page 7. Leave this on display.
● Print copies of the letter for the children's reference, if possible.
● Suggest that Matt needs to decide what to do and get his own solicitor to reply to this letter.

Independent work
● Ask the children to act as Matt's solicitor: they must write a formal letter replying to this one using similar language.
● Support less able learners with a writing frame of paragraph openers.
● As an extra challenge, ask more able learners to involve a third solicitor, writing on behalf of the parents to both children.

Plenary
● Encourage the children to read their letters aloud. Point out the effective use of appropriate language.
● If required, type or write an example page 8.

Conditionals

Learning objective
NLS Term 2
- S5: Use reading to investigate conditionals.

Resources
'Formal and official language' flipchart file; photocopiable page 48 'If'; website **www.kipling.org** (click on *Rudyard Kipling*, then *Some poems*, and browse to 'If').

Links to other subjects
PE
QCA Unit 26 'Net/wall games'
- Link the poem to information about how to improve performance in a sport.

Starter
Display page 9 of the 'Formal and official language' flipchart. Ask the children to use the word *if* in three different complex sentences on their individual whiteboards. Encourage them to discuss their sentences with a partner. They should investigate whether or not they both used *if* in the same way? Record some of the children's sentences on the flipchart.

Whole-class shared work
- Draw attention to the highlighted sentence on page 10: *If this arrangement is continued, my client will require the removal of her property from the garden.*
- Investigate the meaning. Ask: *Is the client going to remove her property?* (Only if the arrangement is continued.)
- Move on to page 11 where the sentence is repeated.
- Explain that the sentence is a *conditional* sentence: one thing depends upon another. Can the children tell you what word makes this a conditional sentence? (*If.*)
- Explain that conditional sentences refer to possible or imaginary situations.
- Read the second sentence. Add the word *if* to the beginning so that it now reads: *If this arrangement is discontinued, my client will require the removal of her property from the garden.*
- Point out that *If* will no longer give the correct meaning. Do the children know which word would? (Unless.)
- Remind the children of the Starter. Ask: *Were any of your sentences conditionals?*
- Go to page 12. Ask the children to write an idea for the second half of the conditional sentence on their individual whiteboards. Type up one of their suggestions on the flipchart.
- Tell the children to work with a partner to make up more conditional sentences linked to Matt and Kylie's argument, always beginning with *If* or *Unless.*
- Display some of their sentences on the interactive whiteboard.
- Read the children the poem 'If' from the Kipling society website (see Resources, above).
- Explain its meaning: a man tells his son all that he must cope with before he will be able to call himself a man. Discuss the construction of the poem. Establish that it is an extended conditional in which the *if* half is most of the poem; the other half is only the last line.

Independent work
- Ask the children to complete the parody of Kipling's poem on the photocopiable sheet.
- Suggest using the subject of a sport.
- Each verse should be an extended conditional, the other half of the conditional being the last line of the verse.
- Support less confident children with suggested phrases.
- As an extra challenge, encourage children to write an *Unless* poem.

Plenary
- Ask some children to present their poems to the class.
- Add interesting examples and features to page 13.

Whiteboard tools
 Pen tool

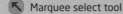 Marquee select tool

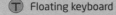 Floating keyboard

Learning objective
NLS Term 2
● T15: To recognise how arguments are constructed to be effective.

Resources
Copies of photocopiable page 49 'Dear Ms Khan'; individual whiteboards and pens; paper and pens; PDF of 'Dear Ms Khan' on the CD-ROM.

Links to other subjects
Citizenship
QCA Unit 9 'Respect for property'
● Use written arguments to emphasise that individuals hold different views and have different needs.
Speaking and listening
Objective 59: To analyse and evaluate how speakers present points effectively through use of language and gesture.
● Give the children oral practice in expressing a viewpoint effectively.

Effective arguments

Starter
Ask the children to think about their opinions of the class timetable. Allow two minutes for them to make notes on individual whiteboards. Encourage them to compare ideas with a partner and agree on one point to make (for 30 seconds) in a debate. Listen to the points.

Whole-class shared work
● Focus on oral arguments, introducing a topic that the children will have views on, such as the timing of the school day.
● Suggest that the school governors could consider these viewpoints. Type them onto a blank flipchart page. For example: start and finish earlier; lengthen the day to include homework time and so on.
● Ask the children to form groups of three with two children adopting different viewpoints and the third child acting as listener.
● Hold group speaking and listening sessions as the children argue their case for one minute. The group listener should decide which argument sounds more convincing.
● Discuss the groups' results. Ask: *Why was one argument successful? What did that speaker do? How important were the points made?*
● Present a new scenario: Town councillors will meet to discuss creating a winter, outdoor ice-skating rink. Letters are sent to the councillors before their meeting.
● Give each child a copy of photocopiable page 49. Explain that this is one of the letters sent to a councillor. Ask them to read the text with a partner.
● Ask questions about the content. For example: *Which side of the argument is supported – for or against the rink?* (Against.)
● Suggest that these features are important in a written argument:
  ● links between points
  ● persuasive examples
  ● evidence
  ● predicting likely objections, answering those objections
  ● appealing to the known views of the audience.
● Display the letter (on the CD-ROM) on the interactive whiteboard and consider each of these features, identifying how they are demonstrated. Analyse the text, highlighting or underlining the examples.
● Ideas include:
  ● persuasive examples: *the rink would interfere with the sleeping habits*
  ● evidence: *Victorian Fayre...I lost two hours every night*
  ● pre-empting possible objections: *young people...need a winter activity*
  ● answering those objections: *there are other leisure pursuits*
  ● appealing to the known sympathies of the audience: *you hold strong views about noise pollution.*

Independent work
● Ask the children to write a letter in support of the ice rink.
● The letter should be written to a different councillor and should use the features listed.
● Support less able learners with helpful phrases.
● As an extra challenge more able learners could to write a letter with a third viewpoint.

Plenary
● Type or write examples of the children's letters onto the interactive whiteboard and encourage the children to read them. Ask: *What makes their arguments effective?*

Whiteboard tools

 Pen tool

 Highlighter tool

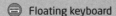 Marquee select tool

▤ Floating keyboard

Spelling mnemonics

Learning objective
NLS Term 2
● W4: Learn and invent spelling rules; invent and use mnemonics for irregular or difficult spellings.

Resources
Individual whiteboards and pens; paper and pens.

Links to other subjects
ICT
QCA Unit 6A 'Multimedia presentation'
● Ask the children to incorporate text, sound and images in creating a spelling-revision activity page for the class.

Starter

Ask the children to look at examples of their recently-corrected writing. Encourage them to list, on individual whiteboards, ten to fifteen of their typical spelling mistakes. Encourage them to compare lists with a partner. Ask: *Have you any problems in common? Do you have a spelling tip to offer?*
   Share results as a class. Try to identify a word that is troubling many children and discuss how others are finding a way to remember it.

Whole-class shared work

● Type *i* and *e* in opposite corners of the whiteboard. Can the children tell you which order is more common – *ie* or *ei* – when the two letters are next to each other? (ie)
● Explain that the usual order rule is *i* before *e*. Ask the children to write an *ie* word on their individual whiteboard and hold it up. Count the different words.
● Divide a blank flipchart page in two using the Lines tool 【▌】. Label one side *ie* and write some of the words on this side. Label the other side of the page *ei*. Which letter, do the children think, makes *i* and *e* break their rule? (c)
● Tell the children this spelling rule: *i before e except after c.*
● Ask the children to write, on individual whiteboards, an example of an *ei* spelling and hold it up. Compare the number of different words this time.
● Use the Shapes tool 【▧】 to make a box on the *ei* side of the flipchart. Label it *c* and write appropriate words in it (such as *receive, conceited, ceiling*).
● Create a second box on the *ei* side, labelling it *ay*. Write *vein* in it, emphasising its long *ay* sound. Agree on and write other appropriate words such as *eight, neighbour* and *reign*.
● Make a third box, labelling it *rule-breakers*. Explain that some words are just awkward! Encourage the children to suggest examples. Add a selection to the flipchart (such as *weird, their, protein*).
● Introduce the term *mnemonic*. Explain that a mnemonic is a device which is designed to aid memory. Mnemonics often use initial letters of words to aid memory. (Explain that the phrase *i before e except after c* is a different type of mnemonic, and that it could be extended with the line: *or when sounded ay as in neighbour and weigh*.)
● Suggest that a spelling mnemonic can be funny, unusual or linked to the word's meaning, but it must be memorable. Collaborate on creating mnemonics, such as:
  ● hippos and lions fight (half)
  ● whales eat in restaurants daily (weird).
● List a mixture of *ie* and *ei* words on the whiteboard (about ten). Be sure to include some of every type, including rule-breakers.

Independent work

● Ask the children to make up mnemonics for the word list.
● Emphasise that they should make the mnemonics memorable.
● Allow less confident children to work with a partner.
● As an extra challenge, ask children to identify their problem spellings and invent mnemonics for them.

Plenary

● Together, annotate a flipchart page to make a poster of memorable mnemonics. You could include images from the Resource library to illustrate further. This can be saved for future reference.

Whiteboard tools
Use the Shapes tool to create boxes.

【▯】 Pen tool

【🔨】 Marquee select tool

【⌨】 Floating keyboard

【▧】 Shapes tool

【▌】 Lines tool

 Resource library

Contracting sentences

Starter
Open the 'Contracting sentences' flipchart and go to page 2. Ask the children to write a sentence of at least 15 words, on individual whiteboards, about their weekend. Ask them to exchange whiteboards with a partner, challenging the partner to reduce the sentence to fewer words.

Repeat the task, giving the children new topics for their sentences. Listen to some *before* and *after* versions. Write or type a few examples on page 2.

Whole-class shared work
● Go to page 3. Explain that there are different reasons for reducing text and different ways to do it. Delete the three panels to reveal these:
  ● Editing
  ● Note-making
  ● Summarising.
● Look at *Wolf News* on page 4 and use it to demonstrate the three ways of reducing the text (referring back to page 3 if necessary):
  1. Editing: Less important information is left out in order to have fewer words. Remind the children of their Independent work, in Lesson 9, when they edited this article to no more than 170 words. If possible, view an edited version (yours or a child's). Ask the children to identify the information that has been kept and information that has been omitted.
  2. Note-making: Complete sentences are not needed. Demonstrate on a new flipchart page, for example:
     ● Wolf Grand – Morecambe – collapses
     ● Victorian hotel
     ● big piece in sea – 3am
     ● local coastal erosion?
  3. Summarising: A sentence is reduced to its core meaning; the outcome must still be a complete sentence. Look at the sentence on page 5. Ask the children, in pairs, to work out the essential meaning and to write a summary sentence on their individual whiteboards.
● Remove the panel to reveal the example. Ask: *Do you agree? Has the essence of the original sentence been retained?*
● Repeat the exercise with the other sentence on the page. Reveal the summary beneath the second panel.

Independent work
● Go to page 6 for a text about Francis Drake. Print copies for the children.
● Ask the children to summarise each sentence in the text.
● Emphasise the need to write complete sentences.
● Support less confident children by highlighting key information.
● As an extra challenge, ask more confident children to reduce the text by note-making.

Plenary
● Write or type examples of the children's summaries in the space provided on page 7.
● Talk about editing. Ask: *Which pieces of information could be edited out of this text to reduce it to 100 words?*

Paragraphs

Learning objective
NLS Term 2
● T2: To analyse how individual paragraphs are structured in writing.

Resources
'Frogs' flipchart file; photocopiable page 50 'Penguins'; individual whiteboards and pens.

Links to other subjects
Science
QCA Unit 6A 'Interdependence and adaptation'
● Write a paragraph of a non-chronological report on the adaptation of animals to their habitats.

Starter
Display page 2 of the 'Paragraphs' flipchart. Tell the children that they have three minutes to make notes for one paragraph, on individual whiteboards, recounting what the class did during a recent school event. Ask them to decide how many sentences they would need and, using numbers and letters, to identify which notes they would use for which sentence.

Let the children compare results with a partner, discussing sentence order. Add some examples to the flipchart.

Whole-class shared work
● Move on to page 3. Revise the term *paragraph.* Encourage suggestions from the children before deleting the panel to reveal a definition: *a group of sentences that fit together well.*
● There is a section of text on Francis Drake on page 4. Discuss the structure of this paragraph and the order in which information is presented. Ask: *Which word links the second sentence to the first sentence?* (This.)
● Go to page 5 for some facts about frogs. Explain that these can be notes for one paragraph of a non-chronological report which the children are going to write on frogs.
● Remove the yellow box to reveal a first attempt at writing the paragraph, Version 1.
● Do the children think the information is in the best possible order? Agree on a better order, annotating the text or moving the sentences around.
● Reveal the second draft, Version 2, on page 6. Ask the children to read and discuss it with a partner, and write a critical comment on their individual whiteboards.
● Compare comments, and add a selection to the flipchart.
● Agree on certain weaknesses, such as dull sentences and sentences that are not connected to one another.
● Work together orally, annotating the text on the whiteboard with the children's suggestions before revealing your final version, Version 3, on page 7.
● Ask: *How has this version been improved?* Remove the yellow box to point out improvements made by the addition of detail (for example, words such as: *powerful, quickly*); and connecting words used to create links within the paragraph (for example: *Because of; This; As a result*).
● Emphasise the improved structure of this paragraph.

Independent work
● Ask the children to construct a paragraph about penguins. The facts which will provide the basis are on page 8.
● Provide each child with a copy of the photocopiable sheet. A first draft has been done. The children should write:
  ● Version 2: with improved sentence order
  ● Version 3: with added detail, improved structure and links.
● Support less able learners by providing the beginning of Version 2.
● As an extra challenge, encourage children to repeat the improvement exercise with a paragraph from one of their own stories.

Plenary
● Write or type some of the paragraphs onto page 9.
● Highlight and discuss good examples of added details and connections in Version 3.

Whiteboard tools
● Pen tool
● Highlighter tool
● Marquee select tool
● Floating keyboard
● Delete button

Connecting paragraphs

Learning objective
NLS Term 3
● T21: To divide whole texts into paragraphs, paying attention to the sequence of paragraphs and to the links between one paragraph and the next.

Resources
'Narratives' flipchart file; individual whiteboards and pens; copy of photocopiable page 51 'Paragraph planning' for each child.

Links to other subjects
History
QCA Unit 15 'How do we use ancient Greek ideas today?'
● Link this story to research on the Greek alphabet and Greek words.

Whiteboard tools
Set the Clock tool's Count down option to three minutes, with a sound to play after timeout, to time the Starter.

 Pen tool

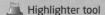 Highlighter tool

Marquee select tool

Floating keyboard

Count down tool

Starter
Open the 'Narratives' flipchart and go to page 2. Allow three minutes for the children to make notes about school yesterday on their individual whiteboards. Use the Clock tool's Count down option to time them. Ask them to decide how many paragraphs they would use if writing the notes into a recount. Then ask them to decide which notes they would need for which paragraph, using numbers and letters. Let the children compare results with a partner.

Whole-class shared work
● Look at the text about Francis Drake on page 3. Ask the children to read the text and to write a single-word label on their whiteboards for the contents of each paragraph.
● Compare results and annotate the whiteboard with the children's suggestions. Remove the yellow rectangles to reveal some examples of labels.
● Ask: *How is the final paragraph linked to the rest of the text?* (*Afterwards*, which is a connective word.)
● Go to page 4. Invite the children to look at a piece of their own writing, for example, a science explanation. Ask them to choose one paragraph from the middle, and to write down why they began that new paragraph at a certain point.
● Compare answers, discussing how they linked the paragraph to the rest of the text. Write or type some examples on the page.
● Point out that decisions about starting a new paragraph are not easy; the progress of a text is not always linear. For example, the second paragraph on page 3 moves *sideways*, rather than *forwards*, chronologically as it expands on the basic information in the first paragraph.
● Look at the text on pages 5 and 6, *Online progress*. Invite the children to read the text with a partner and to think of a single-word label for the contents of each paragraph.
● Share ideas, annotating the text. Remove the yellow rectangles to reveal some examples.
● Ask: *Does the narrative progress chronologically?* Point out how it begins on Monday morning, but moves back in time to explain changes in Henry.
● Encourage the children to identify the connective words that start each paragraph. Highlight these in the text and discuss how they help the reader to make sense of the narrative.

Independent work
● Go to page 7. Ask the children to plan paragraphs for the next part of this story using photocopiable page 51 'Paragraph planning'.
● They should firstly give the paragraphs single-word labels.
● Then, at Stage 2, they should write notes about what will occur in the paragraph, and how it will fit in with the rest of the story. Explain that for Stage 3 they need to provide the opening for each paragraph as well as the connecting words.
● Support less confident children by spending time in initial discussion.
● As an extra challenge, ask more confident children to improve the connections between their paragraphs in a recent story.

Plenary
● Write or type some of the children's ideas in the table on page 8. Save these for a future lesson.

Reading narratives

Learning objectives
NLS Term 3
- S1: To revise the language conventions and grammatical features of the different types of text.
- T7: To annotate passages in detail in response to specific questions.

Resources
'Narratives' flipchart file; individual whiteboards and pens; writing paper and pens.

Links to other subjects
History
QCA Unit 15 'How do we use ancient Greek ideas today?'
- Point out the word *bipeds* in paragraph 5. Identify the Greek origins of *bi*. Ask the children to compile a list of words with Greek roots.

Starter
Click on the button next to Lesson 22 in the 'Narratives' flipchart to go to page 9. Provide individual whiteboards and ask the children to write down the names of three adventure stories or novels. Invite them to compare lists with a partner, justifying their choices to each other.

Ask the children to hold up their whiteboards and look around. Check whether there any titles that are appear more than one whiteboard, and discuss what is special about those books.

Whole-class shared work
- Display page 10. Ask the children to write what they feel the purpose of adventure fiction is.
- Compare their ideas before deleting the panels to reveal two suggestions: a) to entertain the reader; b) to remove the reader from everyday life.
- Ask: *How does the writer achieve these aims?* Most children will focus on plot, but point out the additional importance of story structure, and language and sentence construction.
- Move on to page 11. Discuss the structure of an adventure book, annotating the page accordingly. Adventure novels are consist a build-up of events and complications. Ask: *When does the writer often finish a chapter?* (At a *cliffhanger*, when the reader wonders if danger or problems will be resolved.)
- Now discuss language and sentence construction. Explain that the writer's language and sentence construction may slip by unnoticed. Emphasise that to become effective writers, we need to know the techniques used.
- Establish that the paragraph on page 12 is an extract from an adventure story. Identify writing techniques by making a close analysis of the language and sentences used.
- Draw attention to words by circling, highlighting, or numbering them.
- With the children's help, make annotations in the margin on the whiteboard page.

Example annotations could be:

Words	Annotation
Monday morning	Setting of time and place is established immediately.
Mr Davies; the class	The story is written in the third person.
Mr Davies; Henry	Characters are introduced quickly.
followed; tumbled	Verbs are in the past tense, usual in narratives.
sceptical	This adjective highlights a difference of opinion from his colleagues.

Whiteboard tools
Use the Print button, found in the Teacher tools menu, to provide the children with copies of the text for the Independent work.

- Pen tool
- Highlighter tool
- Marquee select tool
- Print button
- Teacher tools menu

Independent work
- Provide the children with printed copies of page 13, which shows the next three paragraphs of the story. Invite them to read a paragraph, analysing the text, before selecting points to draw attention to.
- Suggest numbering points and then ask the children to make annotations, with corresponding numbers, on separate paper.
- Support less confident children by numbering points in some paragraphs.
- As an extra challenge, encourage children to do a similar analysis of a page from a very different piece of fiction.

Plenary
- Work together on paragraph 2 of the extract. Listen to the children's suggestions, using some to annotate the paragraph on page 14.
- Leave annotation of the remaining paragraphs for a future lesson.

Writing narratives

Learning objectives
NLS Term 3
● **S1:** To revise the language conventions and grammatical features of the different types of text.
● **T7:** To annotate passages in detail in response to specific questions.
● **T21:** To divide whole texts into paragraphs, paying attention to the sequence of paragraphs and to the links between one paragraph and the next.

Resources
'Narratives' flipchart file; Independent work from Lessons 21 and 22; individual whiteboards and pens; writing paper and pens.

Links to other subjects
Speaking and listening
Objective 67: To devise a performance considering how to adapt the performance for a specific audience.
● Let the children work in small groups, scripting a drama of the story to present to other groups.

Whiteboard tools
Use the Recognition tool to convert handwriting to text.

 Pen tool

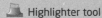 Highlighter tool

🖰 Marquee select tool

⌨ Floating keyboard

🔤 Recognition tool

Starter
Remind the children of their Independent work in Lesson 22. Open page 15 of the 'Narratives' flipchart, showing paragraph 5. Ask the children to note, on individual whiteboards, what they think should be noticed in this paragraph and why.

Whole-class shared work
● Share ideas, agree and annotate the text on-screen. For example:

Words	Annotation
This morning	The time connective links the paragraph to previous ones and signals a return to the immediate present of paragraph 1.
Jim	A new character is introduced. The reader knows that he is Henry's father, referred to at the end of the previous paragraph.
at home	There is a change of setting.
Prime numbers, weather patterns, insulators and bipeds.	The writer emphasises the extent of the work to cover.
tumbled	This is an effective verb, giving a strong visual picture of questions landing quickly on the computer screen.
Nevertheless	This connective structures and links sentences within the paragraph.
Thumbing	The word conveys a clear visual picture of Jim, in an old-fashioned way, turning pages of books, hinting that Jim is happier using books than computers. (The writer hints rather than telling the reader directly.)
Unfortunately	This connective within the paragraph signals that something bad will occur.
hurtling	This word reinforces the earlier images of a lot of work arriving quickly.
computer	Ending the paragraph suggests that a change is coming.
Suddenly	This connective injects drama and suspense into the story. (Ask: *Could this be a place to end the chapter?*)

● Talk about what could happen in the story. (Remind the children about the plans they made in Lesson 21.)
● Use page 16 to revise the important writing techniques mentioned here and in Lesson 22. Click on the button to view a list of some of the techniques used:
  ● creating interesting main characters
  ● using language to create impact on the reader
  ● using effective connectives
  ● creating suspense
  ● hinting at events, rather than telling the reader everything.

Independent work
● Display page 17. Ask the children to read (amending as they wish) their story plans.
● Invite them to write the next section of the story.
● Give the children some test practice with a timed situation.
● Support less confident children by discussing their plans or supplying them with a plan, using page 17 to make any appropriate notes or example plans.
● As an extra challenge, ask more confident children to annotate a piece of personal writing, identifying places for improvement.

Plenary
● Invite children to type or write some paragraph examples on page 18. Point out examples of effective writing techniques.

Non-fiction texts

Learning objectives
NLS Term 3
● S1: To revise the language conventions and grammatical features of the different types of text.
● T19: To review a range of non-fiction text types and their characteristics, discussing when a writer might choose to write in a given style and form.
● T22: To select the appropriate style and form to suit a specific purpose and audience, drawing on knowledge of different non-fiction text types.

Resources
'Non-fiction texts' flipchart file; individual whiteboards and pens; photocopiable page 52 'Identify the text type' for each child; paper and pens.

Links to other subjects
The children's knowledge of non-fiction texts can be applied to reference books for any subject.

Starter
Open the 'Non-fiction texts' flipchart and go to page 2. Ask the children to write on individual whiteboards what they know about non-fiction texts. Encourage them to look in their science, history and geography exercise books to identify the different types of writing they have done. Invite partners to compare findings. Write or type any examples on the flipchart.

Whole-class shared work
● These words are in boxes on page 3: *recount, non-chronological report,* and *instructions.*
● Ask the children to consider what these text types have in common. (They are all non-fiction text types.)
● Remind the children that the text types have particular writing features. Consider text types one at a time, asking the children about important features. Write about five bullet points on each text type in the boxes. Pull the tabs to reveal examples, if required.
● Move on to page 4, which shows the words *explanation, persuasion* and *discussion.* Continue as before, making bulleted notes on these text types and revealing the examples if necessary.
● Save these pages to use in a future lesson. Discuss and compare them to the children's suggestions.
● Point out that selection of text type, and therefore appropriate writing style, involves two factors: the writing's purpose and its audience.
● Click on the image on page 5 to open the *What type of text* quiz. There are six multiple choice questions in which the children must select a text type for each purpose and audience.

Independent work
● Ask the children to read the text extracts on photocopiable page 52 'Identify the text type'.
● Invite them to draw arrows from the text type labels to each text.
● Ask the children to write, on a separate piece of paper, the reasons for their choices.
● Support less able learners with partner work.
● As an extra challenge, encourage more able learners to describe an audience and purpose for each text.

Plenary
● Go to page 7 of the flipchart, which contains some of the text extracts from the photocopiable sheet.
● Use Activote devices, or alternative voting methods, to investigate the children's choices. Annotate the texts and discuss reasons for their choices.

Whiteboard tools

Pen tool

Highlighter tool

Marquee select tool

Floating keyboard

Activote (optional)

Spelling rules

Learning objective
NLS Term 3
● W4: To revise and consolidate work from previous five terms.

Resources
'Spelling rules' flipchart file; individual whiteboards and pens; photocopiable page 53 'A stressful crossword!' for every child.

Links to other subjects
Speaking and listening
Objective 66: To identify the ways spoken language varies according to differences in context and purpose of use.
● Let the children listen to one another speaking naturally, in order to identify unstressed letters.

Starter
Open the 'Spelling rules' flipchart and go to page 2. Provide individual whiteboards and ask the children to write down three words they commonly spell incorrectly. Encourage them to check the spelling in a dictionary. Ask them to compare results with a partner. Do they share any problem words? Suggest that they talk about and underline the parts of the words that present problems before they give each other oral spelling practice.

Write some of the children's words in the yellow box on page 2. Ensure that some of the longer, polysyllabic words are included. Highlight their problem letters.

Whole-class shared work
● Look at the word *similar* on page 3. Invite one child to read it aloud.
● Ask: *What spelling mistake do you think is usually made?* Explain that the second *i* is often left out. Encourage the children to say the word to themselves: do they notice how the second *i* is unstressed, making it easy to forget.
● Ask: *How can you remember the correct spelling?* Discuss ideas, suggesting that emphasising the letter as you say the word to yourself when writing it can be helpful.
● Display page 4. Identify the list of words as words that are commonly misspelled. Each of these words also has an unstressed vowel.
● Invite the children to work with a partner, saying these words to each other and writing the unstressed vowels on individual whiteboards.
● Compare answers, highlighting the unstressed vowels on the whiteboard.
● Play the spelling game on pages 5 to 10. Let the children write a number selection on their individual whiteboards, or vote using Activote devices, before revealing the answer on the interactive whiteboard. Clicking the correct answer will produce a clapping sound.
● Click on *Return to start* to go back to question 1. Repeat the game for the children to beat their scores.
● The correct spellings from the quiz are on page 10 (remove the yellow rectangle to reveal them). Encourage the children to identify and highlight the unstressed vowels.

Independent work
● Ask the children to complete the crossword on their copy of photocopiable page 53.
● Point out that the answers all have a dangerous unstressed vowel!
● Support less able learners with partner work or by filling in some starting letters.
● As an extra challenge, ask more able learners to make a list of words containing an unstressed consonant.

Plenary
● Go to page 12 and view the crossword. Fill in the answers, identifying the unstressed vowels. Click on the button at the top of the page to check answers.

Whiteboard tools
 Pen tool

 Highlighter tool

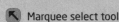 Marquee select tool

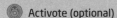 Activote (optional)

Learning objectives

NLS Term 3

● S1: To revise the language conventions and grammatical features of the different types of text.

● T19: To review a range of non-fiction text types and their characteristics, discussing when a writer might choose to write in a given style and form.

● T22: To select the appropriate style and form to suit a specific purpose and audience, drawing on knowledge of different non-fiction text types.

Resources

'Persuasive advertisements' flipchart file; individual whiteboards and pens; computers (optional); paper and pens.

Links to other subjects

PSHE and citizenship

PoS (3a) To learn what makes a healthy lifestyle, including the benefits of healthy eating.

● Link the Independent task to the importance of a healthy diet.

Persuasive advertisements

Starter

Display page 2 of the 'Persuasive advertisements' flipchart. Ask the children to write three advertising slogans they can remember on their individual whiteboards. Invite them to compare results with a partner. Ask: *How can you remember those slogans?* Compare the class results. Identify a slogan chosen by a number of children and dscuss why it is memorable.

Whole-class shared work

● There is a picture of a mobile phone on page 3. What text type, do the children think, should go with this picture? Remove or erase the blue panel to reveal the answer. (Persuasive text.)

● Allow partner discussion as the children share ideas for the text. Suggest questions to consider, for example: *What is the text's purpose? Who is the audience?*

● Encourage the children to make notes of their ideas on individual whiteboards.

● Discuss ideas as a class, adding suggestions to the flipchart.

● Reveal the completed advertisement on page 4. Prompt analysis with the questions written beside the advertisement, annotating the children's responses.

● Go to page 5. Explain that these are stages in an advertisement's planning:
1. Purpose and audience
2. Word level
3. Sentence level
4. Text level.

● Discuss each stage, writing in the boxes as you agree on important questions to consider at that stage.

● Delete the shapes to reveal some examples.

● Return to this page when the children are completing their Independent work.

Independent work

● Display page 6. Tell the children that they are going to plan a magazine advertisement for a healthy food product.

● Explain that the advertisement will be aimed at young people.

● Encourage the children to use either paper or computers for initial drafts.

● Support less confident children with a choice of products.

● As an extra challenge, ask children to advertise the same product for a different audience.

Plenary

● Ask the children to share their advertisements in small groups. Encourage them to read and evaluate each other's work.

● Draw particular attention to effective word-level techniques. Write or type good examples on page 7.

Whiteboard tools

 Pen tool

Delete button

Marquee select tool

Floating keyboard

Recognition tool

Explanations

Learning objective
NLS Term 3
● T15: To secure understanding of the features of explanatory texts from Year 5 Term 2.

Resources
'Explanations' flipchart file; individual whiteboards and pens; paper and pens.

Links to other subjects
Science
QCA Unit 6F 'How we see things'
● Link the Independent work to work on light.

Starter
Display page 2 of the 'Explanations' flipchart. Ask the children to write, on individual whiteboards, the features of an explanation text. Allow them to compare notes with a partner and agree on a list. Ask them to identify the features of explanations in their own science or geography writing. Compare results as a class, writing or typing selected features in the space provided.

Whole-class shared work
● Using page 3, remind the children that an explanation is a non-fiction text type. Look at the explanation circle and talk about the features listed. Ask: *What examples did you find in your writing?* Share results.
● Click on the button to go to the next page. Identify the text here as an explanation.
● Allow the children a few minutes to read the text with partners. Encourage them to identify and note down examples of the five features listed in the circle.
● Share results, annotating the text. For example:
  ● present tense: *flows, is carried*
  ● causal (cause and effect) connectives: *in order to*
  ● time connectives: *After that*
  ● impersonal style with the passive voice: *loose soil is carried*
  ● correct technical terms: *refinery, lubricants.*
● Explain that the circle's list covers only the main features; explanations may have additional characteristics. Allow partners two minutes to identify and note other features they think are typical of an explanation.
● Discuss the children's findings. Highlight and annotate these points:
  ● *title* is a question
  ● *text* answers the title question
  ● *text* tells how something happens
  ● *first sentence* is an introductory statement
  ● *process* is explained in sequential order.
● Use annotation and highlighting to point out the detail of the language, such as: sequential connectives – *once, then*; hypothetical language – *If the presence and location of oil are established, then ...*; complex sentences – *As the mud flows back up to the surface, loose soil is carried with it.* Explain that these features, and diagrams, are all typical of an explanation.
● Return to page 3 and add the above points to the list.
● Click on *Go to Independent work* to continue to page 5.

Independent work
● Ask the children to write an explanation answering a question to suit your current science revision, such as: *How does light travel?* (The questions on page 5 are editable so you can use the Edit text tool ⓣ to change or add to them.)
● Display the list of explanation features by clicking on *Go to explanation circle*.
● Encourage the children to check the required scientific vocabulary.
● Ask them to suggest an accompanying diagram.
● Support less confident children with a writing frame of paragraph openers.
● As an extra challenge, ask more confident children to write an additional explanation for class science revision.
● Click on *Go to plenary* when the children have finished.

Plenary
● Choose some children to type or write their explanations on page 6. Point out where diagrams could support writing.

Whiteboard tools
To change or add to existing text, double-click on the text and select Edit text from the Object edit toolbox.

🖉 Pen tool

🖌 Highlighter tool

🅺 Marquee select tool

ⓣ Edit text tool

🔤 Recognition tool

⌨ Floating keyboard

Book cover blurb

Learning objectives
NLS Term 3
● T10: To write a brief synopsis of a text.
● T11: To write a brief helpful review tailored for real audiences.

Resources
'Book blurb' flipchart file; individual whiteboards and pens; paper and pens; a selection of novels.

Links to other subjects
Speaking and listening
Objective 58: To use a range of oral techniques to present persuasive argument.
● Divide the class into reading clubs. As members present reviews, they must persuade others that their book is the one to read.

Whiteboard tools

📱 Pen tool
🔦 Highlighter tool
🔍 Marquee select tool
abc✓ Recognition tool
⌨ Floating keyboard

Starter
Open the 'Book blurb' flipchart and go to page 2. Ask the children to think of a fiction book to recommend. Hold partner conversations, allowing each child two minutes to present the case for their book. Afterwards, ask the children to make notes on individual whiteboards about:
● what they now know about the other book
● whether they have been persuaded to read it, and the reasons for their decision
● a score out of ten for the speaker's powers of persuasion.
Let the children repeat this for different books. Write or type examples in the space provided on the flipchart.

Whole-class shared work
● Go to page 3. Ask the children to work in pairs to think of questions they would ask before choosing a book as their reading book. Ask them to write their top three questions on individual whiteboards.
● Share results, annotating the flipchart by writing numbered questions in the boxes on page 3.
● Randomly, give partners a paperback novel. Each novel must have a summary book blurb (probably on the back cover).
● Ask the children to read only the blurb. Invite them to check the questions on the flipchart and note, on individual whiteboards, the numbers answered.
● Share results. Write an answer, when supplied, in a different colour under the questions on page 3.
● Investigate the blurb formed by these answers. Ask questions such as: *What sort of picture is built up of this imaginary book? What picture would suit the cover? Did your blurb give additional information?* Discuss the points raised.
● Display page 4. Explain the context: a book review in a magazine for teachers. The review should help a teacher identify if the book will suit a class.
● Read and discuss the review, emphasising that while there is enough information to promote interest in the book, there is not so much of the story that there is no point in reading the book.
● Investigate the text, applying questions from page 3. Point out if and where they are answered.

Independent work
● Move on to page 5. Present the following scenario: you want to compile a resource for next year's Year 6. It will be a collection of reviews to help the children to choose a book.
● Ask the children to write a book review for your collection.
● Suggest that they review a book they have read this year.
● Encourage them to start by writing a brief synopsis of the book to remind themselves of the content.
● Support less able learners with suggested titles or partner discussion.
● As an extra challenge more able learners could write the back cover blurb for a book you have read to the class.

Plenary
● Invite children to write or type their reviews on page 6. Point out how writers offer tempting details without revealing the whole plot.

Linked poems

Learning objective
NLS Term 3
● T13: To write a sequence of poems linked by theme or form.

Resources
Individual whiteboards and pens; paper and pens; poetry anthologies (one for every three children).

Links to other subjects
Speaking and listening
Objective 60: To understand and use a variety of ways to criticise constructively and respond to criticism.
● Once their own poems are written, let the children return to their Starter groups to plan how best to perform their poems.

Starter
Organise the children into groups of three. Give each group access to a poetry anthology, asking the children to select three poems they think could be placed in a separate section of the anthology. On individual whiteboards, they should record the selected titles and how the poems relate to one another. Discuss choices, pointing out how the children have linked poems for different reasons, for example *theme, format* or *vocabulary*.

Whole-class shared work
● Type these lines on a new flipchart page on the whiteboard:
    Winter's freezing cold,
    pulling on an overcoat
    of blinding white snow.
● Explain that the lines form a short poem. Ask someone to read the poem aloud as the rest of the class taps out the syllables on their desks. Repeat this with someone else reading the poem.
● Have the children noticed anything about the tapping? Read the poem again, pausing after each line. Ask the following questions:
    ● *Are you tapping the same number of times for each line?*
    ● *How many syllables are in the first line?* (Five)
    ● *What about the second?* (Seven)
    ● *How many are in the third line?* (Five)
    ● *How many syllables are there altogether?* (17)
● Identify this poem as a *haiku:* a poetry form that always uses 17 syllables.
● Open a new flipchart page and use the Shapes tool 🔷 to create a large circle. Explain that this is an information circle for a haiku.
● Ask: *What information do we have so far to put in the circle?* Agree on and type these points in the circle:
    ● three lines: 17 syllables altogether
    ● five syllables in first line
    ● seven syllables in second line
    ● five syllables in third line.
● Ask the children if they know anything else before you add these points:
    ● originally a Japanese form of poetry
    ● often accompanied by an illustration
    ● originally they were usually about the seasons.
● Read some haikus by well-known poets. For example: 'Haiku' and 'First Haiku of Spring', by Roger McGough; 'Policeman Haiku' and 'Lowku Haiku' by Roger Stevens.
● Point out that poets today sometimes use this poetic form about subjects other than just the seasons.
● Return to the screen with your haiku. Suggest that this should be the first haiku in a series, creating a year's calendar of the seasons.

Independent work
● Challenge the children to work on a haiku poem about the seasons.
● Support less confident children with partner work.
● As an extra challenge, encourage children to write a sequence of haiku poems for the months in a season.

Plenary
● Invite the children to read their haikus aloud. Discuss whether or not they found it a satisfying way to write poetry?

Whiteboard tools
Use the Floating keyboard to type onto the flipchart. Use the Shapes tool to create a large circle.

 Pen tool

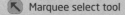 Marquee select tool

 Shapes tool

⊜ Floating keyboard

Learning objectives
NLS Term 3
● W5: To invent words using known roots, prefixes and suffixes.

Resources 💿 🅿
'Word building' flipchart file ; copy of photocopiable page 54 'Unusual people!' for every child; individual whiteboards and pens; paper and pens; computers (optional).

Links to other subjects
History
QCA Unit 15 'How do we use ancient Greek ideas today?'
● Ask the children to identify Greek word roots.

Whiteboard tools
Convert handwriting to text with the Recognition tool.

🖊 Pen tool

⛏ Highlighter tool

◤ Marquee select tool

⌨ Floating keyboard

🗑 Eraser tool

🗑 Delete button

✏ Recognition tool

Word fun

Starter
Open the 'Word building' flipchart and click on the button to go to Lesson 30. Ask the children to choose ten difficult words from two pages of their reading books and write them on individual whiteboards. Ask them to exchange boards with a partner and write (in one word) a meaning for the words listed.

Invite the children to compare results, checking their answers in a dictionary and discussing the construction of each word.

Whole-class shared work
● Go to page 11. Talk about word-building, reminding the children that new words can be constructed from a combination of prefixes, suffixes and roots.
● Demonstrate with the word *conclude* on the whiteboard. Use the Marquee select tool to deconstruct the word into: *con + clude*. Ask: *Which is the root word?* (clude.) *What is* con*?* (A prefix.)
● Ask the children to suggest other words using the same root word (such as *preclude, include* and *exclude*). Share results, writing them on the whiteboard.
● Use the meanings of these words to help the children work out the meaning of the root word. (Shut.)
● Allow partner discussion time as the children investigate the meanings of the prefixes. Suggest thinking of other words with the same prefix. Write the meanings on the whiteboard: *pre* – before; *in* – within; *con* – together; *ex* – outside.
● Explain the game on page 12: the children must combine word parts to create a word to fit a meaning clue. Challenge the partners to identify and write the words on individual whiteboards within a few minutes.
● Demonstrate constructing the answers by dragging and dropping the word parts into the orange rectangles. Focus on the separate word parts, underlining or highlighting them in different colours.
● Move on to page 46 and organise the children into two teams to play another game. Teams take turns to give the correct meaning for a word part. They could designate a representative to either come to the board to write their meaning in a column, or to say the meaning for you to scribe. One point is awarded for a correct answer. Reveal the answer only when the team's answer is correct.
● Display the word *arachnophobia* on page 14. Discuss its make up and what each part means: *arachna* (spider) + *phobia* (fear).
● Have fun by combining word parts to invent new words. For example: *vacca* – cows; *phobia* – fear. Put them together for *vaccaphobia*! (An invented word for *fear of cows*.)

Independent work
● Display page 15. Ask the children to invent new words to complete the poems on the photocopiable page sheet. Discuss the words and their meanings. Finish the sentences and then ask the children to write their own ideas for more poems.
● Support less confident children with partner work.
● As an extra challenge, encourage more confident children to write jokes that involve invented words.

Plenary
● Choose children to type or write their poems on page 16. Encourage them to define the invented words.

The Princess and the Frog

The princess was strolling *in the grounds*.
In the sky, the sun was blazing.
The heat *at midday* felt intense.
The girl *with the golden hair* walked along.
Her feet, *in delicate shoes*, dragged more slowly.
The princess, *on her walk*, paused.
She had spied, *by her side*, a beautiful lake.
She sank, *with weary legs*, upon the bank.
Into the water, her gaze fell.
After a time, her eyes felt heavy.
The girl *near the lake* fell asleep.
Up from the depths, the fish emerged.
They watched, *with glassy eyes*, the sleeping girl.
Out of the reeds, rustled and hopped a frog.
He settled, *without any fear*, *beside the princess*.

Word clusters

▪ Write a word on each petal that is linked to the flower's centre.

Wolf News

MORECAMBE HOTEL COLLAPSE!

Wolf Grand is snatched by the sea

A large section of The Wolf Grand, Morecambe's famous Victorian hotel, disappeared into the sea at 3am this morning. Local coastal erosion was immediately blamed.

The collapse occurred suddenly. There was a rough sea all day yesterday, with waves crashing against the hotel by midnight. Coastguards' opinion was sought, yet the building was given the all-clear. Nevertheless, three hours' later, it was suddenly torn apart.

The west wing was destroyed, but no bedrooms were located in that section. However, a new restaurant, lounges and lobby were all lost. In spite of this building damage, no serious injuries were sustained by guests or staff. Nonetheless, as a precautionary measure, some of the Wolf family were lifted by air ambulance to Lancaster, but casualties were limited to minor sprains, cuts, bruises and shock.

Guests reported being woken by a thundering noise and a juddering movement. Moreover, many talked about the shock of what they felt and saw.

"I don't think I'll ever get over it," said Charlene Lamb, an 80-year-old hotel resident. "I felt my bed going sideways and I thought I would drown."

"Half the staircase had disappeared," reported 10-year-old Dwight Wolf, "so I slid down a banister to escape."

Meanwhile, the hotel's manager, 40-year-old William Wolf, was tearful as he blamed coastal neglect. Furthermore, he believed the problem had been ignored for ten years.

Victorian school life

■ Use these sentences to write a report of two paragraphs. Use connectives to create a linked text.

- ☐ Classes were large.
- ☐ Teachers maintained strict order.
- ☐ Punishments were harsh.
- ☐ There was an emphasis on rote learning.
- ☐ The pupils spoke only when told to.
- ☐ The children answered a register call.
- ☐ The children chanted multiplication tables every day.
- ☐ Monitors worked under the supervision of the teacher.
- ☐ The monitors acted as assistant teachers.
- ☐ The monitors supervised small groups of children.

Name _____

Queen Victoria

Princess Victoria was born on 24 May, 1819; the birth was at Kensington Palace, London. She was the daughter of Edward (the Duke of Kent) and his wife (Victoria).

From early childhood, Victoria was trained for a royal role. She was educated at home by a governess. From an early age she showed particular skills and interests: she enjoyed writing; she kept a diary; she was skilled in drawing; she learned other languages.

On the death of her uncle (William IV) Victoria became Queen. She was still a young woman when her engagement was announced to a member of European royalty: Prince Albert of Saxe-Coburg. In 1840, at the age of 21, Queen Victoria became Albert's wife.

Victoria and Albert had nine children. The eldest was named Victoria, probably after her mother and grandmother; she was born in 1840. The eldest son, Edward, was born in 1841, and became the Prince of Wales, the heir to the throne.

Victoria expanded her kingdom nationally and globally. She bought new British homes, such as Osborne on the Isle of Wight and Balmoral in Scotland. The British Empire expanded dramatically under her reign. New territories included: New Zealand in 1840; Hong Kong in 1842; Natal (in South Africa) in 1843. She encouraged explorers such as David Livingstone, who discovered and named Victoria Falls after the Queen.

Victoria held strong moral views and tried to rule her people wisely. She received strong support from her husband, Prince Albert. He took an active interest in the arts, science and trade, organising the Great Exhibition in 1851. This was a celebration of the country's technical progress and achievements.

Victoria was affected deeply by the death of her husband in 1861. For the remainder of her reign (another 40 years) she wore black, and showed less enthusiasm for public life.

Victoria died on 22 January 1901. Her reign lasted almost 64 years, the longest in British history.

Ship's log

■ Punctuate this text. As well as full stops and capital letters, the writer included:

: colon × 3
; semi-colon × 3
(   ) brackets × 1
,   , parenthetic commas × 3
– dash × 1

15 January 1580

the voyage is tiring danger is everywhere there is much concern about the weather a storm is blowing hard and even more rain looks likely we are close to the land of King Philip of Spain we are watching for Spanish ships Spanish ships have special value they are laden with treasure now is the time to use our best telescope our brave captain is determined that he will be the first seaman to travel around the whole globe if he is successful it will bring so many Elizabeth our Queen will gain great pleasure Drake our captain will win honour and wealth we men his crew may have some reward however small

⚓ S C H O L A S T I C
w w w . s c h o l a s t i c . c o . u k

Poem interpretation

Title

_____

Poet

_____

Mood of poem

_____

_____

_____

The images I see

_____

_____

_____

Examples of word play

_____

_____

_____

Double meanings

_____

_____

_____

My feelings about the poem

_____

_____

_____

If

A poem based on 'If' by Rudyard Kipling

If _____

If _____

If _____

If _____

Then you will be fit to play.

If _____

If _____

If _____

If _____

Then you will have the skill.

If _____

If _____

If _____

If _____

Then you will use the tactics.

If _____

If _____

If _____

If _____

Then you will win the game!

Dear Ms Khan

29 Sunrise Road
Earth Grove
Bowford
BW5 NS4

20 March 2006

Councillor B. Khan
Council Office
The Parade
Bowford
BW1 DC2

Dear Ms Khan

I am contacting you as a worried resident of a flat adjacent to Bowford Gardens: I have read of a proposal to install a winter ice rink on the Gardens. I implore you to oppose this at the next council meeting.

I know from your election speeches that you hold strong views about noise pollution, so I know you will appreciate my concern. You must agree that the ice rink would generate a great deal of intrusive noise. Open from early morning until midnight, the rink would interfere with the sleeping habits of many nearby residents. When the Victorian Fayre was held, I lost two hours every night.

Most of us living in this part of Bowford are elderly, of failing health and in need of our sleep. I am on medication for my arthritis and my doctor insists that early nights are essential to me. I am not alone with such health problems.

Nevertheless, I know that there are young people in the town who need a winter activity. However, there are other leisure pursuits: for example, Gaydon Fields for walking and the new cycle pathways.

I read such good reports of your work on behalf of OAPs that I feel confident of your support. You can understand that an ice rink, only suitable for the able-bodied, will offer people of my age no benefits, only potential medical deterioration.

I hope that I can rely on your help. Neither my friends nor I feel we can cope with a noisy winter.
Yours sincerely
Albert Duke

Penguins

Facts:
downy feathers under waterproof feathers; clumsy movements on land; thick layer of fat; fat keeps it warm; graceful swimmer; streamlined shape is good for swimming; is adapted to cold weather; waterproof feathers on outside.

Version 1
The penguin has waterproof feathers. It has a thick layer of fat and this fat keeps it warm. It has clumsy movements on land. It has downy feathers under its waterproof feathers. It is adapted to cold weather. It has a streamlined shape. This is good for swimming.

Version 2 (Improve sentence order.)

Version 3 (Add detail, improve structure and make links.)

Illustration © Garry Davies

Paragraph planning

■ Plan the next six paragraphs in 'Online progress'.

Stage 1: Labels

Stage 2: Details

Stage 3: Opening words

Identify the text type

persuasion   **instructions**

1. Vitamins
There are about 20 different vitamins. They are usually referred to by a letter of the alphabet. Main ones include:
D – this is found in eggs, butter and fish. It can also be obtained from sunlight. Vitamin D keeps bones and teeth strong. Lack of this vitamin can lead to weak bones.
C – Vitamin C is present in ...

2. Condensation takes place when a gas is turned into a liquid. It is an essential part of the water cycle. As water vapour formed during evaporation rises into the air, so the vapour is cooled. As a result, condensation occurs and water is released from the clouds. Once it is released, it falls as rain.

3. I promise you that our kitchens are second to none. Our team do a brilliant job. The fitters leave no mess, so you have no cleaning-up to do. In order not to inconvenience you, we do everything in one day. In order to help you further, we keep our prices low. Come and check out our showroom so that you can see for yourself.

non-chronological report

explanation

4.
1. First mix the fat and sugar together until soft.
2. Next add the eggs one at a time, beating well.
3. Then stir in the flour and chocolate powder with a metal spoon.
4. Stop when there is no trace of powder.
5. Pour the mixture into the cake tin.
6. Leave the filled cake tin to stand for three minutes.
7. Finally, cook the mixture in a hot oven until set.

5. My holiday last year was the best ever. I went with a group of friends on a golfing holiday to the Algarve in Portugal. We played golf on a different course every day: first we played Vale de Cobo; then Sole Viste; and finally Villamoure Rio. We repeated the cycle three times. By the end of nine days, I felt like a professional!

6. Obviously, there are valid points on both side of the debate. The children need a new sports field and Harbour Fields is a large site. On the other hand, the asking price is high so the school cannot afford that field and new computers. A sensible way forward is to search for a cheaper site, in order that the school can have new computers and a new sports field.

recount

discussion

A stressful crossword!

Clues

Across:

2. wine is ....

4.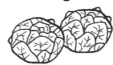

6. a newspaper writer
7. the rules of writing
9. a bony framework
10. sure

Down:

1. a trip away
3. a refreshing citrus drink
5.

8. e is a vowel, f is a ....
9. apart

Unusual people!

My family

My sister is a vaccaphobe,

She won't go in a field.

My Dad has got octophobia

He dreads _____.

My teachers

One teacher takes ambology,

She's always on the move.

Another does finology;

He hates _____.

My friends

Bert has bought a novatele,

The latest remote control;

_____

_____.

Myself

I want to be a monoastra,

The only one on stage;

_____

_____.

vacca – cow
porc – pig
astra – star
nova – new
super – above
        (greater)
photo – light
clude – shut
ambul – walk
geo – earth
tele – far off
graph – to write
hydro/a – water
oct – eight
scope – look
mono – alone
fin – end
graph – to write
scope – look
port – carry
micro – small
port – carry
phobia – fear
graph – write
ology – study
fort – strong
dent – tooth
ped – foot

Mathematics

The lessons in this unit use two types of interactive teaching tool. The first of these is the flipchart. Within some of the flipcharts are the second type of tool, Interactive Teaching Programs (ITPs). ITPs were initially designed by the National Numeracy Strategy (NNS) to support teachers in class who did not have access to interactive whiteboard flipchart programs. They are simple programs that model a small range of objectives, such as data presentation. Their strength is that they are simple and easy to read (all of the programs have a standard blue background enabling children, often boys, who find it hard to distinguish between colours or who find a white screen very bright). The ITPs used in this chapter can be found in Activprimary's Activities explorer (under the heading *KS2 DFES NNS ITP*, along with a complete list of other ITPs developed by the numeracy team. It is not possible to save work from an ITP but if you press the Esc button the ITP will reduce to a window on the computer screen. It can then be enlarged or, usefully, more ITPs can be launched and set up to model further objectives, or simply to extend the objective from that lesson.

Lesson title	Objectives	What children should know	Cross-curricular links
Term 1			
Lesson 1: Equivalent fractions and decimals	• To recognise the equivalence between the decimal and fractions forms.	• Understanding of fractions and decimals.	**Geography** QCA Unit 25 'Geography and numbers'
Lesson 2: Place value of decimal numbers	• To know what each digit represents in a number with up to three decimal places.	• Understanding of place value with whole numbers.	**Geography** PoS (2c) To use maps and plans at a range of scales.
Lesson 3: Multiply by 10, 100 and 1000	• To multiply decimals mentally by 10, 100 and 1000 and explain the effect.	• Understanding of decimals and of multiplying whole numbers by 10, 100 and 1000.	**Geography** PoS (2c) To use maps and plans at a range of scales.
Lesson 4: Simplify fractions	• To reduce a fraction to its simplest form by cancelling common factors.	• Prior knowledge of division, multiplication and fractions.	There are no specific links for this lesson.
Lesson 5: Lying between decimals	• To give a decimal fraction lying between two others, such as 3.4 and 3.5.	• Understanding of decimals.	There are no specific links for this lesson.
Lesson 6: Coordinates	• To read and plot coordinates in all four quadrants.	• Read and plot coordinates in one or two quadrants.	**Geography** QCA Unit 25 'Geography and numbers'
Lesson 7: Percentages (1)	• To understand percentage as the number of parts in every 100.	• Number bonds for 100. • Prior knowledge of addition and subtraction.	There are no specific links for this lesson.

Lesson title	Objectives	What children should know	Cross-curricular links
Lesson 8: Times around the world 💿 🅿	• To appreciate different times around the world.	• Prior knowledge of addition and subtraction. • Read the time on a 24-hour digital clock.	**Geography** QCA Unit 24 'Passport to the world'
Lesson 9: Standard measures 💿 🅿	• To use, read and write standard metric units including their abbreviations and relationships.	• Read numbers in excess of 1000 and know what each digit represents.	**Design and technology** PoS (2d) Measure, mark out, cut and shape a range of materials, and assemble, join and combine components and materials accurately.
Lesson 10: Suitable units of measure 💿 🅿	• To suggest suitable units and measuring equipment to estimate and measure length, mass and capacity.	• Knowledge of different units of measure.	**Design and technology** PoS (2d) Measure, mark out, cut and shape a range of materials, and assemble, join and combine components and materials accurately.
Term 2			
Lesson 11: Finding simple common multiples 💿	• To find simple common multiples.	• Understanding of multiplication.	There are no specific links for this lesson.
Lesson 12: Ordering and rounding decimals 💿	• To order a mixed set of numbers or measurements with up to three decimal places. • To round numbers with two decimal places to the nearest tenth or to the nearest whole number.	• Understanding of decimals. • How to round numbers up or down.	**Geography** PoS (2c) To use maps and plans at a range of scales; QCA Unit 24 'Passport to the world'
Lesson 13: Positive and negative numbers 💿 🅿	• To find the difference between a positive and a negative integer or between two negative integers. • To order a set of positive and negative integers.	• Prior knowledge of addition and subtraction. • Understanding of negative numbers.	**Geography** QCA Unit 15 'The mountain environment'
Lesson 14: Percentages (2) 💿 🅿	• To find simple percentages of small whole number quantities.	• Prior knowledge of multiplication and division. • Number bonds for 100.	**Geography** PoS (2c) To use maps and plans at a range of scales; QCA Unit 24 'Passport to the world'
Lesson 15: Reflection 💿 🅿	• To recognise where a shape will be after reflection: in a mirror line that is touching the shape at a point; in two mirror lines at right angles.	• Understanding of symmetry.	**Design and technology** QCA Unit 6B 'Slippers' **Science** QCA Unit 6F 'How we see things'
Lesson 16: Acute and obtuse 💿 🅿	• To use a protractor to measure and draw acute and obtuse angles to the nearest degree.	• Basic understanding of angles.	There are no specific links for this lesson.
Lesson 17: Rotation 💿 🅿	• To recognise where a shape will be after a rotation through 90° about one of its vertices.	• Understanding of the terms *clockwise* and *anticlockwise*.	**Design and technology** QCA Unit 6C 'Fairground'
Lesson 18: The sum of angles 💿	• Check that the sum of angles of a triangle is 180°.	• Basic understanding of angles. • Prior knowledge of addition and subtraction.	There are no specific links for this lesson.
Lesson 19: Visualising 3D shapes from 2D drawings 💿	• To visualise 3D shapes from 2D drawings. • To identify different nets for a closed cube.	• Understanding of 2D and 3D shapes.	**Design and technology** QCA Unit 6A 'Shelters'

Lesson title	Objectives	What children should know	Cross-curricular links
Lesson 20: Imperial units	• To know imperial units.	• Understanding of different units of measurement. • Prior knowledge of multiplication and division.	**Design and technology** PoS (2d) Measure, mark out, cut and shape a range of materials, and assemble, join and combine components and materials accurately. **Geography** PoS (2c) To use maps and plans at a range of scales.
Term 3			
Lesson 21: Perimeter challenge	• To calculate the perimeter and area of simple compound shapes that can be split into rectangles.	• Prior knowledge of addition and multiplication.	**Geography** PoS (2e) To draw plans and maps at a range of scales.
Lesson 22: Problems with data	• To solve problems by representing, extracting and interpreting data in tables, graphs, charts and diagrams including those generated by a computer.	• How charts can be used and to be able to extract relevant data.	**ICT** QCA Unit 6B 'Spreadsheet modelling'
Lesson 23: Ratio problems	• To solve simple problems involving ratio and proportion.	• Confident in multiplying and dividing up to two-digit numbers including decimals up to two places.	**Design and technology** PoS (1d) to communicate design ideas in different ways.
Lesson 24: Pythagorean numbers	• To use the relationship between multiplication and division.	• All tables up to 10×10. • Good strategies for division.	**History** QCA Unit 15 'How do we use ancient Greek ideas today?'
Lesson 25: Handling data	• To find the mode and range of a set of data. • To begin to find the median and mean of a set of data.	• How to add a sequence of numbers. • How to order a set of numbers from smallest to largest.	**Science** QCA Unit 6A 'Interdependence and adaptation'
Lesson 26: Percentage problems	• To find simple percentages of small whole number quantities (using a calculator).	• Divide by 10, 100. • Multiply by factors of 10.	**Geography** PoS (3d) To explain why places are like they are.
Lesson 27: Triangular numbers	• To identify and use appropriate operations (including combinations of operations) to solve word problems involving numbers and quantities based on *real life*.	• A range of strategies that will enable them to add, subtract, multiply and divide.	**History** QCA Unit 15 'How do we use ancient Greek ideas today?'
Lesson 28: Thales' procedure	• To identify and use appropriate operations (including combinations of operations) to solve word problems involving numbers and quantities based on *real life*.	• Multiply up to 10×10 including up to three decimal places.	**History** QCA Unit 14 'Who were the ancient Greeks?' Unit 15 'How do we use ancient Greek ideas today?'
Lesson 29: Factors	• To factorise numbers to 100.	• Multiply up to 10×10.	**History** QCA Unit 15 'How do we use ancient Greek ideas today?'
Lesson 30: Angles in a triangle	• To calculate angles in a triangle or round a point.	• A semi-circle has 180°.	**History** QCA Unit 15 'How do we use ancient Greek ideas today?'

Equivalent fractions and decimals

Starter
Establish the learning objectives on page 1 of the 'Decimals and fractions' flipchart. Click the button next to Lesson 1 to go to page 2. Working in ability groups, ask the children to think about what the words *decimal* and *fraction* mean.

Invite the groups to share their ideas. Annotate their ideas on the flipchart page. Note that decimals and fractions are linked because they are all worked out from one whole.

Whole-class shared work
● Work through the matching activities on pages 3, 4 and 5 of the flipchart. Discuss how the children can work out the equivalent fractions and decimals.
● Provide the children with individual whiteboards to work out for themselves which fractions and decimals are equivalents.
● Invite the children to swap boards and to share their methods of working out with a partner.
● Place the equivalents next to each other on flipchart pages 3, 4 and 5, discussing how the children worked out each answer. Ask the children to mark their partner's answers.

Independent work
● Keep the children in the ability groups.
● Give each child a copy of the 'Matching decimals and fractions' worksheet, printed on card. (Alternatively, cut out and distribute the relevant sections to the different ability groups.)
● Work with less able learners to complete the top section of the worksheet. Ask them to cut out the selection of fractions and decimals and match them to their equivalents. Help them to work out the solutions on the whiteboard, using page 6 of the flipchart.
● Ask middle-ability groups to complete the top and middle sections of the worksheet. They should cut out the selection of fractions and decimals and match them to their equivalents. All working out should be done on the children's own whiteboards.
● Challenge more able learners to complete all three sections of the worksheet. Invite them to cut out the selection of fractions and decimals and match them to their equivalents. Ask them to use their whiteboards for working out.

Plenary
● Encourage the children to discuss, with their partners, the method they used to check that the fractions and decimals were equivalent.
● Note down the children's ideas on page 7 of the flipchart. Address any misconceptions. Use the *Fractions* Interactive Teaching Program to show fractions, decimals, percentages and ratios alongside each other.
● Pages 8 to 11 can be used to assess the children's understanding of equivalent decimals and fractions.

Place value of decimal numbers

Learning objectives
● To know what each digit represents in a number with up to three decimal places.

Resources ⊙ ℗
'Decimals' flipchart file; individual whiteboards and pens; photocopiable page 89 'Dice template' to create three dice for each group (one dice with the digit positions 10ths, 100ths, and 1000ths (use 1s, 10s, 100s, 10ths, 100ths, and 1000ths for the higher ability groups), and two dice with various numbers with up to three decimal places, differentiated to each group's ability). Page 5 of the flipchart file gives suggestions for the dice template.

Links to other subjects
Geography
PoS (2c) To use maps and plans at a range of scales.
● Test the children's understanding of decimal positions when measuring and recording distances.

Starter
Organise the children into mixed-ability groups. Open the 'Decimals and fractions' flipchart and establish the learning objective. Click on the button next to Lesson 2 to go to page 2. Ask the children to think about decimal numbers and the different features of a decimal number. Thinking of the different parts (hundreds, tens, units, decimal point, tenths, hundredths and thousandths), work with the children to label the number.

Discuss any misunderstandings. Pull down the tab at the top of the page to reveal the different parts of the decimal number.

Whole-class shared work
● Go to page 3. Tell the children that they will be asked a series of questions to identify the position of a digit in a number with up to three decimal places.
● Click on the thumbnail image to start the quiz. There are ten questions for the children to answer.
● Read out the question and the possible answers. Count down from 15 to give the children a time limit to answer each question. Encourage them to answer each question independently before deciding upon a class answer.
● Provide less able learners with a word bank to help with their answers.

Independent work
● Give each child two number dice (which have a variety of differentiated numbers with decimal places) and one digit position dice.
● Display page 4 and ask the children to draw a three-columned table with the headings *Whole number, Digit position* and *Digit.*
● First they need to roll a number dice to get a number with decimal places. They should record this number in the first column of the table. Next, ask them to roll their digit position dice. This position is recorded in the second column. Finally, the children need to work out which digit is in this position in the whole number. For example, if they roll *329.769* on their number dice and *100th* on their digit position dice, then they record *6* in the final column of the table.
● Allow less able learners to work in pairs while the rest of the class work independently. Provide a printout of the annotated page 2 to ensure that they understand the different decimal positions.
● Challenge more able learners by giving them a digital position dice with hundreds, tens and units positions, in addition to the decimal positions (label the sides: *1s, 10s, 100s, 10ths, 100ths* and *1000ths*).

Plenary
● Use the quiz on page 6 to assess the children's understanding of the place value of decimal numbers.
● Again, ask the children to answer each question independently before deciding upon a class answer. Work through as many questions as time allows.
● Check any incorrect answers and discuss any misconceptions that may occur.
● Pages 7 to 10 provide further opportunities to identify the place value of highlighted digits in decimal numbers.

Whiteboard tools
Print out annotated page 2 to provide support in the Independent work.

🖊 Pen tool

🖰 Marquee select tool

🖩 Print button

◉ Activote (optional)

Multiply by 10, 100 and 1000

Learning objectives
● To multiply decimals mentally by 10, 100 and 1000 and explain the effect.

Resources
'Decimals' flipchart file; individual whiteboards; photocopiable page 89 'Dice template' to create three dice for each child: one dice with ×10, ×100, and ×1000 twice (replace one set of numbers with ÷10, ÷100, ÷1000 for more able learners), and two dice with various numbers with up to three decimal places, differentiated to each group's ability; individual whiteboards and pens.

Links to other subjects
Geography
PoS (2c) To use maps and plans at a range of scales.
● Using a map of Great Britain, ask distance questions such as: *If Sheffield is 18 miles from Doncaster, is the distance from Sheffield to Cardiff more likely to be 10, 100 or 1000 times greater?* (Ten times.) *What would the approximate distance be?* (180 miles.)

Starter
Open the 'Decimals' flipchart and click on the button next to Lesson 3 to go to page 11. Click on the link to the *Moving digits* Interactive Teaching Program (ITP) and use it to talk through the place value of each number in a decimal number up to three decimal places. Discuss what happens to the decimal point when the number is multiplied by 10 or 100. Ask the children what would happen if a number were multiplied by 1000.

Whole-class shared work
● Work through the ten questions on pages 12 to 23. The questions provide practice in multiplying numbers with decimals by 10, 100, or 1000.
● Ask the children to work out their answers on individual whiteboards first, and then to share their answers with a partner.
● Invite one child to the whiteboard to drag and drop the lily pads into the correct order, directed by the rest of the class.
● Write the correct answer in the cloud.
● Annotate the place value of the numbers. Encourage the children to explain the effects of multiplying by 10, 100 or 1000.
● Check the answers by moving the frogs at the bottom of the screen.

Independent work
● Give each child two number dice (which have a variety of differentiated numbers with decimal places) and one *multiplier* dice with the numbers ×10, ×100 and ×1000.
● First ask the children to roll a number dice to get a number with decimal places. Next, they must roll their multiplier dice. The children have to calculate and record the results in a number sentence. For example, if they roll 32.019 and ×10, the number sentence is 32.019 × 10 = 320.19.
● Allow less able learners to work in pairs while the rest of the class work independently.
● Challenge more able learners by giving them a *multiplier and divider* dice (see Resources). Alternatively, give them a regular multiplier and challenge them to apply a multiplying action twice to a number. Ask them to explain how the original number has changed.

Plenary
● Go to page 24, and invite the children to offer some of the examples that they used during the Independent work. Which ones did they find particularly difficult?
● Invite individuals to write their difficult number sentences on the flipchart page. Suggest that they use the *Moving digits* ITP to demonstrate what happens to a number when it is multiplied by 10, 100 or 1000.
● Discuss any other difficulties and what methods the children used. Check if their understanding of the vocabulary is secure.
● Assessment questions are provided on page 25 to 27. Ask the children to calculate the answers on their own before deciding upon a class answer. If required, use the *Moving digits* ITP to illustrate the answer.

Whiteboard tools

 Pen tool

 Marquee select tool

 Activote (optional)

Simplify fractions

Learning objectives
● To reduce a fraction to its simplest form by cancelling common factors.

Resources
'Decimals and fractions' flipchart file; photocopiable page 89 'Dice template' to create three dice for each group: on each dice write fractions with the common factors of 2 or 5 (less able), factors of 2, 5, 10, 3 and 4 (middle-ability), a variety of different factors (more able); individual whiteboards and pens, or exercise books for recording.

Links to other subjects
There are no specific links for this lesson.

Starter
Using pages 12 and 13 of the flipchart, ask the children to think about what a fraction is, what is meant by simplest form and what they think a factor is. Encourage them to use vocabulary such as *numerator* and *denominator*. Record their responses on the flipchart page and discuss any misconceptions.

Whole-class shared work
● Go to page 14. This page allows the children to explore what a factor is and how it can be used to cancel fractions down to their simplest form.
● Ask the children what number could be used to divide the numerator and the denominator. (2.) Remind them that this is called the *common factor*.
● Delete the first panel to check the common factor.
● Now ask the children to use this factor to find out how many times it goes into the numerator and denominator. Show the children how to use the common factor to simplify the fraction:
   ● 2 divided by 2 is 1
   ● 4 divided by 2 is 2
   ● so $^1/_2$ is a simplified form of $^2/_4$.
● Delete the panel at the bottom of the page to check the answer.
● Page 15 can be used to reinforce the notion of equivalent fractions. Invite a child to use the Shapes tool ▪● or the Pen tool to colour in $^2/_4$ and $^1/_2$ of the shapes to demonstrate that the two fractions are the same, but that $^1/_2$ is the simplest form.
● Repeat the process for simplifying for the next four fractions on pages 16 to 19.

Independent work
● Give three fraction dice to each group, differentiated to suit the children's abilities (see Resources).
● Ask the children to roll the dice and record the fraction in their books or on individual whiteboards.
● Challenge them to reduce these fractions to their simplest forms.
● Provide support for less able learners, but encourage the rest of the groups to work independently.

Plenary
● Pages 20 and 21 provide further opportunities to identify the simplest form of fractions. Voting methods, such as Activote devices, can be used to decide upon the correct answer. Invite one child to show how the simplest form can be found.
● Go to page 22. Discuss, with the children, how they found the simplest form of a fraction.
● Make a note of any difficulties on the flipchart page and work through the process of simplifying the fraction as a whole class.

Whiteboard tools
Use the Fraction creator tool in the Special tools menu to generate fractions.

🗄 Eraser tool

🗑 Delete button

🢄 Marquee select tool

▪● Shapes tool

▯ Pen tool

✹ Special tools menu

½ Fraction creator tool

◉ Activote (optional)

🔲 **61**

Lying between decimals

Learning objectives
● To give a decimal fraction lying between two others, such as 3.4 and 3.5.

Resources
'Decimals and fractions' flipchart file; photocopiable page 89 'Dice template' to create one decimal dice for each middle- and higher-ability group, and two dice for lower ability groups (on each face, write a decimal number, vary the decimals according to ability: for more able learners use numbers with up to three decimal places).

Links to other subjects
There are no specific links for this lesson.

Starter
Establish the learning objective for the lesson on page 1 of the 'Decimals and fractions' flipchart. Click on the button next to Lesson 5 to go to page 23. Encourage the children to think about what a decimal is. Write their responses on the flipchart page.

   Ask the children to think about what has to happen to the decimal in order to find a decimal fraction that lies between 1.1 and 1.2. Write their responses on the flipchart. Invite children to add one or two examples of decimals to the number line. Address any difficulties.

Whole-class shared work
● Look at the number line on page 24 of the flipchart. Encourage the children to write a number, on their individual whiteboards, that they think will lie between the two given numbers. Invite one child to come to the front to write their response on the number line.
● Ask the children if there are any other numbers that could be used. Invite more volunteers to add their numbers to the number line.
● Challenge the children to add a number between two existing numbers on the number line. Move the numbers along the line to add the new number in the space.
● Examine the place value of the digits in the various numbers. Ask, for example: *Which is closer to 1.1? Is it 1.15 or 1.151? What about 1.149?*
● Continue in this manner for the next five number lines on pages 25 to 29.

Independent work
● Give each group a decimal dice. Ask them to draw a three-columned table in their books, or on individual whiteboards, with the headings *Lowest number, Middle number* and *Highest number*.
● First ask the children to roll the decimal dice and to record the number in the *Lowest number* column of their table. They then need to add 0.1 to this number and record the result in the *Highest number* column.
● Next, in the middle column of the table, ask the children to write a number that lies in between the two decimal numbers.
● Allow less able learners to work in pairs while the rest of the class work independently. Give them two dice and encourage them to write a decimal number that lies between the two different numbers. Support them in identifying which is the higher and lower number.
● Challenge more able learners by giving them a dice with harder decimals. Suggest that they also think of three different middle numbers instead of one.

Plenary
● Use pages 30 and 31 to identify the correct position of a decimal fraction between two numbers. Erase the black line to reveal the answer.
● Encourage the children to think of questions from the Independent work where they had difficulties.
● Work through these as a whole group, addressing any misconceptions that the children have. Use page 32 to make notes.

Whiteboard tools
Change handwriting to text with the Recognition tool, found in the Special tools menu.

 Eraser tool

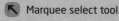 Pen tool

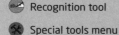 Marquee select tool

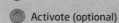 Recognition tool

Special tools menu

Activote (optional)

Coordinates

Learning objectives
● To read and plot coordinates in all four quadrants.

Resources 💿 🅿
'Coordinates' flipchart file; photocopiable page 90 'Plotting coordinates'; prepared 'Plotting coordinates' grids with questions masked (core groups only).

Links to other subjects
Geography
QCA Unit 25 'Geography and numbers'
● Ask the children to locate specific sites using simple coordinates, such as places of interest, a park and so on.

Starter
Go to page 2 of the flipchart and encourage the children to answer the questions: *What is a coordinate? What is a quadrant?* Write their responses onto the flipchart.

Use the *Coordinates* Interactive Teaching Program to demonstrate coordinates to the children. Move the marker around the grid and tell the children to pay attention to how the coordinate changes.

Whole-class shared work
● Using the diagram on page 3 of the flipchart, discuss the four quadrants. Think of a way for the children to remember how to use the x axis before the y axis (for example: *along the corridor and up or down the stairs*).
● Work through pages 3 to 10 of the flipchart, encouraging the children to place the items on the correct coordinates.
● Prompt them with suitable probing questions. For example: *In which quadrant is the comet?* or *How would the coordinate change if we moved the object two places down?*
● Consider what would happen if you read the coordinates the wrong way round.

Independent work
● Give each child a copy of the 'Plotting coordinates' worksheet (photocopiable page 90) and ask them to follow the instructions on the sheet.
● Provide support for less confident children.
● After working through the questions, give each child a blank grid (photocopy the worksheet with the questions blocked out).
● Arrange for the children to work in pairs and challenge them to plot six crosses on their grid without their partner seeing. They should then take turns to guess their partner's coordinates.
● As an extra challenge, invite some children to present their coordinates to the whole class using the blank grid on page 11 of the flipchart.

Plenary
● Go to page 12 and invite the children to answer the questions that were posed at the beginning of the session: *What is a coordinate? Which coordinate comes first in the sequence?*
● Discuss any misconceptions during this section and work out any difficult areas on the board.
● Use pages 13 to 16 to assess the children's understanding of coordinates and quadrants.

Whiteboard tools
Double-click on an object and select Duplicate in the Object edit toolbox to create multiple copies. Select Page reset in the Teacher tools menu to return the page to its last unsaved state.

🖊 Pen tool

🔦 Marquee select tool

🖽 Duplicate function

🔄 Page reset button

◎ Activote (optional)

Percentages (1)

Learning objectives
● To understand percentage as the number of parts in every 100.

Resources
'Percentages' flipchart file; individual whiteboard and pens; photocopiable page 91 'Percentages' for each child.

Links to other subjects
There are no specific links for this lesson.

Starter
Organise the children into mixed-ability groups. Ask them to think about and discuss what a percentage is. Add their suggestions to page 2 of the flipchart. If necessary, reveal the definition on the board (percentage is the number of parts in every 100) and discuss what it means.

Make a link to your work on number bonds to 100. Identify one number and ask the children to write the number bond needed to make 100 on their individual whiteboards. Repeat for two or three examples and write these on the flipchart as a prompt.

Whole-class shared work
● Read out the question on page 3 of the flipchart. Ask the children to vote on the correct percentage using Activote devices or by writing on their whiteboards.
● Erase the red rectangle to reveal the correct percentage. (35%)
● Work through pages 4 to 9 of the flipchart in the same way as above.
● For each question, encourage the children to look at how many parts of 100 have been bought, caught and so on, and from this find the correct percentage or the percentage remaining.
● If necessary, annotate methods of working out on the flipchart page.
● If Activote is not used, make sure that all answers are recorded on individual whiteboards. Identify any common misconceptions ready to discuss during Independent work and the Plenary.

Independent work
● Give each child a copy of the 'Percentages' photocopiable sheet and ask them to work through questions 1-8.
● Provide support for less confident children, as they work through questions 1-4 initially.
● Challenge more confident children to complete questions 9-12 of the worksheet.
● As an additional challenge, ask the children to write their own percentages questions for a partner to answer.

Plenary
● Invite those children who made up some percentages questions (as an extension) to pose them for the whole class to solve.
● Write some of the children's questions on page 10 of the flipchart and use them as starters in subsequent sessions.
● Discuss any difficulties that the children experienced with the worksheet and highlight any common misconceptions.

Whiteboard tools
🗄 Eraser tool

✏ Pen tool

🔍 Marquee select tool

◎ Activote (optional)

Times around the world

Learning objectives
● To appreciate different times around the world.

Resources ◉ 🅿
'Times around the world' flipchart file; paper and pens; sugar paper; individual whiteboards and pens; photocopiable page 92 'World time' for each child; maps or atlases.

Links to other subjects
Geography
QCA Unit 24 'Passport to the world'
● Use information about world time zones to approximate the location of different places in the world. For example, if New York is five hours behind London, then it is most likely to be west of London.

Whiteboard tools
Use the Clock tool in analogue and digital format to establish that children can read the time to the minute on a 24-hour digital clock. Use the Clock tool's Count up option to assist less able learners in working out time difference.

🕐 Clock tool

📟 Count up tool

✏ Pen tool

🔦 Marquee select tool

◉ Activote (optional)

Starter
Go to page 2 of the flipchart and encourage the children to answer the questions. Establish that they can all read the time to the minute on a 24-hour digital clock.
Ask: *Why would different countries have different time zones?* Tell the children to work in small groups and write their thoughts on sugar paper.
Invite one member from each group to explain their group's answers to the rest of the group.
Go to page 3 to show an example of a map that indicates time zones around the world. The red line is the Greenwich meridian line, which is a line of longitude.

Whole-class shared work
● Read out the question on page 4 of the flipchart. Ask the children to vote on the correct time using Activote devices or by writing on individual whiteboards.
● Reveal the answer by moving the flag.
● Provide access to clocks to support less able learners.
● Work through pages 5 to 16. Ask the children to work independently at their tables using their individual whiteboards.
● Annotate methods of working out on the flipchart page and encourage the children to share their methods, before moving the flags to reveal the answers.

Independent work
● Give each child a copy of photocopiable page 92 'World Time' and ask them to work on questions 1–8 initially. (This sheet might also be set as homework.)
● Work with less confident children on questions 1–4 of the worksheet. Allow them to use the Clock tool's Count up option as a device for counting on.
● Challenge more confident children to answer questions 9–12 of the worksheet.
● As an additional challenge, ask the children to prepare their own time zone questions for a partner to answer.

Plenary
● Invite the children to read out some of their time zone questions for the whole class to solve.
● Write some of these on page 17 of the flipchart and use as starter activities for subsequent lessons.
● Discuss any difficulties that the children experienced with the worksheet and highlight any common misconceptions.
● Pages 18 to 21 provide further time zone problems which can be used to assess the children's understanding of times around the world.

Learning objectives
● To use, read and write standard metric units including their abbreviations and relationships.

Resources ● P
'Measurements' flipchart file; photocopiable page 93 'Standard metric units'; a range of objects to measure length, mass and capacity (such as lengths of rope, parcels, non-standard containers filled with water); measuring equipment; individual whiteboards and pens; paper and pens.

Links to other subjects
Design and technology
PoS (2d) Measure, mark out, cut and shape a range of materials, and assemble, join and combine components and materials accurately.
● As the children measure materials for design and technology projects, encourage them to consider the units of measurements and their relationships to other units. For example, 35mm is equivalent to 3.5cm.

Standard measures

Starter
Encourage the children to work in mixed-ability groups. Provide them with paper and pens and invite them to think of the different units of measure for capacity, length and mass, with their abbreviations.
Come back together as a whole class. Using the Fill tool ●, reveal the units for capacity, mass and length by selecting a dark colour to fill the first column of the tables on pages 2 and 3. Repeat in the second column to reveal each of the abbreviations.
Ask the children to think about the relationships between the units of measurement for length, for example. Encourage them to suggest equivalent values by asking questions such as: *How may millimetres make a centimetre?* Fill the third column of each table to reveal a selection of equivalent values.

Whole-class shared work
● Go to page 4 and ask the children: *What is the standard metric unit for temperature? What is its abbreviation?* Encourage the children to record their answers on individual whiteboards before revealing the answers on the screen.
● Remind them of previous science work on changing states of water and ask them: *What is the boiling point for water?* Again, encourage the children to record their responses before revealing the answer.
● Go to page 5 of the flipchart and click on the Interactive Teaching Programs. Explore mass, capacity, length and temperature in turn.
● Set different measures and scales using the buttons on the screen. Ask the children to identify each measure and scale, and to predict the effect of adding or subtracting mass, volume and so on. Experiment with different scales.
● Encourage the children to work in pairs in order to check answers.
● Model the range of equipment available for the children to use in the Independent work. Leave the completed unit and abbreviation charts on the whiteboard for reference.

Independent work
● Set up a carousel of tables with one table for each of the following:
  ● measuring length using rulers, tape measures and metre sticks
  ● measuring mass using kitchen scales and bathroom scales
  ● measuring capacity using measuring jugs.
● Using photocopiable page 93 'Standard metric units' ask the children to explore the range of equipment set out on the tables. They should write down the object to be measured, the unit to measure it in and the actual measurement.
● Rotate the groups around the tables, spending about ten minutes per table.

Plenary
● Work through any misconceptions and difficulties that the children have had, or that you have observed.
● If time is available, work through a selection of assessment pages. Use pages 6 to 12 to read measurements for volume; pages 13 to 15 to read measurements for mass; pages 16 to 19 to read measurements for length.
● Ask the children to suggest suitable units of measurement and their abbreviations. They should write each one on their whiteboards.
● These pages can also be used as starter activities in subsequent lessons.

Whiteboard tools
Use the Fill tool to reveal the units of measurement and abbreviations.

● Fill tool

● Eraser tool

● Pen tool

● Marquee select tool

Suitable units of measure

Learning objectives
- To suggest suitable units and measuring equipment to estimate and measure length, mass and capacity.

Resources
'Measurements' flipchart file; measuring equipment such as rulers, tapes (length), scales, spring balances (mass), measuring cylinders (capacity); small items to measure; photocopiable page 94 'Suitable units of measurement' (one per group).

Links to other subjects
Design and technology
PoS (2d) Measure, mark out, cut and shape a range of materials, and assemble, join and combine components and materials accurately.
- As the children measure materials for design and technology projects, encourage them to consider suitable units of measurements. For example, it is better to measure in millimetres or centimetres for models and to think in terms of metres for larger-scale structures.

Whiteboard tools
Use the Eraser tool to reveal suitable units of measurement. Extend the Maths word bank folder in the Resource library to capture all of the measures and measuring equipment referred to in this lesson (optional).

 Marquee select tool

 Pen tool

 Eraser tool

 Resource Library

 Activote (optional)

Starter
Go to page 20 of the flipchart and match the appropriate equipment to the object to be measured, for example the measuring jug or thermometer can be used for the milk bottle. Encourage the children to give clear reasons for each of their choices.

Discuss the importance of using the correct equipment for measuring. Prompt the children to consider what would happen if the correct equipment was not used. Ask: *What would you use to measure the weight of a paper clip? Could you use bathroom scales? What would you use to measure the thickness of a paper clip? Could you use a ruler with no markings for millimetres?*

Whole-class shared work
- Remind the children about the work in the previous lesson on units of measurement. Explore the terms *length, mass* and *capacity*.
- Go to page 21. Using individual whiteboards, ask the children to write a list of suitable units of measurement for each measure in turn. Invite them to tell you their ideas (including imperial measures) and reveal them on pages 21 to 23 as they are identified.
- Repeat the process, this time asking for ideas on the equipment needed to carry out measurements accurately for each measure. Circle the correct items as the children tell you their ideas.
- Introduce the different objects arranged on the tables (see Resources). Pose the questions: *What measuring equipment is available? What would you use the equipment to measure?*
- Challenge the children to place the objects into three piles: length, mass and capacity.

Independent work
- Give the children, in pairs, time to access the length, mass and capacity tables. Ask them to make notes on the 'Suitable units of measurement' recording sheet (page 94), noting object, estimate and measurement.
- Support less confident children by allowing them to access the words on pages 21 to 23 of the flipchart.
- Challenge the more confident pairs to measure the objects again, this time using imperial measures, if appropriate. (You will need to provide suitable measuring equipment for this.)

Plenary
- Encourage the children to feed back their findings on page 24 of the flipchart.
- Scribe this feedback onto the prepared grid and prompt for any alternative measurements or equipment used. Address any common misconceptions and review the full range of measures and equipment used.
- Use pages 25 to 28 to assess the children's understanding of suitable units of measurement.

Learning objectives
● To find simple common multiples.

Resources
'Multiples' flipchart file; individual whiteboards and pens; five-sided spinners (with the digits 2, 3, 4, 5 and 10); eight-sided dice or spinners (with the digits 2, 3, 4, 5, 6, 7, 8 and 10); 11-sided dice or spinners (with the digits 2-12).

Links to other subjects
There are no specific links for this lesson.

Finding simple common multiples

Starter
Ask the children for the definition of a *multiple*. Write suggestions on the board and if necessary reveal the prepared definition on page 2 of the flipchart. Discuss any misconceptions at this stage.

Roll two dice using the Dice tool 🎲. Ask the children to put the numbers together in either order (for example, dice rolls 3 and 2 = 32). They should write any multiples of that number on paper or on individual whiteboards.

Review the multiples and then repeat up to three times. Ask: *Did we make any numbers that had no factors?* (For example, 11.) *What are these numbers called?* (Prime numbers.)

Whole-class shared work
● Use Activote devices (or individual whiteboards if you do not have access to this facility) to identify multiples on pages 3 to 12. The children have a choice of four answers (a, b, c, and d). They must click on the number that is a multiple of the number given at the top of the page.
● Allow 15 seconds to answer each question. (It is possible to monitor this using Activote devices. You might also wish to allow the children to view their progress).
● As an alternative, ask the children to vote on each answer by putting their hand up or by writing on their whiteboards. Use the Highlighter tool to highlight each correct answer.
● For each question, ask the children to identify the other number that is required to make the multiple.

Independent work
● Show the children page 13 of the flipchart. Provide them, in groups, with a selection of dice or spinners.
● In their groups, the children use an eight-sided dice or spinner with the digits 2, 3, 4, 5, 6, 7, 8 and 10. Ask them to write the first five multiples for the number they have landed on.
● As a variation, ask them to play as above but to roll the dice/spinner a second time. For example, if a 5 is rolled, the children must start from the fifth multiple of the first number rolled. Ask the children to record the starting numbers and the five multiples on paper.
● For less able learners, limit the activity to a five-sided spinner with the numbers 2, 3, 4, 5 and 10. Again, ask the children to spin the spinner and write the first five multiples for the number they have spun.
● Provide more able learners with an 11-sided spinner with the same numbers as above, plus 9, 11 and 12.

Plenary
● Review the Independent work, focussing on any particular areas of difficulty (review Activote feedback where available). Notes can be made on page 14.
● If time is available, roll two or four dice. Invite the children to put two or more numbers together and write any multiples of that number on whiteboards. Alternatively, they could add or subtract numbers to make their starting numbers for this activity.
● Additional multiples questions for consolidating this work have been given on pages 15 to 24 of the flipchart.

Whiteboard tools
Use the Dice tool in the Special tools menu to generate multiples for the Starter and Plenary activities.

🔲 Marquee select tool

✏ Pen tool

🎲 Dice tool

🖍 Highlighter tool

◎ Activote (optional)

Learning objectives
● To order a mixed set of numbers or measurements with up to three decimal places.
● To round numbers with two decimal places to the nearest tenth or to the nearest whole number.

Resources
'Ordering numbers' flipchart file; individual whiteboards and pens. Prepare some sets of cards to order by tenths, hundredths and thousandths.

Links to other subjects
Geography
PoS (2c) To use maps and plans at a range of scales; QCA Unit 24 'Passport to the world'
● Ask the children to approximate distances between places around the world and to compare and order distances. For example, they can investigate foods that have to travel the furthest to reach their local area.

Whiteboard tools
 Eraser tool

 Pen tool

 Marquee select tool

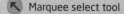Highlighter tool

Delete button

Ordering and rounding decimals

Starter
Go to page 2 of the flipchart and ask the children to round 23.341 to the nearest tenth. Ask them to write the answer on individual whiteboards and then hold them up to show you. If any children have got an incorrect answer, repeat the question and emphasise that you are asking them to round to the nearest tenth. Reveal the answer.

Now ask the children how they would round the next number: 43.461. Show the children the hint if necessary: *We round up if the number is half way between two tenths.* Round up or down the other numbers on page 2. Invite the children to show their answers before checking the answer on screen.

If the children continue to struggle, work with them showing the relative position of the numbers in a simple number line on page 3.

Whole-class shared work
● Discuss the place value of decimals. Ask: *What makes one decimal number larger than another?*
● Go to page 4 of the flipchart. Look at the three numbers and ask the children to rearrange them and write them in the correct order on their individual whiteboards. Ask them to hold up their boards when they have finished.
● Check the children's answers, note any misconceptions and reveal the correct answer, by erasing the panel at the bottom of the page.
● If the children struggle to place the numbers in the correct order, highlight the place value of digits in the numbers.
● Repeat with pages 5 to 10.
● To vary the activity, ask one child to use the Marquee select tool to drag the clouds on the flipchart into the correct number order.
● The other children should write *correct* or *incorrect* on their whiteboards and hold them up. Ask a child holding *incorrect* to come to the board to explain why.
● Check the answers at the bottom of each page.

Independent work
● Give each group a set of number cards and ask them to arrange them in ascending or descending order. Numbers should include different tenths, for example: 24.123, 24.234, 24.345; or hundredths, for example: 24.123, 24.134, 24.145.
● Ask the children to swap sets of cards at regular intervals.
● Limit less confident children to sets in which only the tenths are different (such as: 24.123, 24.223, 24.323).
● Extend more confident children by mixing sets with tenths, hundredths and thousandths. Include some sets with measurements on them.

Plenary
● Discuss any difficulties that have arisen with the Independent work.
● Work through these difficulties as a class, encouraging the children to think of ways to overcome them.
● Finish by going to page 11 of the flipchart to discuss rounding up or down. This will reinforce the work done in the Starter.

Positive and negative numbers

Learning objectives
● To find the difference between a positive and a negative integer or between two negative integers.
● To order a set of positive and negative integers.

Resources 💿 🅿
'Ordering numbers' flipchart file; individual whiteboards and pens; exercise books. Prepare some dice using photocopiable page 89 'Dice template' (see Independent work).

Links to other subjects
Geography
QCA Unit 15 'The mountain environment'
● Ask the children to investigate and compare temperatures at mountain summits and the surrounding areas.

Starter
Show the children the thermometer on page 12 of the 'Ordering numbers' flipchart. Invite individuals to come to the board to identify points on the thermometer such as *negative 3 degrees*, by dragging the temperature gauge.

Discuss the vocabulary used to identify differences in temperature and write the words around the thermometer. (For example: *above zero, below zero, integer, positive, negative, minus.*)

Focus on the order of the numbers on the thermometer and, if necessary, draw a separate number line underneath the thermometer to highlight the position of each integer.

Whole-class shared work
● Work through pages 13 to 20 with the children. Invite individual children to come to the board to move the balloons on these pages into the correct order. Alternatively, ask the children to write the correct order on their individual whiteboards.
● Reveal the correct order on each page.
● Remind the children of the position of the numbers on the thermometer in the Starter activity. Show the thermometer on page 21 and point out the difference between two temperatures. Use the number line to work out the difference.
● Work through pages 22 to 27. Ask the children to look at the two numbers on each page and find the difference between each pair.
● Invite individual children to write their answers on the flipchart using the number line for assistance. Use the Eraser tool to reveal the answers.
● Encourage the children to pay attention as to whether the number is positive or negative.

Independent work
● Arrange the children into small groups and use the blank dice template on photocopiable page 89 to give each group a dice with numbers in the range of –25 to +25.
● Invite the children to take turns to roll the dice and then write the difference between the two numbers using blank number lines in their exercise books.
● Provide less confident children with dice with numbers in the range of –15 to +15.
● Provide more confident children with dice with numbers in the range of –35 to +35.

Plenary
● Discuss the methods that the children used, including their difficulties and what they found easy. Note these on page 28 of the flipchart. Encourage the children to think about how they can overcome their difficulties.
● Use pages 29 and 30 to reinforce ordering positive and negative numbers.
● Use pages 31 to 37 to identify missing numbers on a number line showing particular positive and negative numbers.

Whiteboard tools
Convert handwriting to text with the Recognition tool.

🖊 Pen tool

🖰 Marquee select tool

🗑 Eraser tool

🔤 Recognition tool

🎦 Activote (optional)

Percentages (2)

Starter
Remind the children of previous work done on finding percentages. Talk together about the link with fractions and work through the example on page 11 of the 'Percentages' flipchart: The children need to calculate 50% of 36. Establish that 50% of 36 is the same as $1/2$ of 36, so dividing 36 by two will give us 50% (18).

Show page 12 of the flipchart. Remind children that a percentage is the number of parts in every 100. Relate this to fractions and the problem on page 11: 50% is the same as $50/100$, which can be simplified to $1/2$. The common factor of $50/100$ is 50.

Provide individual whiteboards and ask the children to write a list of common factors for given simple numbers such as 12, 15, 100 and so on.

Whole-class shared work
● Challenge the children to work through the questions found on pages 13 to 22.
● Encourage the children to work together on each question, comparing methods of working out each answer.
● Invite individual children to come to the whiteboard to show their workings out. Ask if anyone had a different way of finding the answer. Invite other children to show the way they worked out the answer.
● Use the Eraser tool to check the answers at the bottom of the page.

Independent work
● Give each child a copy of photocopiable page 95 'Percentages of numbers'. Ask the children to work through the questions 1-10 initially. These questions contain answers of 10%, 50%, 20% and 25%.
● Limit less confident children to questions 1-5 initially. These questions contain answers of either 10% or 50%.
● Challenge more confident children to tackle questions 11-15 where the answers are either 40% or 75%.
● As an additional challenge, ask children to make up their own percentages questions for a partner.

Plenary
● Encourage the children to state what they found difficult and what methods they used. Note these on page 22 of the flipchart.
● Work through any difficulties as a whole class encouraging contributions from all the children.

Reflection

Learning objectives
● To recognise where a shape will be after reflection: in a mirror line that is touching the shape at a point; in two mirror lines at right angles.

Resources
'Shapes' flipchart file; photocopiable page 96 'Reflection'; small mirrors; tracing paper and pens.

Links to other subjects
Design and technology
QCA Unit 6B 'Slippers'
● Encourage the children to design slippers with a reflected pattern, where one shoe is the reflection of the other.
Science
QCA Unit 6F 'How we see things'
● Relate the children's knowledge of reflection to how they see things in mirrors. Discuss why, for instance, some emergency vehicles have signs written in reverse at the front.

Starter
Explain to the children that they will be reflecting shapes in mirror lines but without the use of a grid. Stress that the reflected shape must be identical to the original, and that the distance of the shape from the mirror should stay the same.

Discuss the meaning of the word *congruent* (shapes that are identical in shape and size). Show page 2 of the flipchart and ask where the shape at the bottom of the page should be positioned to show the correct reflection. Ask the children for advice. Can they explain their reasons for positioning the shape?

Whole-class shared work
● Work with the children to complete the activities on pages 3 to 8. Ask them to consider where each shape would be after being reflected in a mirror line.
● Invite individuals to either move or select the shape or object to the agreed position.
● Pause before revealing each shape in its correct position to give the children time to talk about the position with a partner.
● If any guesses were inaccurate, cover the shape with the rectangle and ask another child to try again.

Independent work
● Provide each child with a copy of photocopiable page 96 'Reflection'.
● Provide mirrors to support the children with the activity and, if time is available, ask them to draw their own reflected shapes at the bottom of the page. Encourage them to use shapes of objects from around the room.
● Provide less able learners with some additional adult support. Go through examples in the flipchart or prepare some new examples using the Shapes tool 🔷.
● Suggest that more able learners complete the activity in pairs, with their partners checking the reflections using a mirror. Provide some extra paper and encourage them to draw some more of their own reflected shapes. Challenge them to try examples where the shapes are not parallel or perpendicular to the mirror line.

Plenary
● Ask the children to show their work to a partner. Invite them to put a positive comment about their partner's work on the sheet and one comment for improvement.
● Display page 9 of the flipchart, and encourage the children to consider the two questions: *What is reflection? What difficulties did you have with finding the reflection?* Invite them to give their answers to the class and annotate the page accordingly. Address any misconceptions.
● Use pages 10 to 13 to assess the children's understanding of reflection.

Whiteboard tools
Use the Marquee select tool to move and rotate the shapes to demonstrate the reflections.

🖊 Pen tool

🔲 Rotate function

🔦 Marquee select tool

🔷 Shapes tool

🔘 Activote (optional)

Learning objectives
● To use a protractor to measure and draw acute and obtuse angles to the nearest degree.

Resources
'Angles' flipchart file; photocopiable page 97 'Acute and obtuse'; protractors; pencils; rulers.

Links to other subjects
There are no specific links for this lesson.

Acute and obtuse

Starter
Show the children the angle on page 2 of the 'Angles' flipchart. Ask them whether they think it is an acute or obtuse angle. Ask individual children for definitions of each type of angle. Prompt them if necessary, pulling out the prepared definitions on the flipchart.

Establish with the whole class that the angle is acute. Ask: *How could we prove this is an acute angle?* Introduce the Protractor tool ⊜ on the whiteboard and ensure that the children know how to use it.

Whole-class shared work
● Work through the angles on pages 3 to 10 together. Challenge the children to make an educated guess as to whether each angle is *acute* or *obtuse*.
● Voting methods, such as Activote devices, could be used to decide upon the correct answer.
● Invite individual volunteers to come to the board to check each angle using the Protractor tool. Use the Marquee select tool to rotate the angle, if required.
● Write the measurement at the bottom of the screen.

Independent work
● Give each child a copy of photocopiable page 97 'Acute and obtuse'.
● Encourage the children to use protractors to draw the angles as given on the sheet, and to state whether they are acute or obtuse.
● On the back of the sheet, ask the children to use the protractor to draw three acute and three obtuse angles, giving the measurement of the angles to the nearest degree.
● Support less confident children in their use of the protractor to measure and draw.
● If appropriate, challenge more confident children to draw and measure reflex angles.

Plenary
● Share the results of the measuring activities with the whole class. Congratulate the children on their successes and discuss any points for development.
● Use page 11 of the flipchart to address any difficulties and, if necessary, revise the process of drawing and measuring angles using a protractor on the whiteboard.

Whiteboard tools
Use the Protractor tool from the Special tools menu to measure angles.

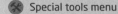 Special tools menu

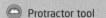 Protractor tool

🖊 Pen tool

�K Marquee select tool

🗄 Eraser tool

◎ Activote (optional)

Rotation

Starter
Explain that the purpose of the lesson is to investigate rotating simple shapes through 90°. Discuss the meaning of the word *rotate* and write any definitions on page 14. If necessary, reveal the prepared definition for rotation.

Invite the children to demonstrate rotation using the shape on page 15. Ask the class to shout *stop* when the shape has been rotated through 90°. Ensure that the children understand the words *clockwise* and *anticlockwise* to further describe the rotation.

Whole-class shared work
● Show the children the starting shape on page 16.
● Explain that you would like them to correctly identify the shape that has been rotated through 90° clockwise. They can do this either by drawing the rotated shapes on their whiteboards or by voting.
● Once the children have all given an answer, click on the most popular selection. You will hear either a cheer for a correct answer or a groan for an incorrect answer.
● Discuss what the shape would look like if it had been rotated:
  ● another 90°
  ● in the opposite direction.
● Repeat for the examples on pages 17 to 20.

Independent work
● Give each child a copy of photocopiable page 98 'Rotation'.
● Ask all the children to draw the rotation of the first two shapes.
● Next, ask the children to find shapes around the classroom or on the whiteboard and challenge them to draw them in the boxes provided and then to draw their rotation through 90°. Can they draw the rotations through 90° clockwise and anticlockwise?
● Support less able learners with the first two shapes and if necessary demonstrate the rotation of these shapes on the whiteboard.
● Challenge more able learners to find more complex 2D shapes to rotate. Are they able to rotate the shapes by 180°?

Plenary
● Review the 'Rotation' activity with the whole class and focus upon the shapes that the children drew.
● Invite one or two children to come to the board to draw their shapes and their rotations. They may find the Pen tool's Point-to-point option 💠 helpful.
● Consolidate the work on rotation by asking individual children to come to the board to rotate one of the four shapes on page 21 through 90° (clockwise or anticlockwise).
● Encourage the whole class to vote whether the rotation is correct or incorrect and ask other children to present alternatives where necessary.

Learning objectives
● Check that the sum of angles of a triangle is 180°.

Resources
'Angles' flipchart file; individual whiteboards and pens; different-shaped triangles made from sugar paper or card; supply of thick paper or card, protractors.

Links to other subjects
There are no specific links for this lesson.

The sum of angles

Starter
Show the children the question on page 12 of the 'Angles' flipchart. Remind them of the work done in Lesson 17 (page 74) on rotating angles through 90°. Ask: *What is a 90° angle called?* (A right angle.) Remind the children also that a straight line is made up of two right angles (180°).

Reveal the isosceles triangle beneath the red rectangle. Look at the diagram on the right-hand side to illustrate how the angles add up to 180°. Use the Protractor tool 🌐 to verify how the angles add up to 180°. Provide a selection of different-shaped triangles and protractors and allow the children some time to explore them. Do they all add up to 180°?

Whole-class shared work
● Go to page 13. Invite the children, in pairs, to work out the missing angle. Ask them to write the answer on their individual whiteboards and display them when you ask them to.
● Check the angle using the Protractor tool. Delete the panel to reveal the correct answer to confirm the children's solutions.
● Work through the other exercises on finding missing angles on pages 14 to 19 in the same way.

Independent work
● Ask the children, in pairs, to make their own large triangles from thick paper or card. Challenge them to measure each angle using a protractor.
● Give less confident children plenty of practice in using the protractor and, if necessary, work with them on the calculations required to find the angles of a triangle. For example, if two of the angles in a triangle are 100° and 50°, the third angle will be 180° – 150° = 30°.
● Challenge more confident children to experiment with a range of different triangles to prove that the same result is always produced. For a further challenge ask them to investigate whether the four angles in a quadrilateral always total 360°.

Plenary
● Encourage the children to share their work with the class. They could use the Shapes 🔵 or Lines tool 🔲 to demonstrate their own triangles on the whiteboard.
● Address any common misconceptions about angles in a triangle or difficulties in measuring angles using a protractor, and write these on page 20.

Whiteboard tools
Use the Protractor tool in the Special tools menu to measure angles on-screen.

🌐 Protractor tool

▤ Eraser tool

🔵 Shapes tool

🔲 Lines tool

◥ Marquee select tool

🗑 Delete button

Visualising 3D shapes from 2D drawings

Learning objectives
● To visualise 3D shapes from 2D drawings.
● To identify different nets for a closed cube.

Resources 💿
'Shapes' flipchart file; models of 3D shapes (including a cube and cuboid); *real life* examples of 3D shapes (such as cereal boxes, drinks cans and balls); interlocking cubes.

Links to other subjects
Design and technology
QCA Unit 6A 'Shelters'
● Encourage the children to visualise their model as they develop their shelter designs.

Starter

Start the lesson by asking the children to complete the 3D shapes labelling activity on page 22 of the 'Shapes' flipchart. Distribute 3D examples of the shapes around the class. In groups, ask the children whether these look different from the 3D images on the flipchart page. Ask questions such as: *How many faces does your 3D shape have? Can you tell this from the 2D drawing? How many vertices? What shape are the faces? Which shapes are regular polyhedra?* And so on.

Whole-class shared work

● Show the children the arrangement of cubes on page 23 and explain that this shows two different views of the same object. Do the children think it is difficult or easy to tell that they show the same object?
● Give the children, in groups, a set of interlocking cubes and ask them to make the shapes shown on page 23. Ask: *Can you see all of the cubes? How many cubes do you need to use?*
● Ask the children to hold up their shape when it is complete. Establish how many cubes were used to make the shape.
● Go to page 24 and ask the children to use their cubes to make the model shown on-screen.
● Ask the children to draw a similar diagram of their model from a different viewpoint and invite them to share their drawings.

Independent work

● Give the children a choice of two different activities:
  ● Ask them to construct their own models using interlocking cubes, then to draw them on grid paper. Challenge more confident children to draw different views of the same model.
  ● Challenge the children to investigate and draw all of the nets of a closed cube. Remind them of work they will have done previously, involving nets of an open cube. Show the children one or two examples on page 25 to start them off. Provide less confident children with cardboard boxes to demonstrate nets.

Plenary

● Review all of the children's work. If time is available, construct one or two of their examples on the whiteboard. Use page 26 to construct a 2D diagram of a model and page 27 to construct nets.
● Highlight any examples where it is not clear how many cubes were used to make a shape and ask: *Are there any cubes we cannot see?*
● Establish that there are eleven different nets of a closed cube.
● Invite volunteers to show their work and reveal the eleven different nets on page 28.
● Use pages 29 and 30 to assess the children's understanding of nets.

Whiteboard tools
Double-click on an object and select Duplicate in the Object edit toolbox to create multiple copies. Select Page reset in the Teacher tools menu to return the page to its last unsaved state.

🖊 Pen tool

🔺 Marquee select tool

🔳 Duplicate function

🔄 Page reset button

Imperial units

Learning objectives
● To know imperial units and to know rough equivalents of lb and kg, oz and g, miles and km, litres and points or gallons.

Resources
'Measurements' flipchart file; equipment for some practical measuring activities (see Independent work); sugar paper; pens.

Links to other subjects
Design and technology
PoS (2d) Measure, mark out, cut and shape a range of materials, and assemble, join and combine components and materials accurately.
● Convert imperial measurements into metric units of measurement.
Geography
PoS (2c) To use maps and plans at a range of scales.
● Many distances are still calculated in miles; ask the children to convert miles to kilometres. Which do they prefer? Why do they think many people still measure distances in terms of miles?

Whiteboard tools
Use the Sound recorder to record some rhymes about imperial to metric conversion.

🖊 Pen tool

🔊 Sound recorder (optional)

🅺 Marquee select tool

◉ Activote (optional)

Starter
Set the children the task of finding out about imperial units before the lesson. They may use work from the previous year, research using books or by asking relatives. Annotate their suggestions on page 30 of the flipchart.

Whole-class shared work
● Organise the children into mixed-ability groups and work through the activities on pages 31 to 34. On each page is a list of imperial and metric measurements. Provide four pieces of sugar paper for each group and ask each group to draw a line down the centre of each piece of paper, marking one half *Imperial* and one half *Metric*.
● Challenge the children to work through the words on the list on each page and write them in the appropriate columns. Ask them to mark each other's work by swapping with another group. Discuss and agree on the right answers.
● Invite volunteers to come and place the words in the correct columns on the flipchart pages.
● Ask if anyone knows the equivalence between any imperial and metric units. The children should know that a mile is about 1600 metres; 2.2 pounds is one kilogram and that a gallon is around 4.5 litres.
● Use page 35 to 37 to establish the equivalent values for metric and imperial units. Ask questions such as: *If one inch is about 2.54 centimetres, how many centimetres is two inches?*
● Point out that the numbers are not exact and have been rounded up to two decimal places. Pose the question: *One pint is approximately equal to 568 millilitres and 5.68 litre. How would you round up the litre measurement to one decimal place?*
● Try to source some common rhymes about imperial unit conversions such as: *A litre of water's a pint and three quarters.* If a microphone is available, use the Sound recorder 🔊 with the children to record some of these rhymes.

Independent work
● Organise a carousel of practical measuring activities. These activities should include measuring using: feet and inches; yards; stones; pounds and ounces; pints and gallons.
● Give the children equal time on each activity to measure using imperial measurements. Set them to work in mixed-ability groups with support as and where needed.

Plenary
● Invite the children to share their thoughts on the measuring activities. Do they prefer to measure in metric or imperial units, or does it not make a difference?
● Discuss whether they had any difficulties with measuring in imperial units. For example, converting inches to feet and inches may have been difficult because it's not a simple case of dividing by 100 (as you would when converting centimetres to metres).
● Use pages 37 to 39 to assess the children's understanding of imperial units and to assess whether they can choose suitable units for a particular task. Encourage them to give reasons for their answers.

Perimeter challenge

Learning objectives
● To calculate the perimeter and area of simple compound shapes that can be split into rectangles.

Resources
'Perimeter challenge' flipchart file; squared paper (1cm); individual whiteboards and pens.

Links to other subjects
Geography
PoS (2e) To draw plans and maps at a range of scales.
● Use the internet to find blueprints of a house (estate agents often have good ones) or locate a map of the school. Explain that most houses are built up of a series of rectangles forming a compound shape similar to the ones studied in this lesson.

Starter
Display page 2 of the flipchart. Ask the children to recite the four-, six- and eight-times tables. Repeat for 40-, 60- and 80- times tables and again for the 0.4-, 0.6- and 0.8- times tables.
    Ask the questions: *What is 3 × 4? What is 3 × 40? What is 3 × 0.4?* Ask the children to write the answers on their individual whiteboards. Reveal the answers by filling the circles on the flipchart with a different colour 🖌.
    Remind the children of the connection between these calculations

Whole-class shared work
● Show the rectangle on page 3. Revise the formulas used to find the area and perimeter of a rectangle or square. Move the rectangle to review the correct formulae:
    ● (Length + breadth) × 2 = Perimeter; Length × breadth = Area.
● Point out the use of the brackets in the first formula. The brackets indicate that the length and breadth are added together before the result is multiplied by 2. Ask: *What would happen if the brackets were removed?*
● Tell the children that they will be creating a number of compound shapes using rectangles of equal size but that the rule of this exercise is that each compound shape created must be different to any other.
● Go to page 4 and explain that these shapes are going to represent the plans for a new Gnome Ville Housing Estate. Ask them to present the most original ideas possible.
● The second diagram on the page shows what happens when two rectangles are compounded.
● Ask the class to consider the effect on the area and perimeter if two rectangles of the same dimensions are joined together. Note that the area doubles (if the rectangles are the same dimensions) but the perimeter does not. Discuss why the perimeter does not double in size.
● Calculate the area and perimeter of the shape on page 5. Reset the page, rearrange the shape, and calculate its area and perimeter.

Independent work
● Ask the children to create compound Gnome Houses using two or three rectangles of equal size on squared paper.
● For less confident children, limit the activity to creating houses with two rectangles of equal size.
● For more confident learners, extend the activity to creating compound houses using three or four rectangles of equal size on squared paper.

Whiteboard tools
To remove an object, double-click on it and select Delete in the Object edit toolbox. Use the Duplicate function to create more rectangles on page 6, if required.

📝 Pen tool

🔦 Marquee select tool

🗑 Delete button

📑 Duplicate function

🔄 Page reset button

🖌 Fill tool

◉ Activote (optional)

Plenary
● Review the houses created. Ask some of the children to demonstrate their designs on the board using the prepared grid and rectangles on page 6. Discuss some of difficulties.
● Explain to the class that it is most likely that the compound shape would consist of different-sized rectangles. Show the house on page 4. Explain that some of the measurements are missing for this compound shape.
● Discuss how these missing measurements could be calculated from the given information (opposing sides would be the same length, parts of short lengths could be used to subtract from known sides and so on).
● Use page 7 to predict which house has the largest perimeter. Move on to page 8 to work out the perimeter (move the mask away to show the measurements). Check whether the children predicted correctly.
● Page 9 offers an opportunity to discuss the effects of the different arrangements on the perimeter.

Problems with data

Learning objectives
● To solve problems by representing, extracting and interpreting data in tables, graphs, charts and diagrams including those generated by a computer.

Resources
Individual whiteboards and pens; access to ICT room; spreadsheet program (such as Microsoft Excel).

Links to other subjects
ICT
QCA Unit 6B 'Spreadsheet modelling'
● This lesson could lead to more extended work exploring the effects of changing data in a spreadsheet.

Starter
Write the following on a blank flipchart page:

Crunch	Bong	Chew 'em	Haywire
29p	39p	49p	99p

Tell the children that these represent the cost of different cereal bars.
Ask: *If I buy a bar of Crunch and a bar of Haywire, how much does this cost?*
   Ask the children to write the answer on their individual whiteboards. Discuss strategies for solving the problem, for example, the rounding up and adjusting strategy. Repeat using different pairs from the table.
   Set a new challenge, such as: *If I buy four bars of Crunch, how much change do I get from £5?* Collect answers and discuss strategies.

Whole-class shared work
● If possible do this lesson in the school computer room or use a set of class laptops if available.
● Ask the children to vote on the snack they would buy from those listed in the Starter. Record their responses on the whiteboard, explaining that they are going to investigate how best to represent this data.
● Explain that the data is presented as a simple table. Ask for suggestions as to how it could be presented differently (such as in a spreadsheet).
● Switch to Desktop mode and open a spreadsheet program, such as Microsoft Excel. Enter the details:

Cereal Bar	Number of votes
Crunch	12
Bongo	4
Chew 'em	14
Haywire	6

● Highlight all of the text and click on the Chart wizard. Select a standard bar chart and click finish. This will present a bar chart of the information given. Ask the children: *What does this type of chart show?* (It shows the most popular brand instantly.)
● Follow the procedure again; this time select pie chart from the Chart wizard. *What does this form of presentation tell us?* (It shows what rough fraction or percentage of people liked each type of bar.)

Independent work
● If possible provide a computer per pair of children and ask them to enter the table onto a spreadsheet in order to generate a chart.
● As an additional challenge, task the children with using the data to answer questions such as: *What percentage liked Haywire bars?*

Whiteboard tools
Switch to Desktop mode to use the annotation tools on the class spreadsheet. Enter data into the spreadsheet with the Floating keyboard or the Handwriting tool.

🖵 Desktop mode

⌨ Floating keyboard

✏ Pen tool

✎ Handwriting tool

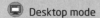 Return to main screen

Plenary
● Agree that tables can be shown in different ways and that often more than one set of data can be presented. Demonstrate using the data below to create a bar chart.

Cereal Bar	Class 1	Class 2
Crunch	12	10
Bongo	5	8
Chew 'em	14	14
Haywire	6	3

● Ask the children how we can identify which class is which. (They should include a key or chart labels.)
● Could the details for a third class be input? Add the details and show that, with a third class, not only can the overall data be analysed, but that trends can be identified. (For example, Chew 'ems seem to be generally liked by all the classes.)

Ratio problems

Learning objectives
● To solve simple problems involving ratio and proportion.

Resources
'Model cars' flipchart file; tape measure; calculators; paper and pens.

Links to other subjects
Design and technology
PoS (1d) To communicate design ideas in different ways.
● Explain that architects and designers often create a scale model of the final product in order to show what the final design will look like and to discuss any potential design flaws.

Starter
Open page 2 of the 'Model cars' flipchart. Explain that a number of coloured marbles have been put into the container: four red, three green, two blue and one yellow marble. Highlight the key vocabulary: *likely, certain, unlikely, equal chance.* Ask: *If you were to pick a marble from the bag, what is the most likely colour to be picked?* Agree it is red. Drag a marble out and see.

Ask the children to make statements about the probability of selecting the colour of cubes using the words on the flipchart. What other words might be added to the list? Ensure that *equally likely, even chance* and *some* are added. With each word, encourage the children to make a statement about the marbles in the container.

Add or remove marbles from the container at intervals to change the probability. Ask: *How many marbles should we add to the container so that picking each colour is equally likely?* Ensure that the children understand the idea of equally likely outcomes.

Whole-class shared work
● Explain that the children are going to investigate proportion. Where would they use the word *proportion*? Collect answers, ascertaining that proportion is relative to an object's real size. Reveal the definition on page 3.
● Explain that you will be looking at the relationship between normal cars and model cars and that this is expressed as a ratio.
● Go to page 4. Explain that the ratio of the model car is 1:20. (The car is $\frac{1}{20}$ of the size of the original.)
  ● Draw attention to the equation for working out the original size:
    ● 12cm × 20 = 250cm.
● Encourage the children to discuss if they think this is accurate.
● Ask what would happen if the model car was 8cm long. Explain that to increase the ratio size the number after the colon increases (so it would be 1:8). Compare and investigate the ratios 1:10 and 1:30. Which, can the children tell you, would be a realistic car size. Use a metre stick to demonstrate the agreed length.

Independent work
● Show the class the six different ratios and the cars with their sizes indicated, on page 5.
● Explain that the toy company have mixed up the ratios and have asked you to pair up cars with correct ratios.
● In mixed-ability groups ask the children to work out the answers on paper.
● Invite representatives from each group to come to the board to drag and drop one ratio alongside a car. Use the spyglass to see if the ratio is correct.

Plenary
● Share lists and discuss any disagreements. Ask the group representatives to show their workings out on pages 6 and 7.
● Agree that the larger the original object is, the larger the ratio is likely to be. Explain that the ratio can be found by dividing the size of the model by the original size of the object.
● Set the Plenary activity on page 8 as homework.

Whiteboard tools
 Marquee select tool

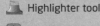 Highlighter tool

Pen tool

 Delete button

Pythagorean numbers

Learning objectives
● To use the relationship between multiplication and division.

Resources
'Pythagorean numbers' flipchart file; photocopiable page 99 'Square and triangular numbers chart'; individual whiteboards and pens.

Links to other subjects
History
QCA Unit 15 'How do we use Ancient Greek ideas today?'
● Explain that Pythagoreans (those who followed the teachings of Pythagoras) believed that there were only whole numbers and that parts of numbers (decimals, fractions) did not occur in the natural universe. It was not until a scholar attempted to find the square root of two that this came into question and was then hidden, becoming known as the *Great Cover Up*.

Starter
Show page 2 of the whiteboard on which a rectangle is presented.

Draw attention to the side measurement. Challenge the children to work out, using individual whiteboards, what the other side measurement will be if one side is 8cm and the perimeter is 30cm.

Collect the children's answers and erase the red boxes on the flipchart to reveal the correct answers. Ask: *What is the area of this rectangle?* Share answers and discuss strategies.

Now consider whether a rectangle with this perimeter could have other dimensions? Collect and record the children's suggestions and ask them to work out the areas in their heads.

Repeat the activity using 42cm for the perimeter. Discuss answers, addressing any misconceptions.

Whole-class shared work
● Explain that the ancient Greeks represented whole numbers as geometric shapes, often with pebbles on the sand.
● Go to page 3 which shows the standard five Pythagorean number-shapes. Explain that these represent number-shapes. Use the Reveal tool 🖵 to focus on the name and definition of one number-shape at a time.
● Ask the children to discuss the triangular number and its definition. Agree that a triangular number is the number of pebbles in a triangular array.
● Go to page 4 and explain that the numbers in the chart have been shown up to the third shape. Using the square number, give the next shape (4 × 4) and the next (5 × 5). Repeat with the triangular number, giving the fourth and fifth triangle shapes. Use small shapes or the Pen tool to show the pattern of triangular numbers.

Independent work
● Provide each child with a copy of photocopiable page 99. Complete the first row on the whiteboard, showing the pattern for the first square and triangular number.
● Challenge the children to find the square and triangular numbers up to the tenth shape and to complete the table on the photocopiable page.
● Give less confident children some counting beads (or similar) for support. Work with the children at the whiteboard to demonstrate how the pattern builds.
● Challenge more confident children to develop a pattern for rectangular numbers to the tenth number. Display page 5 of the flipchart which shows how the pattern begins. Use the pattern to develop a formula for the twentieth and fiftieth shape in this pattern.

Plenary
● Discuss the patterns created and the types of numbers produced.
● Use the large multiplication grid on page 6 to show where the numbers fall for square, triangular and rectangular numbers.
● Explain that these numbers are called family members and that each family shape is called a figurative shape. So three is a figurative number in the *triangle family* and nine is a figurative number in the *square family*.

Whiteboard tools
Use the Shapes tool to show the pattern of triangular numbers.

 Eraser tool

 Shapes tool

 Pen tool

 Marquee select tool

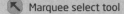 Reveal tool

Handling data

Learning objectives
● To find the mode and range of a set of data.
● To begin to find the median and mean of a set of data.

Resources
'Handling data' flipchart file; books; individual whiteboards and pens.

Links to other subjects
Science
QCA Unit 6A 'Interdependence and adaptation'
● Ask the children to consider why temperatures for countries close to the equator are less extreme. Investigate where the hottest and coldest climates are and how this impacts on habitats.

Starter
Display page 2 of the flipchart. Ask the children to state division facts derived from this number sentence. Record these facts and prompt the use of patterns to extend the range of facts.

Go to page 3 and repeat the activity, this time stating multiplication facts. Ask the children to work in pairs and record answers on their whiteboards. Identify some patterns used and ask the children to explain them.

Whole-class shared work
● Explain to the children that they will be looking at the average monthly temperatures during the year for London. From this data they are going to find:
  ● the mean (the average number when all the data is added together, then divided by the total number of entries)
  ● the range (the difference between the lowest and highest numbers)
  ● the mode (the number that appears most often)
  ● the median (the central number when all the data has been put into order from smallest to largest).
● Revise these meanings on page 4 of the flipchart. Then display page 5, which shows the average monthly temperature for one year in London.
● Using the four definitions, the class should begin to organise the temperatures from coldest to warmest in order to find the *range*, then the *mode, mean* and *median* temperatures.
● Identify the *range* by finding the difference between the coldest and warmest temperatures. How would the children calculate this if the coldest temperature was -4°C?
● Next, identify the *mode*. Explain that if two sets of numbers appear equally then they are both the mode numbers.
● Identify the *mean* number by adding all twelve entries and dividing by twelve.
● Identify the *median* number. When there is an odd set of figures, seven for example, then the middle number is the median number. In this case there are two median numbers; to find the absolute median they need to be added together and divided by two.

Independent work
● Explain that the children are going to be presented with a range of temperatures taken from several countries (using flipchart page 6). Their task is to find the mean, mode, median and range of each country and to present this as a table in their books.

Plenary
● Discuss the strategies used and identify the most efficient ways of finding the four results.
● Remind the children that it is very important to organise the list of numbers before starting the activity, as this will help with finding the median, range and mode.
● If time permits, use page 7 to compare the data from the Independent work (on New York) with the data from the Whole-class shared work (on London).
● Review the children's work, making notes on page 8 if necessary.

Whiteboard tools

 Highlighter tool

 Pen tool

Marquee select tool

Percentage problems

Learning objectives
● To find simple percentages of small whole number quantities (using a calculator).

Resources
Photocopiable page 100 'The Grand Sale'; calculators; individual whiteboards and pens.

Links to other subjects
Geography
PoS (3d) To explain why places are like they are.
● Investigate your local high street: how could it be improved? Are there any shops that are particularly attractive? Are there any types of shop that you do not have that would improve the high street? Why?

Starter
Ask the class to recite the eight- and nine-times tables. Repeat the eight-times table, but this time stop at a particular multiplication fact. Invite one child to write a related division fact on an empty flipchart page on the whiteboard. Continue until six division facts have been recorded.

Invite the rest of the class to confirm that the facts are correct and, in pairs, ask them to use each of the six facts to derive another fact. Collect some responses quickly and record these on the flipchart page.

Repeat, using other facts from the eight- and nine-times tables until the board is full of division facts. Use these for subsequent oral and mental starter sessions.

Whole-class shared work
● Explain to the class that in today's lesson they are going to investigate which of four clothes shops offers the best value for money during their sales. State that while all the prices of products are different, so are the percentage discounts and that although some products may appear to be initially more expensive if the reduction is large enough they may be cheaper.
● Explain that they will need to:
1. identify the percentage reduction
2. subtract that figure from the original cost to find the sale price.
● Write on the whiteboard: *£25, £40, £50* and *£80*. On individual whiteboards, ask the children to find 10%, 25% and 50% of each amount.
● Discuss the children's strategies for finding these figures. Ask them to use their whiteboards to work out the answers. Remind the children that 50% is equivalent to $\frac{1}{2}$ and that halving a number will produce its 50% sale price. Ask what equivalent fraction there is for 25% and how that could be used to find the sale price (ideas could include dividing by four, or halving and halving again, then subtracting that number from the original). Do the same for 10%.
● Invite children to come to the board to check their calculations using the Floating calculator 🖩.

Independent work
● Give each child a copy of 'The Grand Sale' photocopiable sheet. Using this sheet remind the children that they have to identify the reduced prices of each item of clothing. Ask questions such as: *Which stores offer the cheapest items? Which stores offer the best value?*

Plenary
● Discuss which stores offer the best value and the greatest reductions.
● Ask: *Would any of the stores tempt you to buy from their sale even if they did not offer the cheapest clothing? What other factors would you take into consideration?*
● Change the percentage reduction for one of the stores and ask the class for the new prices. For example, Top Togs now offers a 60% reduction. What are the new prices? Check using the Floating calculator.

Whiteboard tools
Use the Floating calculator from the Special tools menu to check calculations.

🖊 Pen tool

🔄 Recognition tool

✳ Special tools menu

🖩 Floating calculator

Triangular numbers

Learning objectives
● To identify and use appropriate operations (including combinations of operations) to solve word problems involving numbers and quantities based on *real life*.

Resources
'Triangular numbers' flipchart file; individual whiteboards and pens.

Links to other subjects
History
QCA Unit 15 'How do we use ancient Greek ideas today?'
● Give the children a little bit of background information: *Pythagoras was so excited by his discoveries that he wanted to share them with other people. In fact, he offered to pay his first student a daily wage so that he could teach him. Eventually Pythagoras ran out of money but by then the student was so interested in the subject that he offered to pay him, and the first school was formed.*
Ask the class how much you should pay them to teach them mathematics!

Whiteboard tools
Use the Clock tool's Count down option to count down two minutes for the Starter activity. Use the Shapes tool to demonstrate the pattern of triangular numbers.

🡖 Marquee select tool

▨ Shapes tool

▤ Eraser tool

⏱ Count down tool

▯ Pen tool

Starter
Open the 'Triangular numbers' flipchart and go to page 2. Read the number sentence: 7 × 8 = 56. Ask the children to state facts which can be derived from this fact. Record their suggestions, for example:
● 56 ÷ 8 = 7
● 5.6 ÷ 8 = 0.7.
Check the Hints box for further examples.
Prompt the children to identify, extend and explain particular patterns of facts. For example: *If you know 7 × 8 = 56, you also know that 56 ÷ 8 = 7.*
Move on to page 3, which shows the number sentence 6 × 9 = 54 and ask the children to derive as many related facts as they can in two minutes. Use the Clock tool's Count down option ⏱ to time them. Collect examples to identify patterns.
Repeat using another multiplication fact, with the children recording only division facts.

Whole-class shared work
● Display page 4 to remind the children about triangular numbers.
● Use page 5 to demonstrate that if two consecutive triangular numbers are placed together they produce a square number. For example: 1 + 3 = 4; 3 + 6 = 9.
● Invite the children, in pairs or small groups, to choose any two consecutive triangular numbers to prove this.
● Ask the class to investigate what happens when a triangular number is doubled. (A rectangular number is created.) Use page 4 to test these rules.
● Explain that for the remainder of the lesson the class are going to be investigating other formulas.

Independent work
● Look at the grid on page 6. Ask more confident learners to work out how many numbers between 1 and 40 can be identified as pentagonal numbers. (See page 7 for an explanation.)
● For middle-ability children, explain that square numbers can be made up from triangular numbers using two different formulas - the one that the class has already investigated and another which states that eight times any triangular number, plus one, is a square number. Ask the children to investigate this by using triangles that are made up of either three or six cubes plus one.
● Challenge the children to test out the formula with a range of triangular numbers. Compare square numbers and patterns.
● For less confident learners, use bricks to show that an odd number plus an odd number makes an even number and that an even number plus an odd makes an odd. Explain that when they represent the numbers they can have no more than two rows of bricks. For example: three would be shown as one row with two and the other row with one; nine would be shown as one row with four and the other row with five.

Plenary
● Ask each group to explain their formula to the class. Have their investigations proven their formulae? Make notes on page 8.
● Display the chart on page 9 of the flipchart.
● Number shapes (or figurative numbers) extend beyond triangular numbers and square numbers. They can be shown as hexagons, pentagons, octagons and so on. Explain that figurative numbers can have relations with one another, for example 6 is a triangular and hexagonal number.

Thales' procedure

Starter
Type the following on a blank flipchart page:
- 25% of 50
- 60% of 70
- 33$\frac{1}{3}$% of 120
- 5% of 94
- 30% of 3200
- 23% of 150
- 47% of 250
- 99% of 800.

Ask the children to work in pairs to find the percentages. Invite them to decide which percentages they can find mentally or with jottings and which they would need a calculator to find. Provide individual whiteboards for the children to record their work.

Encourage the children to use their knowledge of equivalents. For example, that finding 25% is the same as finding $\frac{1}{4}$, and to use methods that build on from finding 10%, 5% and 1%. Draw attention to amounts such as 47%, highlighting that this is almost 50% (or half) and so a guess close to half would be a good approximation.

Collect the children's answers and methods. Use the Floating calculator 🖩 to check answers.

Whole-class shared work
- Explain that Thales used five simple steps to solve the problem of finding the height of an object by calculating the size from its shadow. The procedure is as follows:
  - Place a stick in the ground and measure its height (in centimetres), making a note of it on the board.
  - Measure the length of the shadow cast by the stick (in centimetres) and note that length. (Discuss what will happen to the length of this shadow at different times of the day. Explain that because of the indoor lighting this measurement should remain constant.)
  - Measure the length of the shadow cast by the object (a bookcase, for example) and note this on the board.
  - Multiply the stick's height by the length of the object's shadow.
  - Divide this result by the length of the stick's shadow. This final result is the height of the object.
- Consider if it would be better to measure the object in centimetres or metres (dependent on the size of the object). Remind the children that they will need to adjust the measurement if they have opted to show the result in metres.

Independent work
- Explain that, in groups, the class are going to use this procedure to calculate the size of the largest tree in the school, a car, and the school building.
- Provide the groups with copies of the procedure and administer the activity so that each group is given the same access to each item.
- Additional adult support will be required for this activity.

Plenary
- Gather together the groups' results. Do they differ, and if so why? Have the formulas been followed correctly? Discuss any problems with the procedure (such as, accurate measurement and the changing length of the shadows).
- Discuss the effective use of this procedure. Write both the difficulties and effective uses on the flipchart and save the page for future use.

Learning objectives
● To factorise numbers to 100.

Resources 🅿
Photocopiable page 101 'Find the factors'. Prepare a flipchart with a 100-square and multiplication square.

Links to other subjects
History
QCA Unit 15 'How do we use ancient Greek ideas today?'
● Explain to the children that Pythagoras believed that all numbers could be shown figuratively and that all factors could be displayed in the same way.

Factors

Starter
Write the numbers 3 and 7 on a blank flipchart page. Quickly rehearse the multiplication tables for 3 and 7 with the whole class.

Ask: *What numbers appear both in the three- and the seven-times tables?* Divide the class into two groups. Set one group to count in threes and the other to count in sevens to generate the sequence: 3, 6, 7, 9, 12, 14, and so on. Ask: *What numbers do not appear in the sequence? Why?*

Establish that only multiples of 3 or 7 (or both) can be in the sequence. Draw coin shapes on the board with 3p and 7p inside them. Tell the children to imagine that, as from today, there will be only 3p and 7p coins. Ask: *What sums of money can we make using only 3p and 7p coins?* Collect the children's responses and record them on the board.

Whole-class shared work
● Explain that in today's lesson the children are going to investigate which numbers have the most factors and which numbers are least likely to have a factor. Explain that some numbers have no factors at all and that these are called *prime numbers*.
● On the whiteboard, display your prepared multiplication square and 100-square.
● Ask the children to discuss which numbers they can see that are cross-referenced from the multiplication square with the 100-square. Share some of the answers by highlighting the 100-square where there is a number from the multiplication chart. Explain that each highlighted numbers is a factor. For example: 12 has the paired factors 2 and 6; 3 and 4; 6 and 2; 4 and 3.
● Other numbers (such as 36) have more than two pairs of factors.

Independent work
● Give each child a copy of photocopiable page 101 'Find the factors'. They must use it to identify all numbers with at least two pairs of factors.
● Focus less able learners on finding as many factors as they are able.
● Challenge more able learners to identify numbers which either have the most numbers of factors or no factors at all (prime numbers).

Plenary
● Encourage the children to share those numbers which have more than one pair of factors and highlight them on the 100-square.
● Ask the more confident group to identify some of the prime numbers and explain their particular property (that they can only be divided by one and themselves).
● Play the *Factor Game*: write a number, such as 42, in the centre of a circle and ask the children to guess the pairs of factors used to make that number. The person who guesses correctly then becomes the lead person and chooses a new number (one that has factors) and the game continues.

Whiteboard tools
Prepare a 100-square and a multiplication square for the main activity. Examples can be found in the Resource library under mathematics, in the Grids and graphs folder.

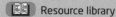 Resource library

 Highlighter tool

 Pen tool

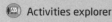

Angles in a triangle

Starter
Write the following on a blank flipchart page:

A 168 ÷ 2	**E** 168 ÷ 5
B 168 ÷ 6	**F** 168 ÷ 10
C 168 ÷ 4	**G** 168 ÷ 8
D 168 ÷ 3	**H** 168 ÷ 9

Ask the children to work in pairs to decide which calculations they can do mentally or with jottings, and which require a written method.

Discuss their responses and ensure that they can carry out at least A, C and F mentally (provide individual whiteboards for the rest of the calculations). Remind the children of the tests of divisibility and discuss how they can be used to establish if each division is exact.

Whole-class shared work
● Go to Activities explorer ⓐ and then KS2 DFES NNS ITP.
● Open the *Calculating angles* Interactive Teaching Program and select one triangle. Remind the children that there are four types of triangle:
  ● isosceles – where two sides are of equal length
  ● scalene – where all sides are of unequal length
  ● right angled – where one of the angles is a right angle (this could be a scalene triangle)
  ● equilateral – where all of the angles are of equal size.
● What all of these shapes have in common is that their angles add up to 180°. The simplest example is that an equilateral triangle has three 60° angles.
● By selecting one triangle and the protractor within the ITP, demonstrate how to find one angle of a triangle. Explain that as the angles always add up to 180°, only two corners need to be measured. The third one can be found by adding the first two angles and taking them away from 180. 180 – (Angle A + Angle B) = Angle C
● Explain that a protractor usually has numbers running in two directions, and ask why this is the case? Ensure that the children know how to use *common sense judgement* when measuring the size of each angle: if it is small then it is unlikely to be 125° instead of 65°. Make sure that the children understand the difference between obtuse and acute.

Independent work
● Provide individual copies of the 'Triangle angle mangle' photocopiable sheet and ask the children to work out the missing angles.
● Reinforce the fact that once we know two of the three angles we can work out the missing angle.
● Challenge more confident children to investigate a range of angles in the *Calculating angles* ITP. In some shapes, lengths and angles can be generated randomly to extend the activity further.

Plenary
● Ask the children to share their work and to discuss any challenges. Explain that quadrilaterals, such as squares and rectangles, have angles that total 360°, which is double the size of the angles of a triangle. Also, note that whenever two triangles are placed together they always make a quadrilateral.
● Explain that this occurs in many places including with triangular numbers; two consecutive triangular numbers, such as 6 and 10, will always make a square number.

Matching decimals and fractions

0.10	0.70	0.30	0.20	0.50
0.80	0.40	0.60	0.90	$\dfrac{1}{10}$
$\dfrac{3}{10}$	$\dfrac{9}{10}$	$\dfrac{1}{5}$	$\dfrac{3}{5}$	$\dfrac{4}{5}$
$\dfrac{7}{10}$	$\dfrac{4}{10}$	$\dfrac{1}{2}$		

0.05	0.15	0.25	0.35	0.45
0.55	0.65	0.75	0.85	0.95
$\dfrac{1}{4}$	$\dfrac{11}{20}$	$\dfrac{17}{20}$	$\dfrac{3}{20}$	$\dfrac{9}{20}$
$\dfrac{7}{10}$	$\dfrac{3}{4}$	$\dfrac{1}{20}$	$\dfrac{19}{20}$	$\dfrac{13}{20}$

$\dfrac{7}{25}$	$\dfrac{17}{25}$	$\dfrac{3}{25}$	0.80	$\dfrac{3}{5}$
0.48	$\dfrac{4}{5}$	0.60	0.24	$\dfrac{24}{50}$
0.40	0.12	0.68	$\dfrac{11}{25}$	0.28
$\dfrac{6}{25}$	0.44	$\dfrac{2}{5}$		

100 Activprimary™ WHITEBOARD LESSONS • YEAR 6

Dice template

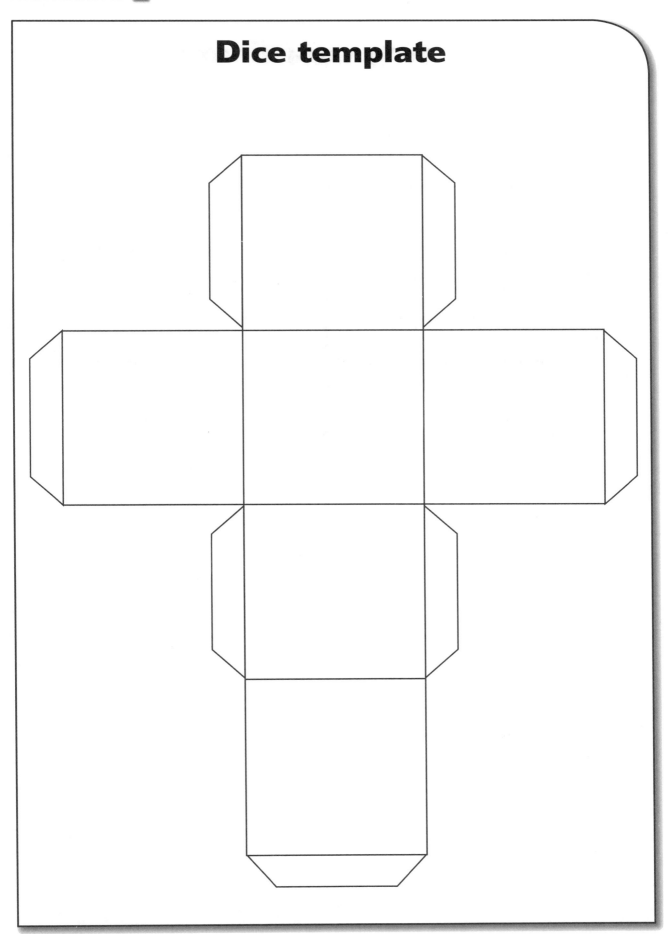

Plotting coordinates

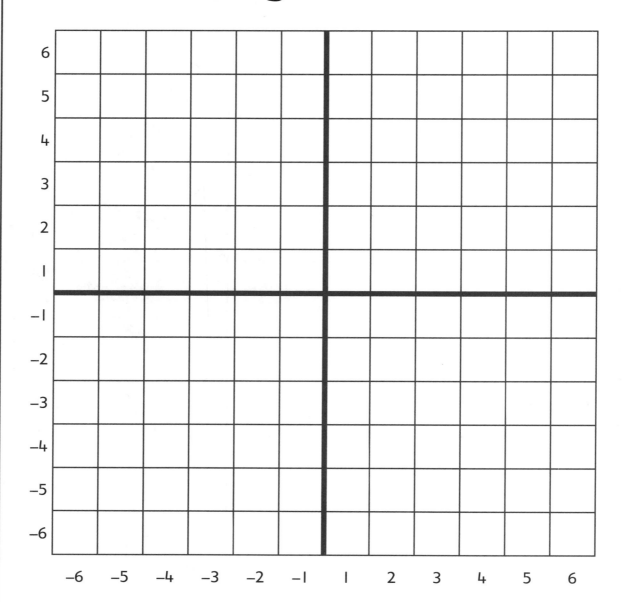

Draw a circle in (1, -1).
Write the letter 's' in (2, -2).
Colour (-3, -6) in yellow.
Put a blue cross in (-4, 4).

Draw a heart in (3, -4).
Put a cross in (-4, 5).
Colour (-1, 6) in red.
Put a green triangle in (-2, 6).

Now put your initials into three coordinates.
Write the coordinates in the spaces below.

_____ ; _____ ; _____ .

▮ S C H O L A S T I C
w w w . s c h o l a s t i c . c o . u k

Percentages

1. There are 100 strawberries. Ali eats 23%.
How many strawberries did he eat?

2. There are 100 fish in the river. James catches 85 of them.
What percentage is this?

3. Homesh has 100 stamps. He gives 73 to a friend.
What percentage is this?

4. There are 100 deer in a forest. 65% run away.
How many deer run away?

5. Lucy has 100 pencils. She breaks 16%.
How many pencils does she have left?

6. 100 butterflies are in a garden. 37 of them land on flowers.
What percentage of butterflies is not on flowers?

7. There are 100 flowers in a field. Emma picks 41%.
What percentage of flowers are left in the field?

8. There are 100 cars on a motorway. 19% of the cars come
off the motorway. How many cars stay on?

9. Navid has 100 newspapers. He gives 27 to Carl and 47% to
Mohammed. What percentage of newspapers does he have left?

10. The bus has 100 seats. 43% of the bus seats are filled. Kendra
and her 12 friends get on. What percentage of seats are empty?

11. Simon has 100 rolls of turf. He lays 22 rolls vertically and 39%
horizontally. How many rolls of turf does he have left to lay?

12. There are 100 ducks on a pond. 64% fly off and then 19
new ducks land. How many ducks are left on the pond?

World time

1. It is 7pm in England. Belgium is one hour ahead. What time is it in Belgium?

2. It is 3.15am in England. Lithuania is two hours ahead. What time is it in Lithuania?

3. It is 13.25 in England. The Bahamas are five hours behind. What time is it in the Bahamas?

4. It is 18.45 in Japan. Japan is nine hours ahead of England. What time is it in England?

5. It is 3.34am in Kazakhstan. Japan is 3 hours ahead. What time is it in Japan?

6. It is 22.57 in England. Ireland is in the same time zone. What time will it be in Ireland two hours?

7. It is 5.23am in England. Samoa is eleven hours behind. What time is it in Samoa?

8. It is 13.05 in England. Tonga is 13 hours ahead. What time is it in Tonga?

9. Guatemala is six hours behind England. If it is 04.13 in England what time is it in Guatemala?

10. Afghanistan is four and a half hours ahead of England. If it is 21.13 in England what time is it in Afghanistan?

11. Tuvalu is 12 hours ahead of England. If it is 13.13 in England what time is it in Tuvalu?

12. Haiti is five hours behind England. If it is 03.54 in England what time is it in Haiti?

Standard metric units

Object	Unit of measurement	Measurement

Suitable units of measurement

Object	Estimate	Measurement

Percentages of numbers

1. There are 48 strawberries in a field. Alice ate 24 of them. What percentage is this?

2. There are 50 cars in a car park. Five of the cars are blue. What percentage is this?

3. There are 90 books in a library. Declan reads nine of them. What percentage is this?

4. There are 26 cream cakes in the window. 13 are chocolate éclairs. What percentage is this?

5. There are 30 CDs in Gita's music collection. Three of the discs are rock music. What percentage is this?

6. There are 12 lions in a zoo. Three of them are male. What percentage is this?

7. Branimir had a bird sanctuary holding 35 birds. Seven of these are doves. What percentage is this?

8. There are 25 horses in a race. Five of these are white horses. What percentage is this?

9. Heather has 24 pets. Six of these are goldfish. What percentage is this?

10. There are 36 fish in an aquarium. Nine are angel fish. What percentage is this?

11. Cameron has 96 stamps in his collection. 72 of these stamps are from different countries. What percentage is this?

12. There are 25 people in a circus. Ten of these are clowns. What percentage is this?

13. There are 36 butterflies in a field. 27 of them are cabbage whites. What percentage is this?

14. There are 50 ice-creams in a parlour. 20 of them are mint choc chip. What percentage is this?

15. There are 35 apples on a tree. 14 fall to the ground. What percentage is this?

Reflection

■ Draw the reflection of these shapes. Use a mirror to help you.

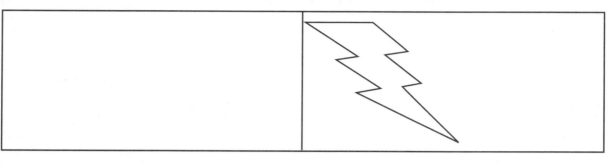

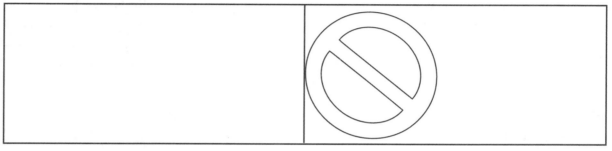

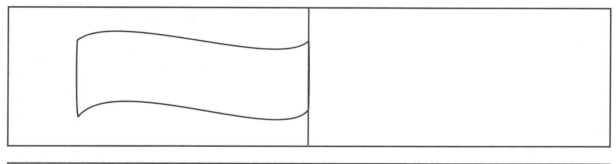

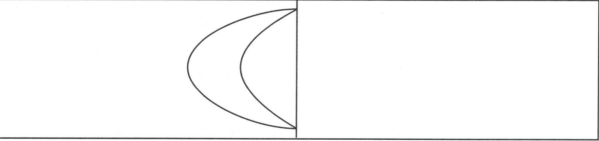

■ Now choose a picture of your own and draw its reflection.

Acute and obtuse

Draw a 34° angle. Is it obtuse or acute?

Draw a 124° angle. Is it obtuse or acute?

Draw a 72° angle. Is it obtuse or acute?

Draw a 92° angle. Is it obtuse or acute?

Rotation

◾ Draw a picture of what these shapes will look like after a 90° clockwise rotation.

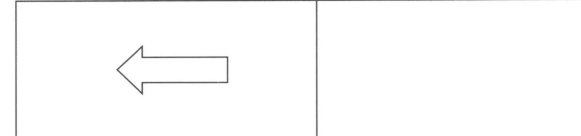

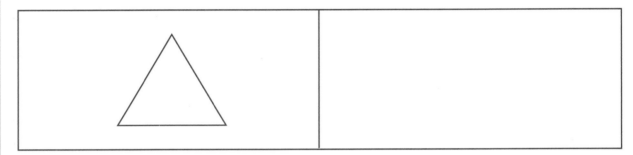

◾ Choose a shape and then draw it after it has been rotated 90° clockwise.

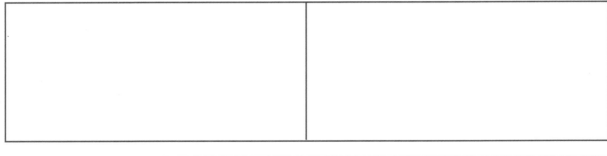

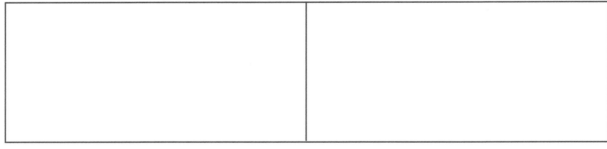

Name _____

Square and triangular numbers chart

	Triangle	No. of pebbles	Square	No. of pebbles
1st				
2nd				
3rd				
4th				
5th				

The Grand Sale

Item	Bargain Benny's 10% off	Top Togs 50% off	Trendz 25% off	Classic Casuals 30% off
Shoes – original price	£20	£40	£28	£46
Reduced price				
Jumper – original price	£15	£45	£26	£50
Reduced price				
Trousers – original price	£38	£60	£32	£55
Reduced price				
Hat – original price	£12	£22	£10	£20
Reduced price				
Sports Bag – original price	£30	£50	£26	£45
Reduced price				

◀ Which shop offered the cheapest of the following items in the sale?

Jumper _____   Shoes _____

Trousers _____   Sports bag _____

Hat _____

Find the factors

×	1	2	3	4	5	6	7	8	9	10
1	1	2	3	4	5	6	7	8	9	10
2	2	4	6	8	10	12	14	12	18	20
3	3	6	9	12	15	18	21	24	27	30
4	4	8	12	16	20	24	28	32	36	40
5	5	10	15	20	25	30	35	40	45	50
6	6	12	18	24	30	36	42	48	54	60
7	7	14	21	28	35	42	49	56	63	70
8	8	16	24	32	40	48	56	64	72	80
9	9	18	27	36	45	54	63	72	81	90
10	10	20	30	40	50	60	70	80	90	100

1	2	3	4	5	6	7	8	9	10
11	12	13	14	15	16	17	18	19	20
21	22	23	24	25	26	27	28	29	30
31	32	33	34	35	36	37	38	39	40
41	42	43	44	45	46	47	48	49	50
51	52	53	54	55	56	57	58	59	60
61	62	63	64	65	66	67	68	69	70
71	72	73	74	75	76	77	78	79	80
81	82	83	84	85	86	87	88	89	90
91	92	93	94	95	96	97	98	99	100

◖ Numbers with one or more pairs of factors:

◖ Numbers with the most pairs of factors:

◖ Numbers with no factors (prime numbers):

Triangle angle mangle

■ Using a protractor, find two of the angles from each of these triangles.

■ Use your knowledge that all three angles add up to 180° to estimate what the final angle is before asking your partner to measure it.

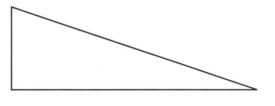

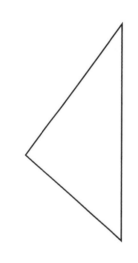

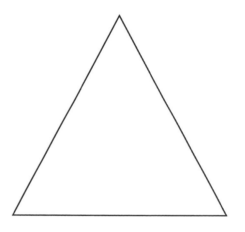

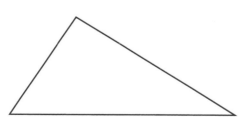

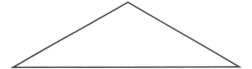

Illustration © Garry Davies

■SCHOLASTIC

www.scholastic.co.uk

Science

This chapter provides 20 lessons based on the Year 6 units in the QCA Schemes of Work for science. The key objectives from each unit have been deliberately chosen because teaching will be particularly aided and enhanced by the use of an interactive whiteboard. The lessons and associated flipchart files are designed to encourage the whole class to discuss and demonstrate ideas, plan investigations effectively, record and evaluate results and make substantiated conclusions. In this way, many of the lessons actively support teaching and evaluating key scientific enquiry skills (Sc1 National Curriculum). The flipchart files are also designed to enhance the children's ICT skills through, for example, creating and manipulating objects on screen, using writing and drawing tools and entering data into tables and spreadsheets.

Lesson title	Objectives	What children should know	Cross-curricular links
Lesson 1: Identification keys	**QCA Unit 6A** 'Interdependence and adaptation' • To make and use keys to identify animals in a particular habitat.	• Familiarity with the ideas of habitats and feeding relationships.	**ICT** PoS (2a) How to develop and refine ideas by bringing together, organising and reorganising text, tables, images and sound as appropriate; (4a) Review what they and others have done to help them develop their ideas.
Lesson 2: Food chains	**QCA Unit 6A** 'Interdependence and adaptation' • To understand that food chains can be used to represent feeding relationships in a habitat. • To know that food chains begin with a plant (the producer). • To construct food chains in a particular habitat.	• Familiarity with the ideas of habitats and feeding relationships.	**Speaking and listening** Objective 60: To understand and use a variety of ways to criticise constructively and respond to criticism.
Lesson 3: Plant roots	**QCA Unit 6A** 'Interdependence and adaptation' • To understand that water and nutrients are taken in through the root. • To know that roots anchor the plant in the soil.	• What plants need in order to grow well.	**Geography** QCA Unit 15 'The mountain environment ' QCA Unit 23 'Investigating coasts'
Lesson 4: Mouldy bread investigation	**QCA Unit 6B** 'Micro-organisms' • To know that micro-organisms are often too small to be seen. • To make suggestions about observing food, bearing in mind the need for safety. • To know that micro-organisms can cause food to decay. • To know that food needs to be handled and stored with care. • To know that micro-organisms which cause decay are living organisms.	• Living things feed, grow and reproduce.	**Design and technology** QCA Unit 5b 'Bread'
Lesson 5: Beneficial decay	**QCA Unit 6B** 'Micro-organisms' • To know that micro-organisms bring about decay. • To understand that decay can be beneficial.	• Living things feed, grow and reproduce.	**PSHE** PoS (3b) That bacteria and viruses can affect health and that following simple, safe routines can reduce their spread.
Lesson 6: Dissolving investigation	**QCA Unit 6C** 'More about dissolving' • To turn ideas about helping solids dissolve more quickly into a form that can be investigated and decide how to carry out a fair test. • To decide what apparatus to use and to make careful observations and measurements. • To use a line graph to present results. • To make comparisons and draw conclusions.	• Some solids dissolve in water and others do not. • Solids, liquids and gases can be separated.	**Mathematics** NNS: Use, read and write standard metric units; suggest suitable units and measuring equipment.

Lesson title	Objectives	What children should know	Cross-curricular links
Lesson 7: Solutions and evaporation ⚫	**QCA Unit 6C** 'More about dissolving' • To make and test predictions about which types of water contain dissolved materials. • To know that when solids dissolve, a clear solution is formed (which may be coloured); the solid cannot be separated by filtering. • To make and test predictions about what happens when water from a solution evaporates. • To know that when the liquid evaporates from a solution the solid is left behind.	• Undissolved solids can be separated from liquids by filtering, and that solids, liquids and gases can be separated.	**PSHE** PoS (3e) To recognise the different risks in different situations and then decide how to behave responsibly.
Lesson 8: Mixing materials ⚫	**QCA Unit 6D** 'Reversible and irreversible changes' • To know that mixing materials can cause them to change. • To know that some changes that occur when materials are mixed cannot easily be reversed. • To make careful observations, record and explain these using scientific knowledge and understanding.	• Know about dissolving, evaporating, condensing, melting and freezing as changes which can be reversed.	**Mathematics** NNS: Suggest suitable units and measuring equipment to estimate or measure length, mass or capacity.
Lesson 9: Heating and cooling materials ⚫ 🅿	**QCA Unit 6D** 'Reversible and irreversible changes' • To know that heating some materials can cause them to change. • To know that cooling some materials can cause them to change.	• Know about dissolving, evaporating, condensing, melting and freezing as changes which can be reversed.	**PSHE** PoS (3e) To recognise the different risks in different situations and then decide how to behave responsibly.
Lesson 10: Burning materials ⚫	**QCA Unit 6D** 'Reversible and irreversible changes' • To know that when materials are burned, new materials are formed. • To know that the changes that occur when most materials are burned are not reversible.	• Know about dissolving, evaporating, condensing, melting and freezing as changes which can be reversed.	**Speaking and listening** Objective 59: To analyse and evaluate how speakers present points effectively through use of language and gesture. **PSHE** PoS (3g) School rules about health and safety, basic emergency aid procedures and where to get help.
Lesson 11: Balanced and unbalanced forces ⚫ 🅿	**Unit 6E** 'Forces in action' • To know that several forces may act on one object. • To represent the direction of forces by arrows. • To understand that when an object is stationary, the forces on it are balanced. • To know that unbalanced forces change the speed or direction of movement of an object.	• Forces can be measured in newtons (N). • Recognise a variety of forces and understand that forces act in particular directions.	**Geography** QCA Unit 15 'The mountain environment ' QCA Unit 23 'Investigating coasts'
Lesson 12: Upthrust of liquids ⚫	**Unit 6E** 'Forces in action' • To know that when an object is submerged in a liquid, the liquid provides an upward force (upthrust) on it. • To take careful measurements of force using a forcemeter. • To use tables to present results, identifying patterns and drawing conclusions. • To evaluate repeated measures.	• Forces can be measured in newtons (N). • Recognise a variety of forces and understand that forces act in particular directions.	**Mathematics** NNS: Use, read and write standard metric units; record estimates and readings from scales to a suitable degree of accuracy.
Lesson 13: Air resistance investigation ⚫ 🅿	**Unit 6E** 'Forces in action' • To know that air resistance slows moving objects. • To know that when an objects falls, air resistance acts in the opposite direction to the weight. • To check measurements by repeating them • To interpret a line graph and use it to describe the motion of spinners falling.	• Forces can be measured in newtons (N). • Recognise a variety of forces and understand that forces act in particular directions.	**Mathematics** NNS: Solve a problem by representing, extracting and interpreting data in tables, graphs, charts and diagrams.
Lesson 14: Light and eyes ⚫ 🅿	**QCA Unit 6F** 'How we see things' • To know that light travels from a source. • To understand that we see light sources because light from the source enters our eyes. • To use knowledge about light to explain observations.	• Light is needed in order to see. • There are many light sources and that the main source of light in daytime is the Sun.	**Speaking and listening** Objective 58: To use a range of oral techniques to present persuasive argument. Objective 59: To analyse and evaluate how speakers present points effectively through use of language and gesture.

Science Chapter 3

Lesson title	Objectives	What children should know	Cross-curricular links
Lesson 15: Reflecting light in mirrors	QCA Unit 6F 'How we see things' • To know that light from an object can be reflected by a mirror – the reflected light enters our eyes and we see the object. • To know that the direction of a beam or ray of light travelling from a light source can be indicated by a straight line with an arrow. • To understand that when a beam of light is reflected from a surface, its direction changes. • To make careful observations and comparisons.	• Light is needed in order to see. • There are many light sources and that the main source of light in daytime is the Sun.	Design and technology QCA Unit 6A 'Shelters'
Lesson 16: Shadow investigation	QCA Unit 6F 'How we see things' • To identify factors which might affect the size and position of the shadow of an object. • To investigate how changing one factor causes the shadow to change. • To consider trends in results and to decide whether there are results which do not fit the pattern. • To check measurements by repeating them. • To recognise differences between shadows and reflections.	• Light is needed in order to see. • There are many light sources and that the main source of light in daytime is the Sun. • When light is blocked by some materials, shadows are formed.	English NLS Term 1 T9: To plan a short section of a story as a script.
Lesson 17: Changing circuits	QCA Unit 6G 'Changing circuits' • To know that the brightness of bulbs, or speed of motors, in a circuit can be changed. • To appreciate that care needs to be taken when components in a circuit are changed to ensure that bulbs/motors do not burn out.	• Know which common appliances use electricity and the dangers associated with mains electricity. • Understand why some circuits work and others do not.	Speaking and listening Objective 58: To use a range of oral techniques to present persuasive argument.
Lesson 18: Conventional circuit symbols	QCA Unit 6G 'Changing circuits' • To know that there are conventional symbols for components in circuits and that these can be used to draw diagrams of circuits • To appreciate that circuit diagrams, using these symbols, can be understood by anyone who knows the symbols and can be used for constructing and interpreting circuits.	• Know which common appliances use electricity and the dangers associated with mains electricity. • Understand why some circuits work and others do not. • A complete circuit is required for a device to work and switches can be used to control devices.	Geography PoS (2c) To use atlases and globes, and maps and plans at a range of scales.
Lesson 19: Burglar alarm (1)	PoS Sc1 'Scientific enquiry' and Sc4 'Physical processes' • To construct circuits, incorporating a battery or power supply and a range of switches, to make electrical devices work. • To test ideas using evidence from observation and measurement. • To use simple equipment and material appropriately. • To use scientific knowledge and understanding to explain observations and conclusions. • To review their work and the work of others and describe its significance and limitations..	• A complete circuit is required for a device to work. • Switches can be used to control devices.	Design and technology PoS (4c) How mechanisms can be used to make things move in different ways, using a range of equipment; (4d) How electrical circuits, including those with simple switches, can be used to achieve results that work.
Lesson 20: Burglar alarm (2)	PoS Sc1 'Scientific enquiry' and Sc4 'Physical processes' • To construct circuits, incorporating a battery or power supply and a range of switches, to make electrical devices work. • To test ideas using evidence from observation and measurement. • To use simple equipment and material appropriately. • To use scientific knowledge and understanding to explain observations and conclusions. • To review their work and the work of others and describe its significance and limitations.	• A complete circuit is required for a device to work. • Switches can be used to control devices.	Design and technology PoS (4c) How mechanisms can be used to make things move in different ways, using a range of equipment; (4d) How electrical circuits, including those with simple switches, can be used to achieve results that work.

Identification keys

Learning objectives
QCA Unit 6A 'Interdependence and adaptation'
● To make and use keys to identify animals in a particular habitat.

Resources
'Identification keys' flipchart file; lists of plants and animals (see Independent work); large sheets of paper.

Links to other subjects
ICT
PoS (2a) How to develop and refine ideas by bringing together, organising and reorganising text, tables, images and sound as appropriate; (4a) Review what they and others have done to help them develop their ideas.
● Investigate minibeasts in the local area and ask the children to create an identification key for them. Encourage them to exchange their keys with other children to see whether their completed keys are effective.

Whiteboard tools
Erase or delete shapes to reveal answers (double-click and select Delete in the Object edit toolbox). If required, use the Print button in the Teacher tools menu to print pages 6 to 11 for children to cut up and classify the animals.

⬉ Marquee select tool

✎ Pen tool

⌨ Floating keyboard

🗑 Delete button

🗄 Eraser tool

🖶 Print button

📖 Resource library

🖊 Highlighter tool

◉ Activote (optional)

Starter
Go to page 2 of the 'Identification keys' flipchart and discuss the features of each animal. Look at the similarities and differences between these animals and begin to discuss ways of classifying them. Talk about how this could be displayed. Invite the children to move animals around the screen to classify them. The children may group the animals according to type, but point out that another way to group the animals is by habitat. Ask: *Could any of these animals live in the same habitat? In what kind of habitat would they live?*

Whole-class shared work
● Work through pages 3 and 4, talking about the layout of the identification key and the different questions that could be placed in each box.
● Ask the children to answer each question or statement, placing the animals correctly on the key. Support and model this process as necessary.
● Erase the boxes (and the animals placed on top) to reveal the answers.
● For page 4, discuss what the octopus, whale and turtle have in common. (They all live in the sea, so they are from the same kind of habitat.)
● Move on to page 5. Invite the children to look at each animal and think about how they can make a key to classify them. Encourage them to use the resources on the page to make an identification key, and to write a question or statement on each block to classify the animals.
● Discuss the kind of habitat in which these animals may be found. Ask: *What other animals could be found in this habitat?* If time is available, explore the Resource library 📖 for animals that could be added to the key.
● Discuss why identification keys are helpful. For example, you could use a key when investigating minibeasts in a local habitat. It should be possible to identify any number of animals as the questions are based on identifying differences and all animals are different.

Independent work
● Provide the children with a list of animals with illustrations and large sheets of paper. Ask them to sort the animals by habitat and then to create identification keys for them.
● Support less able learners by helping them to identify common habitats, and by providing some questions for their identification keys. Work with a small group of three or four children on the interactive whiteboard, using page 6 to 11. (These pages can also be printed out for the children to cut out the animals and sort them into a key.)
● Challenge more able learners with a list of plants as well as animals (with illustrations if appropriate) so that they can begin to classify different kinds of living organisms, noting the different scientific features of each and grouping them in a suitable manner.

Plenary
● Discuss any misconceptions and problems that may have arisen.
● Look at one of the completed keys on pages 6 to 11 and encourage the children to note positive points of the work.
● Using page 12 of the flipchart, discuss and list some of the questions and statements that the children used to classify the animals and plants in their identification key. Highlight the most effective ones.
● Pages 13 to 17 offer questions to assess the children's understanding of keys. Ask them to identify the mystery animal behind the question mark, only revealing the other animals if they struggle to work out the answer.

Food chains

Starter
Open the 'Food chains' flipchart and go to page 2. Discuss each animal and what it eats. Use this information to group the animals on the page.

Talk about how this information can be displayed in a formal way. Move on to page 3 and look at the food chain displayed on this page. Explain how the food chain starts with a *producer*, and has a *primary consumer* and *secondary consumer*. Tell the children that a food chain represents the feeding relationships between organisms. The arrows represent the idea that something *is eaten by* the next link in the food chain. (Another way to remember this is that the arrow points towards the stomach.)

Invite individuals to come to the board and label the parts of the food chain. Continue this work on page 4. Point out that humans can also be primary consumers. Draw attention to the fact that humans can eat meat (primary consumers) and vegetables (primary producers).

Whole-class shared work
● Go to page 5. Explain that a food chain starts with a primary energy source, such as the Sun. (Plants use the Sun's energy to make food through photosynthesis.) Plants are then the first link to be eaten in the food chain; they are the producers. Point out that both food chains on pages 3 and 4 started with a plant (grass).
● Invite a child to drag the animals, labels and arrows on page 5 to create an accurate food chain. Point out that food chains usually represent the feeding relationships between plants and animals in a particular habitat. For instance, a lion may be able to eat a fox, but it would not be appropriate to add it to this food chain.
● Continue this work on pages 6 to 8 to enable the children to become confident in constructing a food chain.
● Talk about the differences in each food chain as appropriate. Discuss how it is possible for more than one primary consumer to eat the primary producer, and for more than one primary consumer to be eaten by a secondary consumer. Remind the children that humans can be secondary consumers as well as primary consumers.

Independent work
● Arrange for less able learners to work in pairs. Provide a variety of pictures and ask them to place them onto sugar paper using an appropriate format for a food chain.
● Arrange for middle-ability groups to work on the photocopiable activity sheet 'Food chains'. Work through the worksheet placing the correct energy source, primary producer, primary consumer and secondary consumer into the boxes in the tables.
● Provide the children in higher-ability groups with their own copies of the photocopiable sheet and encourage them to complete it unaided. As an extension, ask the children to design their own food chains. Ensure that they have at least four items in each chain.

Plenary
● Discuss any misconceptions and problems that may have arisen.
● Encourage the children to present their food chains.
● Work through the quiz on pages 9 to 16, inviting individuals to click on an answer. A cheer signifies a correct answer.
● Once the quiz has been completed, invite the children to complete the table on page 17, placing each illustration in the correct column.

Plant roots

Learning objectives
QCA Unit 6A 'Interdependence and adaptation'
● To know that water and nutrients are taken in through the root.
● To know that roots anchor the plant in the soil.

Resources
'Plant roots' flipchart file; photocopiable page 127 'Plant roots'; variety of plants with different roots (for example, root vegetables, onions, pot plants).

Links to other subjects
Geography
QCA Unit 15 'The mountain environment ' QCA Unit 23 'Investigating coasts'
● Investigate plants that are found in mountain and coastal environments. If possible, find out about the root systems of these plants and think about how the plants are anchored into the mountain side or sandy areas.

Starter
Open the 'Plant roots' flipchart and go to page 2. Review the children's knowledge of what plants need to grow well. (For example: light, water and nutrients.) Like humans and animals, plants need food and water to stay healthy. Lead the children to consider how water and nutrients (in the form of dissolved minerals) in the soil are absorbed by plants. (Through the roots.)
Move on to page 3 to sort the true and false statements about plants and roots.

Whole-class shared work
● Use page 4 to annotate class thoughts about why plant roots are so important. Not only do plant roots absorb water and nutrients from the soil, they also anchor the plant into the ground. Ask: *What would happen if the roots didn't anchor the plant?*
● Go to the diagram of a dandelion and its roots on page 5. This is an example of a *tap root*. Point out how the primary root is a lot thicker than the secondary branching roots. These roots store food; some tap roots can be eaten (root vegetables). Encourage the children to name examples of root vegetables, such as carrots, parsnips, beets and radishes.
● A diagram of the *fibrous roots* of grass is on page 6. This is a system of slender roots with many smaller branching roots. Many flowers have a similar root system.
● Page 7 illustrates oak *tree roots*. Point out that although the root system is similar to the grass roots, the roots of a tree spread further and are much thicker because they need to anchor the weight of the tree.
● Spring onion roots are illustrated on page 8. This diagram shows *adventitious roots*, which grow directly from a stem. In this case, the roots grow out of a bulb, which is a special kind of stem. Roots that are produced from plant cuttings are another example of adventitious roots.
● Use page 9 to compare and contrast the different roots.
● Go to page 10. Discuss whether the roots of a pot-bound plant would spread in a different way from the roots of a plant in the ground. With the children, draw what the roots might look like.

Independent work
● Give each child a copy of photocopiable page 127 'Plant roots' to investigate the plant roots that they have been given.
● Ask the children to produce a labelled drawing of the plant and its roots, showing where the plant is most likely to take in water and nutrients.
● Encourage the children to write a sentence to describe how the roots anchor the plant.
● Display page 9 to support less confident children in their drawing.
● Encourage more confident children to write further sentences about the roots of the plant that they have been given.

Plenary
● Invite the children to share their drawings. Discuss any misconceptions that may have arisen during this exercise. Page 11 can be used for notes.
● Although soil contains a lot of nutrients, fertiliser can be added to it to give plants more nutrients and to provide nutrients that are not commonly found in that particular type of soil. Use page 12 to identify the ingredients that can be found in fertilser (nitrogen; phosphorus; potassium; sulphur; calcium; magnesium; water).
● Page 13 provides an opportunity to remind the children of the vocabulary used in this lesson.

Whiteboard tools
 Pen tool

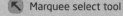 Marquee select tool

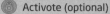 Activote (optional)

Mouldy bread investigation

Learning objectives
QCA Unit 6B 'Micro-organisms'
● To know that micro-organisms are often too small to be seen.
● To make suggestions about observing food, bearing in mind the need for safety.
● To know that micro-organisms can cause food to decay.
● To know that food needs to be handled and stored with care.
● To know that micro-organisms which cause decay are living organisms.

Resources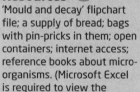
'Mould and decay' flipchart file; a supply of bread; bags with pin-pricks in them; open containers; internet access; reference books about micro-organisms. (Microsoft Excel is required to view the embedded spreadsheet in the flipchart.)

Links to other subjects
Design and technology
QCA Unit 5b 'Bread'
● Find out what the children know about the rules for basic food hygiene and other safe practices when preparing food.

Whiteboard tools
Activprimary will switch to Desktop mode when the spreadsheet is opened. Click on Return to main screen to return to the flipchart. Use the Handwriting tool or Floating keyboard to add data to the spreadsheet cells.

🔲 Pen tool

🅡 Marquee select tool

🖵 Desktop mode

🔝 Return to main screen

✎ Handwriting tool

⌨ Floating keyboard

Starter
Encourage the children to carry out research, using books and the internet, into what a micro-organism is. Compile their findings and comments and write them onto page 2 of the 'Mould and decay' flipchart.
   Ask questions such as: *Are micro-organisms alive? Are they good or bad?*

Whole-class shared work
● Explain to the children that they are going to investigate the effects of micro-organisms on bread, by observing how quickly bread becomes mouldy depending on heat or light.
● Using page 3 of the flipchart, ask the children what they have to remember when observing food. Write down their ideas.
● Click on the skull icon at the top of the page to view safety advice in Page notes. The text can be selected and added to the page. It is important to refer to your school's health and safety guidance on handling micro-organisms. For further guidance on safe microbiology, see *Be Safe* (ASE) and *Studying Micro-organisms in Primary Schools* (CLEAPSS guide L190).
● Go to page 4 of the flipchart and consider the questions that should be asked. Think about the area or focus of the investigation, the hypothesis and variables, and annotate the table accordingly.
● Move on to pages 5 and 6 and encourage the children to think about what equipment they will need and how they can ensure a fair test.
● Ask the children how much mould grows on bread over a period of a week, for example. Discuss how they will record and measure the results (without handling the bread). One possible way to measure the mould is to draw a square-centimetre grid on the food bag with a fine marker pen before placing the bread in it, so that the children can measure the area of mould on the bread.

Independent work
● Support lower-ability groups with their investigation of mouldy bread by providing a given hypothesis and materials.
● The middle-ability group should investigate mouldy bread with a given hypothesis but should decide on what materials they require as a group.
● The higher-ability group should design their own fair test, deciding what hypothesis they will focus on, as well as what materials and methods they require.
● Once the children have carried out their fair test, go to page 7 and encourage them to discuss which graph would be best for plotting their results.

Plenary
● Enter the results in the spreadsheet embedded on page 7, as a whole class. (The spreadsheet can be adjusted to suit the investigation.)
● Discuss any misconceptions that may have arisen during this exercise. Talk about any problems the children came across and how they overcame them.
● Use the questions on page 8 to encourage the children to analyse their results. Ask them which conditions are best for slowing down the rate of mould growth.
● Discuss how the children can tell that the mould is a living organism (because it grows). Point out that the individual spores (the micro-organisms) are invisible to the naked eye but when a lot of the spores grow in one place they can look extremely unpleasant.

Beneficial decay

Learning objectives
QCA Unit 6B 'Micro-organisms'
● To know that micro-organisms bring about decay.
● To understand that decay can be beneficial.

Resources
'Mould and decay' flipchart file; books about decay; access to the internet; digital cameras; clipboards, pens and paper; paper, glue and materials for making posters or collages; extra adult support for Whole-class shared work.

Links to other subjects
PSHE
PoS (3b) That bacteria and viruses can affect health and that following simple, safe routines can reduce their spread.
● Discuss ways to prevent viruses and infections being spread.

Starter
Go to page 9 of the 'Mould and decay' flipchart and ask the question: *What is decay?* Invite them to research this question using books and the internet.

Move on to page 10 and ask the children to use the information found at the start of the session to answer the question: *What are the benefits of decay?* Write their ideas onto the flipchart.

Next, go to page 11 and prompt the children to consider what would happen if materials did not decay. Encourage them to think about the waste from the kitchen, for example. Ask: *What would happen if vegetable peelings and leftover food did not decay after they were thrown away?* Make notes of the children's ideas.

Whole-class shared work
● Display page 12 of the flipchart. Invite volunteers to come to the board and move the objects to the appropriate side depending on whether or not they think they decay.
● Arrange to go for a walk around the school grounds. Split into small groups to look for evidence of items that are decaying or not decaying.
● Help the children to collect evidence by taking digital photos, collecting samples (ensuring safety), and taking notes. Explain that they will be using this information during their Independent work (see below).
● Back in class, use the children's notes and page 13 of the flipchart to make lists of things that do and do not decay.
● Discuss the lists that have been compiled. Ask the children if they notice anything about the lists. They should notice that natural materials decay, while most objects that do not decay are made from plastics and metals. Explain that natural materials decay because micro-organisms grow and feed on them.

Independent work
● Display page 14. Invite less able learners to make a collage or poster about things that decay, addressing the benefits of decay. Use the Resource library 📖, and Shapes 🔷 and Lines tool | to draft a poster on this page to support the children.
● Invite the middle-ability group to make a collage or poster of things that do not decay. Ask them to note the difficulties that this may cause.
● Suggest that more able learners make a collage or poster which incorporates both things that do and do not decay. Challenge them to include notes as to the benefits and problems that arise with objects that do and do not decay.

Whiteboard tools
Use the Resource library and Lines and Shapes tools to help draft a poster on page 14 of the flipchart.

🖊 Pen tool

⌨ Floating keyboard

🢤 Marquee select tool

📖 Resource library

| Lines tool

🔷 Shapes tool

Plenary
● Discuss any misconceptions that may have arisen during this exercise. Talk about any problems the children came across and how they overcame them.
● Invite the children to present their collages or posters and explain why they have arranged them the way they have. What are the benefits of decay? What would happen if nothing decayed?
● Use page 15 of the flipchart to check the children's understanding of what they have learned today.

Dissolving investigation

Learning objectives
QCA Unit 6C 'More about dissolving'
● To turn ideas about helping solids dissolve more quickly into a form that can be investigated and decide how to carry out a fair test.
● To decide what apparatus to use and to make careful observations and measurements.
● To use a line graph to present results.
● To make comparisons and draw conclusions.

Resources
'Solutions' flipchart file; clear containers; spoons or sticks for stirring; measuring jugs; water (cold, tepid and warm); solids to test for whether or not they dissolve (such as different types of sugar, stock cubes and salt). (Microsoft Excel is required to view the embedded spreadsheet in the flipchart.)

Links to other subjects
Mathematics
NNS: Use, read and write standard metric units; suggest suitable units and measuring equipment.
● Discuss whether a test would be fair if the types of measurement used were inconsistent.

Whiteboard tools
Activprimary will switch to Desktop mode when the spreadsheet is opened. Use the Handwriting tool or Floating keyboard to add data to the spreadsheet.

- Pen tool
- Marquee select tool
- Desktop mode
- Return to main screen
- Handwriting tool
- Floating keyboard
- Highlighter tool

Starter
Discuss what is meant by the word *dissolving*. Using page 2 of the 'Solutions' flipchart, ask volunteers to come and write, inside the jug, some things that they think dissolve.

Move on to page 3 and discuss what would help the solids to dissolve. This list could include: size of particles of the solid; temperature of water; volume of water; stirring. This discussion will help the children to form ideas when planning their test.

Whole-class shared work
● Ask the children to discuss and decide what is meant by the term *a fair test*. Make some notes on page 4 of the flipchart.
● Split the children into ability groups and begin to plan a fair test for finding out what makes solids dissolve more quickly.
● Encourage the children to feed back their ideas to the whole class. If possible, arrange for each group to consider and talk about one of the following: *size of particles of the solid, temperature of water, volume of water and stirring.*
● Using the table on page 5 of the flipchart, and suggestions from the class, plan a fair test for the area that the lower-ability group will investigate.
● Point out that the dissolved solid must result in a relatively clear liquid; otherwise it will be very hard to see whether it has fully dissolved. Discuss ideas for solids that could be used in the investigation.

Independent work
● Arrange for the lower-ability group to plan a fair test using the notes discussed during the Whole-class shared work. They should then carry out the test, counting the number of stirs. Help the children to record their findings in a table, and then write a conclusion.
● Encourage the middle-ability group to plan a fair test using the information from earlier in the lesson. Allow them to choose from size of particles of the solid, temperature of water and volume of water. They should then carry out the test counting the number of stirs. Ask the children to record their findings in a table and then write a conclusion.
● The higher-ability group should complete the same work as the middle-ability group but with less support and guidance.

Plenary
● Invite the children to feed back their results and to enter their data into a spreadsheet. An embedded spreadsheet on page 6 contains a number of results tables and graphs. Select an appropriate results table; it can be altered to suit the children's investigations. The sheets can also be copied to enable other groups to input their results: right-click on the tab at the bottom of the sheet; select Move or Copy from the pop-up menu; select the option Create a copy and click OK.
● Discuss the children's results and look at how they answer their investigation questions. Were the children's hypotheses correct? If not, discuss why the results were not as expected.
● Use page 7 of the flipchart to reinforce the children's knowledge and understanding of this activity. Encourage them to discuss answers in pairs or groups before contributing their ideas to the whole class.
● Go to page 8 and encourage the children to search for some of the vocabulary used during this session. Invite individuals to come and highlight the words that they spot.

Solutions and evaporation

Learning objectives
QCA Unit 6C 'More about dissolving'
● To make predictions about which types of water contain dissolved materials and test these predictions.
● To know that when solids dissolve, a clear solution is formed (which may be coloured); the solid cannot be separated by filtering.
● To make predictions about what happens when water from a solution evaporates and to test these predictions.
● To know that when the liquid evaporates from a solution the solid is left behind.

Resources
'Solutions' flipchart file; a selection of five clear liquids for each group (some should have material dissolved within it and some should not).

Links to other subjects
PSHE
PoS (3e) To recognise the different risks in different situations and then decide how to behave responsibly.
● Discuss the dangers of drinking unidentified liquids. Which liquids should be kept well away from children? Why are safety lids important?

Whiteboard tools
Convert handwriting to text using the Recognition tool.

[Pen] Pen tool

[T] Text editor tool

[K] Marquee select tool

[Highlighter] Highlighter tool

[abc] Recognition tool

Starter
Before you begin, make sure that the children understand that they must not taste the liquids that you are going to give them.

Provide each (ability-based) group with a selection of five clear liquids in beakers labelled *1, 2, 3, 4* and *5*. Ask the children to decide whether each liquid has material dissolved in it or not. Ensure that they understand that when a solid is dissolved, it remains in the liquid (the solution) but cannot be seen: one example could be sugar that is added to tea.

Complete the chart on page 9 of the flipchart together. This chart will serve as a prediction of the test carried out during the main section of this lesson.

Whole-class shared work
● Display the question on page 10: *How can you find out if your predictions are true?* Remind the children of any work that they have done on filtering. Establish that it will not be possible to separate dissolved solutions by filtering so another method needs to be used.
● Encourage the children to suggest other ways to get rid of the water. Lead them to think of methods of evaporation: for example, they could leave quantities of each liquid in a warm place to evaporate. Invite the children to write their suggestions on how to check their predictions (without tasting the solution) on the flipchart.
● Discuss how they could check whether an evaporated liquid was a solution or whether it was pure water. For example, they could feel whether any residue was left; if the liquid were a solution, the solid would be left behind in some form as the water evaporates. Point out that the solid would probably look different from its original form.
● Use this information to plan a fair test using the grid on page 11, and to list the materials required on page 12. Encourage the children to work in their groups to complete the plan and to decide what materials will be required to carry out their fair test.

Independent work
● Ask the children to test their predictions using evaporation. Encourage them to think of a way to record their results using a table or chart.
● Support the lower-ability groups by showing them how to create a table or chart for their results and by working with them to form a conclusion about their results.
● Challenge the higher-ability group to decide on how to display their results and to analyse their results to draw conclusions, without any adult support.

Plenary
● Invite the children to present their results to the rest of the class. Make notes on page 13.
● Ask the children to complete the quiz on page 14. Suggest that they discuss the questions in their groups before answering; then discuss their ideas as a whole class.
● Finish by completing the word search on page 15 to reinforce the knowledge and vocabulary from this lesson. Invite volunteers to come and highlight the words that they spot. Use the spyglass to check answers.

Mixing materials

Learning objectives
QCA Unit 6D 'Reversible and irreversible changes'
● To know that mixing materials can cause them to change.
● To know that some changes that occur when materials are mixed cannot easily be reversed.
● To make careful observations and to record and explain these using scientific knowledge and understanding.

Resources
'Mixing materials' flipchart file; a range of materials such as: sand, powder paint, salt, plaster of Paris, flour, Andrews salts, baking powder; paper and pens.

Links to other subjects
Mathematics
NNS: Suggest suitable units and measuring equipment to estimate or measure length, mass or capacity.
● Discuss the importance of using standard measures in order to carry out a fair test.

Starter
Display the science challenge on page 2 of the flipchart and discuss it with the children.

Provide a range of materials including sand, powder paint, salt, plaster of Paris, flour, Andrews salts and baking powder. Invite the children to work in groups to predict if these materials will dissolve in water, not dissolve in water, or change in another way.

Ask the children to combine their predictions and invite individuals to come and drag and drop the items onto the chart, explaining the reasons for their choices.

Whole-class shared work
● Split the class into mixed-ability groups. Ask the children to discuss how they can plan a fair test to explore their predictions.
● Display page 3 to provide guidance for the children's group discussions.
● Come back together as a class and encourage the children to discuss what question should be asked, the area of focus and the hypothesis. Encourage them to consider the controlled, independent and dependent variables. Annotate the page with their ideas.
● Once the plan is complete, invite the class in their mixed-ability groups to discuss the materials that they will require to carry out their fair test. List these on page 4 of the flipchart.

Independent work
● Before you begin, make sure that the children understand that they must not eat or drink any of the materials that they are testing.
● Ask the children to remain in their groups and invite them to test each of the materials by adding water.
● Encourage the children to measure accurately and make careful observations. Invite them to record their results into a table devised by the group.
● As the children work, encourage them to use relevant vocabulary to broaden their knowledge and understanding of this task.

Plenary
● Invite the children to take turns in presenting their results to the rest of the class. Encourage them to use scientific knowledge and understanding in their explanations. Make notes on page 5.
● If there is time, go to page 6 of the flipchart for a vocabulary test. The test requires the children to match the scientific definition to the correct word by dragging them from the red box at the bottom of the page.
● Remind the children of previous work on evaporation and filtering, and of separating liquids and solids. Discuss whether the processes of evaporation and filtering could be applied to the solutions that they created in this investigation. They should realise that these processes will not reverse the mixing process for some of the solutions, such as the plaster of Paris. Emphasise that these solids and liquids have undergone an irreversible change; solutions that can be evaporated and filtered have undergone a reversible change.

Whiteboard tools
 Pen tool

 Floating keyboard

 Marquee select tool

Heating and cooling materials

Learning objectives
QCA Unit 6D 'Reversible and irreversible changes'
● To know that heating some materials can cause them to change.
● To know that cooling some materials can cause them to change.

Resources
'Changing materials' flipchart file; photocopiable page 128 'Heating and cooling materials'; a range of pictures (or real) materials such as: raw egg, cake mix, ice, jug, bar of chocolate, water, dough, fried egg, bread, unfired clay, cake and liquid chocolate; individual whiteboards and pens.

Links to other subjects
PSHE
PoS (3e) To recognise the different risks in different situations and then decide how to behave responsibly.
● Discuss the dangers surrounding heat and electricity. Draw up a set of guidelines for conducting science experiments.

Starter
Discuss ways of changing materials. Think about changes in the home that the children will be familiar with (such as freezing water to make an ice-cube or boiling an egg for breakfast).
Go to page 2 of the 'Changing materials' flipchart to make a list of items that the children think can be changed by heating and/or cooling.

Whole-class shared work
● Before you begin, make sure that the children understand that they must not eat or drink any of the materials that they will be working with.
● Provide a range of pictures or materials for the children to look at including raw egg, cake mix, ice-cubes, jug, bar of chocolate, water, dough, fried egg, bread, unfired clay, cake and liquid chocolate.
● Invite the children to discuss each material in turn, asking what change may happen if the material is heated or cooled.
● Allocate each child a partner of similar ability, and provide each pair with a copy of photocopiable page 128 'Heating and cooling materials'. Ask the children to cut out and place each object in the object column, then discuss the change that may happen if the object is heated or cooled and note whether the change is reversible or not.
● Display page 3 and invite the children to present the predictions that they have made. Plan a fair test together.

Independent work
● Combine pairs of children to create groups of similarity. Invite less able learners to carry out a test on three of the materials. Provide adult support and supervision.
● Arrange for middle-ability groups to carry out a test on four of the materials. Provide some adult guidance. Please note that adult supervision will be required for safety reasons when heating materials.
● Invite more able learners to carry out a test on five of the materials (with adult supervision for safety reasons only).
● Each set of results should be presented in a chart.

Plenary
● Arrange for each group of children to present their results to the rest of the class. Make notes on page 4. This information should be used to form conclusions and indicate any misconceptions that may have arisen.
● Play the quiz on pages 5 to 11 of the flipchart. Click on the letter to hear a sound effect indicating whether or not the answer is correct.

Whiteboard tools
Use the Pen tool to write the list in the Starter.

 Pen tool

 Activote (optional)

Burning materials

Starter
Open the 'Changing materials' flipchart and click on the button next to Lesson 10. This takes you to page 12. Have a class discussion about objects that can be burned and the new material that is made as a result. Write the children's ideas onto the page.

Show the children some pictures of a piece of paper, a slice of bread, a match and a candle. Organise them into small mixed-ability groups to discuss what changes may occur when these objects are burned and whether the change is reversible.

Whole-class shared work
- Invite each group to state their prediction for what would happen when a piece of paper is burned.
- Display page 13 of the flipchart. Explain that the children need to watch the video clip of a piece of paper being burned. Invite them to discuss whether the change is reversible or not.
- Now watch the video clips of the slice of bread, candle and match being burned. Before each clip is played, ask the children to state their prediction.
- Make sure you spend some time discussing the dangers of this type of test. As well as the obvious dangers of using matches and setting things on fire, the children need to know that some objects give off poisonous gases when burned. Stress the importance of never playing with matches or creating fires.
- Invite the children to record their observations in a table format.

Independent work
- Rearrange the children into groups of similar ability. Invite the lower-ability group to make a poster about the changes that occurred with the bread. Was the change reversible? Ask the children to state the safety issues. Provide adult support while the children work.
- Ask the middle-ability group to make a poster about the changes that occurred with the wooden match. Was the change reversible? Encourage the children to discuss safety issues and comment on the new materials that are formed as a result of burning.
- Challenge the higher-ability group to make a poster or slideshow presentation showing the changes that can occur when materials are burned, and the safety issues around this topic. Encourage the children to pay particular attention to noting the new materials that can be formed as a result of burning. Suggest to the children that they may use other sources of information including outside reading and internet resources to inform their work.

Plenary
- Invite the children to present their slideshow presentations and/or posters to the rest of the class. Encourage them to explain their posters using their scientific knowledge and understanding.
- Encourage the children to note the new materials made as a result of burning the material, the dangers that surround this area of investigation and whether the change caused by burning materials is reversible. Use page 14 to write notes as required.

Learning objectives
QCA Unit 6D 'Reversible and irreversible changes'
- To know that when materials are burned, new materials are formed.
- To know that the changes that occur when most materials are burned are not reversible.

Resources
'Heating and cooling materials' flipchart file; pictures of a piece of paper, slice of bread, a match and a candle; paper and materials to make posters; slideshow presentation software such as Microsoft PowerPoint (optional).

Links to other subjects
Speaking and listening
Objective 59: To analyse and evaluate how speakers present points effectively through use of language and gesture.
- Encourage the children to listen to how others present their posters or slideshows and how they make clear the dangers of burning materials.
PSHE
PoS (3g) School rules about health and safety, basic emergency aid procedures and where to get help.
- Discuss the school's health and safety policy. Could the children improve or add anything to the policy?

Whiteboard tools
Switch to Desktop mode to view the children's presentations. Click on Return to main screen to return to the flipchart.
- Pen tool
- Floating keyboard
- Marquee select tool
- Desktop mode
- Return to main screen

Balanced and unbalanced forces

Learning objectives
QCA Unit 6E 'Forces in action'
● To know that several forces may act on one object.
● To represent the direction of forces by arrows.
● To understand that when an object is stationary, the forces on it are balanced.
● To know that unbalanced forces change the speed or direction of movement on an object.

Resources
'Investigating forces' flipchart file; photocopiable page 129 'Balanced and unbalanced forces'; sugar paper; pens.

Links to other subjects
Geography
QCA Unit 15 'The mountain environment' QCA Unit 23 'Investigating coasts'
● Investigate the different winter and water sports that take place in mountain and coastal environments, respectively. Ask the children to identify the different forces at work. In each case, discuss the consequence if a force is unbalanced: for example, *What difficulties would a swimmer face if the waves in the sea are very strong?*

Starter
Using page 2 of the 'Investigating forces' flipchart, make a list of forces that the children are aware of. Show them the selection of pictures on pages 3 and 4. Label the pictures with the different forces acting upon the object in the picture.

Whole-class shared work
● Use page 5 to discuss the term *balanced force*. Explain that when an object is stationary the forces on it are balanced, as illustrated on the flipchart.
● Go to page 6 and introduce the term *unbalanced force*. Explain that an unbalanced force changes the speed, position or direction of movement of an object.
● Display page 7. Provide some sugar paper and pens and divide the children into small groups. Invite them to think of different situations where they have seen a balanced and unbalanced force. Ask them to take notes on the pieces of sugar paper. (They could perhaps use one piece for the balanced forces and one for the unbalanced forces.) Update the flipchart accordingly.
● Working in pairs, ask the children to choose one of the scenarios from the balanced forces list and one from the unbalanced forces list. Provide adult support and encourage the children to perform these scenarios safely.

Independent work
● Give each child a copy of photocopiable page 129 'Balanced and unbalanced forces' and ask them to work individually.
● Encourage less confident children to use the scenarios they have just acted out to inform their drawing. Suggest they draw one unbalanced force picture and one balanced force picture. Provide a word bank and adult support to enable the children to label their work effectively.
● Encourage middle-ability children to work without adult support.
● Challenge more confident children to use scenarios of their choosing, including scenarios that were not acted out. Encourage these children to work independently on this activity without additional support.

Plenary
● Invite the children to present their diagrams to the rest of the class.
● Discuss the forces acting on the object and whether it is balanced or unbalanced. Address any misconceptions. Make any notes on page 8.
● If time allows, invite some of the children to act out their scenarios safely.

Whiteboard tools
Use the Pen or Lines tool to add arrows to mark the forces at work on the object.

 Pen tool

 Line tool

Upthrust of liquids

Learning objectives
QCA Unit 6E 'Forces in action'
● To know that when an object is submerged in a liquid, the liquid provides an upward force (upthrust) on it.
● To take careful measurements of force using a forcemeter.
● To use tables to present results, identifying patterns and drawing conclusions.
● To evaluate repeated measures.

Resources
'Investigating forces' flipchart file; forcemeter; a selection of materials to use with the forcemeter, none of which will float (see page 12 of the flipchart); bowl of water. (Microsoft Excel is required to view the embedded spreadsheet in the flipchart.)

Links to other subjects
Mathematics:
NNS: Use, read and write standard metric units; record estimates and readings from scales to a suitable degree of accuracy.
● The children will explore the use of a forcemeter and develop an understanding of the units that it can measure.

Whiteboard tools
Activprimary will switch to Desktop mode when the spreadsheet is opened. Use the Handwriting tool or Floating keyboard to add data to the spreadsheet. To change existing text select Edit text from the Object edit toolbox.

⊡ Pen tool

⬉ Marquee select tool

▢ Desktop mode

▦ Return to main screen

✑ Handwriting tool

⌨ Floating keyboard

Ⓣ Edit text tool

◉ Activote (optional)

Starter
Remind the children of work that they have done on forces. Open the 'Investigating forces' flipchart and go to page 9. Show the children a forcemeter and ask them what units of measurements the forcemeter uses. (Newtons.)

Tell the children that weight is a force and it is measured in newtons with a forcemeter. Demonstrate how to use the forcemeter to take a reading of an object's weight.

Whole-class shared work
● Go to page 10 and record the weight of the object in newtons. Invite the children to work in pairs or small mixed-ability groups using the forcemeter to measure one object. Allow time for them to get used to using the forcemeter and help them to make accurate readings.
● Delete the shape on page 10 to reveal the next part of the investigation.
● Show the children a bowl of water (that is big enough to contain the object being measured). Tell them that you are going to place the object in the water and use the forcemeter to measure the weight of the object again. Using page 10, encourage the children to predict what will happen to the measurement.
● Submerge the object in water and then record the reading on the forcemeter on the bottom of page 10. Check the children's predictions. Ask: *Is the result unexpected? Why?*
● Go to page 11. Explain why the weight of the object appears to decrease when it is placed in water. Tell the children that upthrust is an upward force exerted on an object, so when an object is placed in water, the water provides an upward force (upthrust) on it.
● With the children, work out the upthrust of the liquid using the readings on page 10. Record the result on page 11.

Independent work
● Provide the children with a selection of objects. Invite them to take turns to measure each object out of the water, and then in the water, to calculate the amount of upthrust acting on the object.
● Display page 12. Ask the children to record the results in a grid using the following headings: *weight in air; weight in water; upthrust.*
● Suggest that they repeat the measurements of some of the objects to increase the accuracy of their results.
● Invite the children to present their results to the rest of the class, discussing any patterns that appear. Encourage them to explain their observations using scientific knowledge and understanding.
● Compare the results of all the groups.
● Go to page 13 of the flipchart and display a sample of results using the embedded spreadsheet; the results will also be displayed in a bar chart.
● Invite the children to transfer their own results from the table into a bar chart using spreadsheet software or graph paper.

Plenary
● Invite the children to present their results to the rest of the class. Encourage them to use their bar chart and scientific knowledge to explain their observations to the rest of the class.
● Discuss the possible reasons for differences in results and list these ideas on page 13.
● Invite the children to discuss which results are the most reliable and why this is the case.

Air resistance investigation

Learning objectives
QCA Unit 6E 'Forces in action'
- To know that air resistance slows moving objects.
- To know that when an object falls, air resistance acts in the opposite direction to the weight.
- To check measurements by repeating them.
- To interpret a line graph and use it to describe the motion of spinners falling.

Resources
'Investigating forces' flipchart file; photocopiable page 130 'Air resistance'; scissors.

Links to other subjects
Mathematics
NNS: Solve a problem by representing, extracting and interpreting data in tables, graphs, charts and diagrams.
- Choose another similar investigation such as testing paper aeroplanes. Encourage the children to reuse the data-handling and measuring skills that they used in the previous work.

Starter
Encourage the children to think about air resistance. Write down their ideas on page 14 of the 'Investigating forces' flipchart.

Whole-class shared work
- Provide each pair, or small mixed-ability group, with a copy of photocopiable page 130 'Air resistance'.
- Invite the children to make and explore the spinners. Encourage them to think about possible questions to investigate. Provide adult support if necessary.
- Ask the children to give some feedback to the rest of the class about their ideas for questions to investigate. Record their suggestions on page 15 of the flipchart.
- Areas of possible investigation could include; the size of the spinner; the amount of paper clips attached to the spinner; the height the spinner is dropped from; the material used to make the spinner, and so on. The time taken to reach the ground should be measured in every instance.
- Show the children the grid on page 16. Choose one of the children's questions/ideas for investigation and set up a fair test, filling out the grid. Encourage the children to think about the controlled, independent and dependent variables for the given situation.
- Arrange for the children to work in ability groups and choose an area for investigation. Invite them to plan a fair test using the model on page 16 of the flipchart.
- Provide additional support for less able learners to help them to design their fair test. Alternatively, allow them to use the model on the board.

Independent work
- Work with less able learners, supporting them as they carry out their spinner test. Encourage them to repeat their measurements and help them to transfer their results into a line graph.
- Arrange for the middle-ability group to carry out the spinner test with minimal support. Suggest that they repeat their measurements and record them on a line graph.
- Allow more able learners to carry out their chosen spinner test independently. Ask them to repeat measurements and record their results on a line graph.

Plenary
- Discuss any misconceptions that have arisen during the investigation.
- Invite each group to present their results to the rest of the class using their scientific knowledge and understanding.
- Identify and discuss any patterns in the results using page 17.

Whiteboard tools
Use the Pen tool and Eraser tool to write on pages and to erase answers when required.

 Pen tool

 Eraser tool

 Floating keyboard

Light and eyes

Learning objectives
QCA Unit 6F 'How we see things'
● To know that light travels from a source.
● To understand that we see light sources because light from the source enters our eyes.
● To use knowledge about light to explain observations.

Resources
'Light and shadow' flipchart file; photocopiable page 131 'Light and eyes'; torch or other light source for each group of children.

Links to other subjects
Speaking and listening
Objective 58: To use a range of oral techniques to present persuasive argument.
Objective 59: To analyse and evaluate how speakers present points effectively through use of language and gesture.
● Invite the children to make polished presentations using a variety of resources to enhance their contributions. Encourage excellent listening skills.

Whiteboard tools
Use the Pen or Lines tool to draw arrows.

 Pen tool

⊜ Floating keyboard

◥ Marquee select tool

❘ Lines tool

◉ Activote (optional)

Starter
Open the flipchart at page 2. Invite individuals to come to the board and click on the sources of light. Correct answers will be cheered and mistakes greeted with a groan.

Ensure that the children understand the difference between a light source and light that is reflected. To emphasise the point, darken the room and switch a torch on: a torch is a light source. Switch off the torch and hold up a reflective material; emphasise that it only *seems* to light up when a light shines on it.

Whole-class shared work
● Tell the children they will be investigating how light allows us to see objects. The organ of sight is the eye, and it is very sensitive. Show the children the diagram of the eye of page 3.
● Because the eye is a sensitive organ, emphasise that it is very important that the children do not shine torches directly into someone's eyes. Similarly they should never look directly look directly at the Sun.
● Go to page 4 and discuss how people are able to see objects. Referring back to the diagram on page 3, point out that light enters the eye via the pupil and through the lens. The children should begin to understand that they can see when light enters the eyes.
● Look at the second question on page 4. Ask the children what happens when they enter a dark room. How easily can they see objects? What will help them to see objects?
● Arrange for the children to work in a darkened room. Remind them about using torches safely: never shine a torch into a person's face.
● Group the children in mixed-ability pairs and ask them to investigate what happens to a beam of light when it is stopped by a piece of card.
● Encourage them to think about how people are able to see objects in the light and how visibility decreases as the amount of light decreases.
● Ask the groups to present their ideas to the rest of the class for discussion. Any misconceptions should be addressed.
● Invite children to come and draw their ideas on page 4. Place emphasis on drawing arrows to indicate the direction in which the light travels.

Independent work
● Provide each child with a copy of photocopiable page 131 and ask them to label the eye diagram. They must then draw and label a diagram of what happens when a light source is stopped by a piece of card.
● Ask the children to draw arrows to show the direction of the rays. In the third box they should draw a diagram showing how people are able to see objects.
● Provide a word bank for lower- and middle-ability children to use and provide plenty of adult support for lower-ability children.
● Higher-ability children should be encouraged to work independently.

Plenary
● Invite the children to present their work to the rest of the class, using scientific knowledge and understanding to explain their diagrams. Any misconceptions should be discussed. Use page 5 to make notes.
● Discuss the use of arrows in the diagrams.
● Pages 6 to 8 offer questions to assess the children's knowledge of the parts of the eye.
● Use pages 9 and 10 to consolidate the children's understanding of light and materials.

Reflecting light in mirrors

Learning objectives
QCA Unit 6F 'How we see things'
● To know that light from an object can be reflected by a mirror: the reflected light enters our eyes and we see the object.
● To know that the direction of a beam or ray of light travelling from a light source can be indicated by a straight line with an arrow.
● To understand that when a beam of light is reflected from a surface, its direction changes.
● To make careful observations and comparisons.

Resources
'Light and shadow' flipchart file; a torch for each group; mirrors; sugar paper and pens; photocopiable page 132 'Reflecting light in mirrors'.

Links to other subjects
Design and technology
QCA Unit 6A: Shelters
● Challenge the children to design a lighting system using mirrors for a shelter that can only have one or two lights.

Whiteboard tools
You will need to be in Design mode to insert links for scanned work. You can also upload scanned images via the Resource library.

🅰 Pen tool

🔦 Marquee select tool

❘ Lines tool

◎ Activote (optional)

🛠 Design mode

📖 Resource library

◆ Categories

⬭ Other location

⊞ Browse other location

Starter
Ask the children if they can find ways of seeing behind them. Develop a discussion about reflecting and mirrors. Record the children's suggestions on page 11 of the flipchart.
   Next, invite the children to see if they can move a beam of light around the classroom. Can they explain what is happening to the light? Make a note of their thoughts and explanations on page 12.

Whole-class shared work
● Look at the diagram on page 13 of the flipchart together.
● The diagram provides a challenge for the children to complete. They are asked to shine the torch in a way to make the beam of light touch each mirror and return to the source of light. Discuss how this might be achieved by angling the mirrors.
● Remind the children not to shine the torches into people's faces.
● Ask volunteers to use the Lines tool ❘ or Pen tool to add arrows to the diagram showing the direction of the beam.

Independent work
● Arrange for the children to work in a darkened room in ability groups of various sizes. Remind them of the challenge: they need to bounce the light off each mirror and return the light back to the source without adult intervention, where possible.
● Help the children to allocate tasks within the group: one child holds the torch, one maps the direction of the beam on sugar paper and all the others hold mirrors.
● Provide the children in the lower-ability group with copies of photocopiable page 132 and encourage them to draw a diagram of what would happen if three children had mirrors (circle the number three on the sheet). Remind them to take care to draw the direction of the beam of light with an arrow.
● The children in the middle-ability group should do the same as the lower-ability group, but with five mirrors.
● The higher-ability group should work independently and do the same as the other two groups but with seven mirrors.

Plenary
● Display page 14. Invite the children to present and explain their diagrams using scientific knowledge and understanding. Are their results the same as predicted?
● Encourage the children to compare their diagrams to others in the class.
● Check that they have used arrows to show the direction of the beam of light. Make sure that any misconceptions are addressed.
● The children's diagrams can be added to page 14 as hyperlinks or as scanned images.
● Use pages 15 and 16 to consolidate the children's knowledge and understanding of light.

Shadow investigation

Learning objectives
QCA Unit 6F 'How we see things'
● To identify factors which might affect the size and position of the shadow of an object.
● To investigate how changing one factor causes the shadow to change.
● To consider trends in results and to decide whether there are results which do not fit the pattern.
● To check measurements by repeating them.
● To recognise differences between shadows and reflections.

Resources
'Light and shadow' flipchart file; photocopiable page 133 'Shadow investigation'; a torch for each group and a darkened room.

Links to other subjects
English
NLS Term 1 T9: To plan a short section of a story as a script.
● Encourage the children to write a short script for a shadow puppet play.

Starter
Begin by asking the children to consider what a shadow is. Write their thoughts on page 17 of the 'Light and shadow' flipchart.
Encourage the children to think about what could affect the size and position of a shadow. Suggest that they investigate this question, using a darkened room. Remind the children to take care not to shine the torch in people's eyes and to keep safe in the darkened room. Ask them to give feed back to add their ideas to page 18 of the flipchart.

Whole-class shared work
● Go to page 19 and pose the problem to the children. Ask volunteers to move the light source on the page to where they consider the optimal position to be. Ask them to explain their reasons.
● Encourage the children to investigate the optimal conditions for a shadow puppet show. Discuss what a shadow puppet show is and why the lighting is important.
● Invite the children to use the plan on photocopiable page 133 'Shadow investigation'. Arrange for them to work in ability groups (providing support for less able learners as required).
● Encourage the children to think about what controlled, independent and dependent variables they will need. They will also need to list any materials they will require and explain the method of investigation.
● Arrange for the children to spend some time listening to each other's ideas and plans. At this point, iron out any misconceptions and encourage the children to modify their plans if necessary.

Independent work
● Enable all the children, in their ability groups, to carry out the planned investigations. Ensure that all groups attempt to find the optimal position for light in a shadow puppet show.
● Ask the children to write measurements and results on a table stating what effect the light has on the puppet.
● Vary the level of support to suit the different abilities. More able learners should work unaided.

Plenary
● Display page 20 and invite the children to share their findings with the rest of the class. Address any misconceptions.
● Suggest that the children compare their results with those of the rest of the class to check if the same result has been reached.

Whiteboard tools
Use the Pen tool to write the children's ideas on the board. Use the Marquee select tool to move the light source behind the shadow puppet.

 Pen tool

 Marquee select tool

Changing circuits

Learning objectives
QCA Unit 6G 'Changing circuits'
● To know that the brightness of bulbs, or speed of motors, in a circuit can be changed.
● To appreciate that care needs to be taken when components in a circuit are changed to ensure that bulbs/motors do not burn out.

Resources
'Circuits' flipchart file; photocopiable page 134 'Changing circuits'; a selection of working circuits; circuit boards and equipment; individual whiteboards; paper and pens.

Links to other subjects
Speaking and listening
Objective 58: To use a range of oral techniques to present persuasive argument.
● Suggest that the children prepare a short talk to make to the younger children in the school about the dangers of electricity.

Starter
Go to page 2 of the flipchart and pose the question: *What do we need circuits for?* Write the children's responses on the page.

Continue to page 3 and ask the children what components they would need to make a circuit. This should reinforce their prior knowledge of circuits. Make a list of the components on the page. Now go to page 4 and invite volunteers to construct circuits using the pictures on the board. Discuss the purposes for each circuit and any misconceptions the children may have.

Whole-class shared work
● Show the children a selection of working circuits. Ask them to think about the changes that could be made to the circuits to alter the brightness of the bulb and to write these down on individual whiteboards or paper.
● Invite the children to present their ideas to the rest of the class. List the best ideas on page 5 of the flipchart and discuss any misconceptions that may arise.
● Challenge the children to use their knowledge and understanding to plan an investigation to see if their ideas work. Arrange for them to work in ability groups and assign tasks to each group.
● Suggest that the lower-ability group plan to change the brightness of a bulb. Provide a word bank and some adult support.
● Challenge the middle-ability group to plan to change the brightness of a bulb or the speed of a motor. Provide a word bank and minimal adult support.
● Set the higher-ability group the challenge of planning to change the brightness of a bulb or the speed of a motor with little or no adult support.

Independent work
● Display page 6 and provide each child with a copy of photocopiable page 134.
● Ask the children to design circuits for:
    ● a bright bulb or a fast motor
    ● a dim bulb or a slow motor
    ● a circuit that can switch a bulb on and off.
● Provide the children with circuit boards and equipment to allow them to investigate.
● Support the lower-ability groups with visual stimulus on the interactive whiteboard, and ask them to make circuits for bulbs only.
● Challenge the higher-ability groups to investigate how they can create circuits with varying degrees of motor speed or bulb brightness.

Plenary
● Invite each group to present one of their circuits and explain how it works, using scientific knowledge and understanding. Write notes on page 7 addressing any misconceptions.
● Encourage the children to discuss any difficulties that they have experienced and how they overcame these. How did they ensure that the bulb or motor did not burn out?

Whiteboard tools
Use the Lines tool to link components in circuits. Use the Duplicate function in the Object edit toolbox to create multiple copies of an object.

⬚ Pen tool

◥ Marquee select tool

▮ Lines tool

▦ Duplicate function

Conventional circuit symbols

Learning objectives

QCA Unit 6G 'Changing circuits'

● To know that there are conventional symbols for components in circuits and that these can be used to draw diagrams of circuits.

● To appreciate that circuit diagrams, using these symbols, can be understood by anyone who knows the symbols and can be used for constructing and interpreting circuits.

Resources

'Changing circuits' flipchart file; photocopiable page 135 'Circuit symbols'.

Links to other subjects
Geography

PoS (2c) To use atlases and globes, and maps and plans at a range of scales.

● Relate the use of symbols in science to those used in geography on maps to represent items.

Starter

Ask the children about the difficulties they had with drawing the circuits for the last lesson. Ask: *Why is it important to have conventional symbols for drawing circuits?* Encourage the children to voice their opinions and add them to page 8 of the flipchart.

Introduce the children to the different types of symbols on page 9. Do they recognise any of the symbols?

Whole-class shared work

● Display page 10 of the flipchart and look at the diagram. It shows a circuit drawn without the use of conventional symbols. Demonstrate how to redraw it with conventional symbols by dragging the symbols and using the Lines tool ▢ to link them.

● Now invite the children to find a diagram they have drawn without the use of conventional symbols. Challenge them to redraw it using conventional symbols. Display the list of symbols on page 11 of the flipchart for reference while they work.

● Spend some time comparing these new diagrams with groups of similar ability. Encourage the children to use their scientific knowledge and understanding. Address any misconceptions.

Independent work

● Provide each child with a copy of photocopiable page 135. Encourage the children to label each symbol accurately, using the word bank at the bottom of the page for reference and to check spelling.

● Challenge the children to draw a circuit using the symbols they have just learned on the reverse of the sheet.

● Next ask the children to redraw the circuits that they designed in the previous lesson, using the conventional circuit symbols.

Plenary

● Invite the children to present their work to the rest of the class. Encourage them to identify the different parts of their circuits and to explain how they work together.

● Ask volunteers to draw their circuits on the whiteboard using the symbols on page 11 and the Lines tool ▢. Address any misconceptions.

● Use the quiz on pages 12 to 18 to consolidate the children's knowledge and understanding of circuit symbols. Invite them to take turns to click on their choices. They will either hear a cheer or a groan depending on their answer.

Whiteboard tools

Use the Lines tool to link components in circuits.

▢ Pen tool

▢ Marquee select tool

▢ Lines tool

▢ Activote (optional)

Burglar alarm (1)

Learning objectives
PoS Sc1 'Scientific enquiry' and Sc4 'Physical processes'
● To construct circuits, incorporating a battery or power supply and a range of switches, to make electrical devices work.
● To test ideas using evidence from observation and measurement.
● To use simple equipment and material appropriately.
● To use scientific knowledge and understanding to explain observations and conclusions.
● To review their work and the work of others and describe its significance and limitations.

Resources
'Burglar alarm' flipchart file; circuit equipment including switches, wire, batteries and buzzers; a selection of carpet, sponge, foam and aluminium foil; paper; pens; pencils.

Links to other subjects
Design and technology
PoS (4c) How mechanisms can be used to make things move in different ways, using a range of equipment; (4d) How electrical circuits, including those with simple switches, can be used to achieve results that work.
● Find out about a range of devices used in the home that rely on the use of mechanisms. Make a class collection.

Starter
Display a selection of circuit equipment including switches, wire, batteries and buzzers. Arrange the children in mixed-ability groups and encourage them to explore how to make a circuit with a switch.

Go to page 2 of the 'Burglar alarm' flipchart and invite volunteers to demonstrate how they might create a circuit with a switch.

Whole-class shared work
● Display page 3 of the flipchart and explain to the children that their task is to make a pressure-pad burglar alarm. The burglar alarm should activate when trodden on, thereby making the circuit complete and causing the buzzer to sound. Write the children's ideas on the flipchart page.
● Let the children work in ability groups to design a circuit that is capable of this action. Care must be taken so that the switch will not be too sensitive, as it should only activate when trodden on.
● Invite the children to bring their circuit designs to show to the rest of the group. Encourage them to explain the design of their alarms using scientific knowledge and understanding. Any misconceptions should be addressed at this point.
● Explain that the circuit should be incorporated into a mat.

Independent work
● Provide each group with a selection of carpet, sponge, foam and aluminium foil in addition to all their circuit materials.
● Encourage the children to spend some time exploring the available materials.
● Ask them to include samples of their chosen materials on their design sheet, along with the circuit diagram.
● Differentiate the work to suit the full range of abilities in your class. For example, provide word banks and adult support for less able learners. Middle-ability groups will require less adult support and more able learners should be encouraged to work independently.

Plenary
● Invite the children to present their diagrams to the rest of the class.
● Encourage them to give each other constructive feedback, with the aim of improving their designs and making them more effective. Write some of the main points on page 4 of the flipchart.
● Explain that the children will carry out any improvements to their designs in a later session.

Whiteboard tools
Use the Lines tool to link components in circuits.

 Pen tool

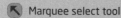 Marquee select tool

| Lines tool

Burglar alarm (2)

Learning objectives

PoS Sc1 'Scientific enquiry' and Sc4 'Physical processes'
● To construct circuits, incorporating a battery or power supply and a range of switches, to make electrical devices work.
● To test ideas using evidence from observation and measurement.
● To use simple equipment and material appropriately.
● To use scientific knowledge and understanding to explain observations and conclusions.
● To review their work and the work of others and describe its significance and limitations.

Resources

'Burglar alarm' flipchart file; circuit equipment including switches, wire, batteries and buzzers; a selection of pieces of carpet, sponge, foam and aluminium foil; paper and pens.

Links to other subjects

Design and technology
PoS (4c) How mechanisms can be used to make things move in different ways, using a range of equipment; (4d) How electrical circuits, including those with simple switches, can be used to achieve results that work.
● Make a class collection of toys and gadgets that are operated using switches. Use the collection as an inspiration for work on designing and making items that incorporate a switch.

Whiteboard tools

Upload scanned images via the Resource library.

🖊 Pen tool

🖱 Marquee select tool

▎ Lines tool

📖 Resource library

✦ Design mode

Starter

Open the 'Burglar alarm' flipchart and click on the button next to Lesson 20 to go to page 5. Look at the designs from the previous lesson, focussing on some of the positive aspects of each design. Recall aspects for development from page 4.

Arrange for the children to work in the same groups as in the previous session. Give them time to complete the modifications of their designs. Ensure that all modifications are written in a different colour to show improvements to the design.

Whole-class shared work

● Invite volunteers to demonstrate their amended designs, using the symbols on page 6.
● Provide the materials necessary for the children to follow their designs.
● Invite the children to begin making their alarms. Encourage them to take care to follow their design accurately, taking note of any modifications made from the presentations.
● Provide different levels of adult support to suit the different abilities. (Less confident children may need lots of support but more confident children should be encouraged to work as independently as possible.)
● Arrange for the children to present their mats to the rest of the class.

Independent work

● Ask the children to make a large, fully annotated diagram of their final design. Encourage them to think about the reasons for each choice made and make notes of these reasons on their final design.
● Provide support to less confident children and help them to write reasons for their choices.

Plenary

● Present the final designs to the rest of the class. Encourage the children to evaluate their own designs and those of others, using scientific knowledge and understanding.
● Add the children's designs to page 7. To insert hyperlinks for scanned work you will need to be in Design mode ✦. Right-/barrel-click and select Insert Link Object from the pop-up menu. Alternatively, upload scanned images from a specific folder via the Resource library 📖 (go to Categories, then Other location and Browse to other location).

Name _____

Food chains

■ Complete the grids below. Take care to put the correct item in the correct position in the food chain.

1. Ant, leaf, anteater

Primary producer	Primary consumer	Secondary consumer

2. Grass, human, sun, cow

Energy source	Primary producer	Primary consumer	Secondary consumer

3. Owl, wheat, mouse

Primary producer	Primary consumer	Secondary consumer

4. Hedgehog, leaf, slug

Primary producer	Primary consumer	Secondary consumer

5. Honeysuckle, robin, fox, sun

Energy source	Primary producer	Primary consumer	Secondary consumer

■ Make your own tables on a piece of paper or on the back of this sheet for the following:

6. Frog, leaf, aphid, snake, mongoose

7. Bird, leaf, spider, aphid, cat

Illustration © Garry Davies

Plant roots

◀ Draw a labelled diagram of your plant and its roots.
Remember to show where the plant is most likely to take in water and nutrients.

My plant and its roots

◀ Write a sentence to describe how the roots anchor the plant.

◀ If there is time, write a few more sentences about the importance of roots.

_____
_____
_____
_____
_____
_____
_____
_____

Name _____

Heating and cooling materials

■ Cut out the words below and place them in the table in the correct place.

■ Write **Yes** in the third box if the change is reversible, or **No** if it is not.

✂

raw egg	cake mix	ice	jug
bar of chocolate	water	dough	fried egg
bread	unfired clay	cake	liquid chocolate

Object	Change	Is it reversible?

100 Activprimary™ WHITEBOARD LESSONS · YEAR 6

◣ S C H O L A S T I C
w w w . s c h o l a s t i c . c o . u k

Balanced and unbalanced forces

◖ In the box below, draw and label a picture of a balanced force.
   Draw arrows to show the direction of each force.

Does your picture show a balanced force? _____

Why? _____

_____

◖ In the box below, draw and label a picture of an unbalanced force.
   Draw arrows to show the direction of each force.

Does your picture show an unbalanced force? _____

Why? _____

_____

Air resistance

◼ Cut out spinners 1, 2 and 3. Use them to perform your air resistance test.

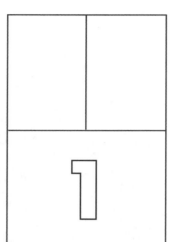 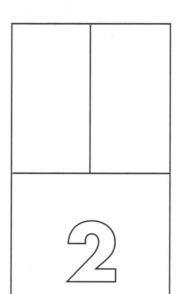 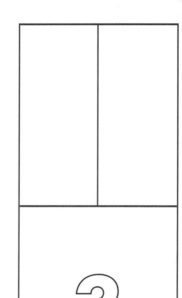

◼ Use the table below to record your results.

Variable	Spinner 1	Spinner 2	Spinner 3

▪SCHOLASTIC
w w w . s c h o l a s t i c . c o . u k

Name _____

Light and eyes

◀ Label this diagram of the eye.

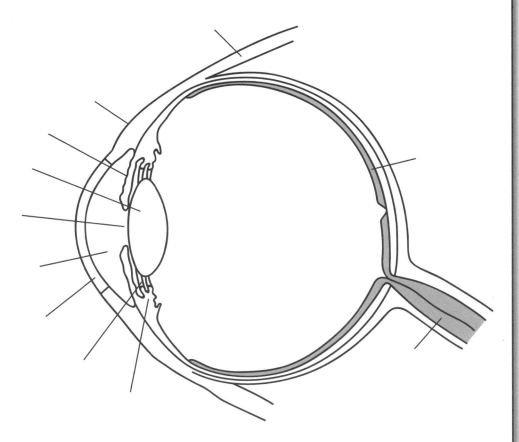

◀ Draw a picture of what happens when light is stopped by a piece of card.

◀ Draw a diagram of what happens to enable us to see an object.

Reflecting light in mirrors

◼ Draw a diagram of what happens to a beam of light when it is bounced off three, five or seven mirrors and returned to its original source.

Did the angle of the mirror make a difference to this task? Why?

_____

_____

Why is it important to show the direction of the beam of light with an arrow?

_____

_____

Illustrations © Garry Davies

◖SCHOLASTIC
w w w . s c h o l a s t i c . c o . u k

Name _____

Shadow investigation

◧ What is the best position for the light in a shadow puppet show?

My hypothesis is _____

_____

My controlled variable is _____

_____

My independent variables are _____

_____

My dependent variable is _____

_____

The materials I will need are _____

_____

_____

The method for this experiment is _____

_____

_____

_____

_____

_____

_____

_____

_____

_____

Illustration © Garry Davies

Changing circuits

■ Draw diagrams for the following circuits.

A circuit for a bright bulb or fast motor

A circuit for a dim bulb or slow motor

A circuit for a bulb or motor with a switch

Circuit symbols

▪ Label the circuit symbols. Use the words at the bottom of the page to help you.

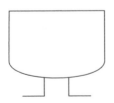

closed switch   battery   open switch

buzzer   bulb   ammeter   voltmeter

Foundation subjects

Although foundation subjects cover a multitude of learning experiences, addressing objectives from seemingly disparate curriculum areas, something they all share is their readiness for enhancement with ICT. As educators grow in their experience and confidence with computers, so does their ability to identify opportunities for technology to improve the learning experience.

Modern children are at home with technology and regard it as a natural and exciting part of school life. They are also readily engaged by visual stimuli, and this is where the interactive whiteboard can make a spellbinding contribution. Used simply, it opens up a world of images, photographs and films that can be shared with the whole class. However, the tools and software that accompany the whiteboard can enrich and broaden experiences across the curriculum, showing learners people, places, artefacts, works of art and concepts in an accessible and motivating way.

All of the tools, applications and techniques described in the lessons that follow are easily learned and applied. They are also transferable to other curriculum areas, where they can be used to focus attention, model processes, refine ideas, generate interest and generally breathe new life into teaching and learning.

Lesson title	Objectives	What children should know	Cross-curricular links
History			
Lesson 1: On a plate	QCA Unit 12 'How did life change in our locality in Victorian times?' • To select and record information relevant to a chosen topic. • To identify and record characteristic features of Victorian life. • To organise and communicate their knowledge.	• How to use artefacts and pictures to ask and answer questions about the past. • They should have made a study of life in Victorian times and know about some of the important changes that took place.	**Speaking and listening** Objective 60: To understand and use a variety of ways to criticise constructively and respond to criticism. **Art and design** PoS (2c) To design and make images and artefacts; (4c) To consider the roles and purposes of artists, craftspeople and designers working in different times and cultures.
Lesson 2: All at sea	QCA Unit 19 'What were the effects of Tudor exploration?' • To find out about Drake's voyage around the world. • To apply understanding of chronology. • To infer reasons why the voyage took place.	• Considered the way that the past is represented. • Looked at the lives of other people and societies. • The reasons for, and the difference between, invasion and settlement.	**Geography** PoS (2c) To use atlases and globes, and maps and plans at a range of scales; (3b) To learn about the location of places and environments they study and other significant places and environments.
Lesson 3: Recording artefacts	QCA Unit 16 'How can we find out about the Indus Valley civilisation?' • To use pictures of artefacts to find out about a particular aspect of life in Mohenjo-Daro. • To answer a historical question in an organised and structured way.	• How to use artefacts to ask and answer historical questions. • The convention of AD and BC dates.	**English** NLS Term 1 T17: To write a non-chronolgical report.
Lesson 4: It's Greek to me	QCA Unit 15 'How do we use ancient Greek ideas today?' • To know that many English words have Greek origins. • To identify some of the words, prefixes, suffixes and letter strings that indicate a word has Greek origins.	• When the ancient Greek civilisation flourished. • That the Ancient Greeks spoke a different language and used a different alphabet from us.	**English** NLS Term 3 W5: To invent words using known roots.

Lesson title	Objectives	What children should know	Cross-curricular links
Geography			
Lesson 5: Make a map [P]	• To use and draw maps. • To identify physical and human features.	• Some knowledge of map symbols and compass direction. • Be able to sort features into human and physical.	**History** QCA Units 6A–C 'Why have people invaded and settled in Britain in the past?' **ICT** QCA Unit 5A 'Graphical modelling'
Lesson 6: Features of a river	**QCA Unit 14** 'Investigating rivers' • To use maps at different scales. • To be able to identify the main features of a river. • To use secondary sources.	• Know some water features in the local area. • Some experience of drawing a sketch map or geographical diagram.	**Geography** QCA Unit 15 'The mountain environment' QCA Unit 22 'A contrasting locality overseas' QCA Unit 23 'Investigating coasts' **Science** PoS Sc3 (2e) The part played by evaporation and condensation in the water cycle.
Lesson 7: Looking at mountains	**QCA Unit 15** 'The mountain environment' • To identify physical and human features of mountains. • To identify land use.	• Some introductory work on mountains and know some of the main mountain ranges. • Be able to identify nouns, verbs, adjectives and adverbs.	**English** NLS Term 3 T13: To write a sequence of poems linked by theme or form.
Lesson 8: What time is it? [P]	• To identify time differences around the world. • To use maps at different scales. • To use secondary sources.	• To use an index and coordinates in an atlas to locate places. • Awareness that there is a time difference between different locations in the world.	**Science** PoS Sc4 (4a) To know that the Sun, Earth and Moon are approximately spherical.
Art and design			
Lesson 9: Sketching action figures	**QCA Unit 6A** 'People in action' • To develop accuracy in selecting and recording from first hand observation. • To compare methods and approaches used by others to show figures and forms in movement.	• Where body parts are jointed. • Know names such as wrists, elbows, shoulders, waist and so on.	**Science** PoS Sc2 (2e) To know that humans have skeletons and muscles to support and protect their bodies and to help them to move. **Physical education** QCA Unit 28 'Gymnastic activities (6)'
Lesson 10: Creating a hat [disc] [P]	**QCA Unit 6B** 'What a performance' • To evaluate a product, its design and construction. • To analyse products to generate ideas for their own design.	• How shape, materials and colours can be used to communicate meaning.	**English** NLS Term 1 T9: To prepare a short section of story as a script.
Lesson 11: Drawing a detailed landscape	**QCA Unit 6C** 'A sense of place' • To record a variety of features in a landscape showing understanding of relative size, distance and shape.	• Which elements of the environment are man-made and which are natural. • How elements of compositions can be arranged in the foreground, mid-ground or background.	**ICT** QCA Unit 6A 'Multimedia presentation' **History** QCA Unit 18 'What was it like to live here in the past?' **Geography** QCA Unit 15 'The mountain environment'
Design and technology			
Lesson 12: Shelters [P]	**QCA Unit 6A** 'Shelters' • To relate the way things work to their intended purpose. • To produce a detailed design for a structure.	• Structures have a specific purpose. • Names of different materials and their properties.	**Geography** QCA Unit 15 'The mountain environment' **Mathematics** NNS: To use, read and write standard metric units.
Lesson 13: Fantastic footwear [disc] [P]	**QCA Unit 6B** 'Slippers' • To understand that products are designed for a particular purpose and are suitable for different users. • To evaluate products, relating their materials and construction to their intended use.	• How to evaluate a product, describing features using appropriate vocabulary.	**Science** PoS Sc3 (1a) To compare everyday materials on the basis of their material properties. **English** NLS Term 1 T6: To produce a modern retelling.

Lesson title	Objectives	What children should know	Cross-curricular links
Religious education			
Lesson 14: How do people of different faiths worship? ⊙ 🅿	**QCA Unit 6A** 'Worship and community' • To describe the key aspects of religions. • To understand that there are similarities and differences within and between religions.	• The names of different world faiths. • Some of the basic beliefs and rituals of the religions studied.	**Geography** PoS (2c) To use atlases and globes. **English** NLS Term 1 T17: To write non-chronological reports.
Lesson 15: What is a mosque and what is it used for? ⊙ 🅿	**QCA Unit 6B** 'Worship and community: what is the role of the mosque?' • To know the key features of a mosque, its purpose and significance for Muslims.	• Religions have a community centre or place for worship and know about some of their features.	**ICT** QCA Unit 6A 'Multimedia presentation' **English** NLS Term 1 T17: To write non-chronological reports.
Lesson 16: How do people express their religious beliefs through art?	**QCA Unit 6F** 'How do people express their faith through the arts?' • To appreciate that art can be very sacred and spiritual for believers.	• That each of the world religions has iconic figures who are often represented in art.	**Art and design** PoS (4c) To learn about the roles and purposes of artists working in different times and cultures. **English** NLS Term 1 T17: To write non-chronological reports.
Physical education			
Lesson 17: Evaluating and refining gymnastic actions	**QCA Unit 28** 'Gymnastic activities (6)' • To combine and perform gymnastic actions, shapes and balances. • To evaluate their own work and suggest ways of making improvements	• Experience of incorporating a variety of actions into a routine, both alone and with a partner for the purpose of display. • How to safely set up and use a variety of apparatus at high, intermediate and low level.	**ICT** QCA Unit 6A 'Multimedia presentation' **English** NLS Term 1 T17: To write non-chronological reports.
Lesson 18: Peer-group coaching in games	**QCA Unit 24** 'Invasion games (4)' **QCA Unit 25** 'Striking and fielding games (2)' **QCA Unit 26** 'Net/wall games (2)' • To evaluate their own and others' strengths and weaknesses in performances and to suggest areas for improvement.	• Experience in playing the three types of game: invasion, net/wall, striking and fielding. • The basic principles of attack and defence for the three types.	**ICT** QCA Unit 6A 'Multimedia presentation' **Speaking and listening** Objective 60: To understand and use a variety of ways to criticise constructively and respond to criticism. **PSHE** PoS (3a) To understand the benefits of exercise; (5b) To feel positive about themselves.
PSHE and citizenship			
Lesson 19: What's in the news? ⊙ 🅿	**QCA Unit 11** 'In the media - what's the news?' • To research, discuss and debate topical issues, problems and events. • To evaluate how the media present information.	• How to skim and scan for information.	**English** NLS Term 1 T15: To develop a journalistic style; T16: To use the styles and conventions of journalism to report on, for example, real or imagined events.
Lesson 20: Moving on	**QCA Unit 12** 'Moving on' • To understand that transition and change are a natural part of everyone's life.	• How to construct a concept map.	**Speaking and listening** Objective 64: To improvise using a range of drama strategies and conventions to explore themes such as hopes, fears, desires.

On a plate

Learning objectives
QCA Unit 12 'How did life change in our locality in Victorian times?'
● To select and record information relevant to a chosen topic.
● To identify and record characteristic features of Victorian life.
● To organise and communicate their knowledge.

Resources
'On a plate' flipchart file; copies of the letter printed from page 4 of the flipchart and outline of a plate printed from pages 5 or 6; several pictures and other examples of commemorative ware; pencils; crayons; paper for notes on evaluations.

Links to other subjects
Speaking and listening
Objective 60: To understand and use a variety of ways to criticise constructively and respond to criticism.
● Speaking and listening skills will be developed during the Plenary session as children listen to and question other's ideas.
Art and design
PoS (2c) To design and make images and artefacts;
(4c) To consider the roles and purposes of artists, craftspeople and designers working in different times and cultures.
● In a subsequent art lesson ask the children to develop the ideas planned in this lesson to create a finished artefact.

Starter
Ask the children to recall what they already know about changes during the Victorian period. List their ideas on page 2 of the flipchart. Encourage them to classify the changes under the headings: *Home and family life; Transport; Work and industry*. Add new headings as required.
   Discuss with the children what had caused these changes and what impact they had on Victorian society.

Whole-class shared work
● Share the examples of commemorative ware with the children and discuss what they show, for example: the date; special events (such as marriages or jubilees); achievements; pictures of famous people (usually royalty).
● Encourage the children to talk about any examples of commemorative ware at home.
● Explain to the children that commemorative china is made at the time of the event and can often tell us what the people thought was important.
● Display the picture of the commemorative plate on page 3.
● Explain that this plate was made to celebrate Queen Victoria's Golden Jubilee. How do we know this? Highlight these facts.
● Ask the children to tell you what else the plate depicts. Enlarge the image if necessary. Annotate the picture with the children's suggestions.
● Ask questions such as: *What can you tell about Queen Victoria? What statistics are given? What can you tell about life in Britain? What was important to the Victorians about Queen Victoria's reign?*

Independent work
● Give out the *design brief* letters and templates printed from pages 4, 5 and 6 of the flipchart. Read through the letter together to ensure full understanding.
● Display the plate on page 3 and ask the children to point out elements of design. For example, how many main pieces of information are included?
● Refer back to the information on page 2 and ask the children to identify the most important events or changes that they will want to include.
● More able learners could select at least one from each list, while those who are less able may prefer to focus on only one aspect of change.
● Invite the children to create a draft design using sketches and annotations.

Plenary
● Divide the designs into sets and display them around the room.
● Organise the class into groups. Ask each group to focus on evaluating one set of designs.
● When the children have evaluated the designs, one spokesperson for each group should report back on his or her group's observations and comments. Suggest to the children that they should be willing to justify their decisions.
● Annotate page 7 with the children's observations.

Whiteboard tools
 Highlighter tool

 Text editor tool

Pen tool

 Print button

 Floating keyboard

All at sea

Learning objectives
QCA Unit 19 'What were the effects of Tudor exploration?'
● To find out about Drake's voyage around the world.
● To apply understanding of chronology.
● To infer reasons why the voyage took place.

Resources
'All at sea' flipchart file; blank sheets of A3 paper; photocopiable page 159 'Drake's voyage'; pencils; scissors and glue for less able learners. Full copies of Francis Pretty's narrative can be found at: **www.bartleby.com**

Links to other subjects
Geography
PoS (2c) To use atlases and globes, and maps and plans at a range of scales; (3b) To learn about the location of places and environments they study and other significant places and environments.
● The children will develop their knowledge and understanding of places using map work.
● The children could use the idea of scale in maps to work out the distances travelled, particularly across oceans.

Whiteboard tools
Use the Floating keyboard, in the Text editor tool tray, to type sentences.

 Highlighter tool

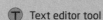 Text editor tool

 Pen tool

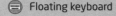 Floating keyboard

Starter
Ask the children to recall facts about exploration in Tudor times and note these on page 2 of the 'All at sea' flipchart.

Encourage them to consider the following things: when the Tudor period was; what the ships were like; what the food was like and how ships were provisioned; navigation; fears and superstitions.

Ask the children to suggest how we know about Tudor exploration. (For example, through diaries, maps, drawings and so on.)

Whole-class shared work
● Explain to the children that they are going to read simplified extracts from a narrative written by one of the men on Drake's ship. Do the children think that this will give accurate information about the journey? Why or why not?
● Read through pages 3 to 7 with the children, explaining any difficult vocabulary or expressions. Highlight dates and locations.
● Discuss the problems and dangers that the men would have encountered on the journey, in particular crossing large oceans. Would these dangers have been different to those faced on coastlines? How?
● Point out the locations on the large world map on page 8.
● Discuss what these extracts suggest to us about reasons for the voyage. (Reasons include the desire for wealth, the desire to conquer new lands and the desire to defeat the Spaniards.) Which particular extracts support these ideas?
● Relate the reasons to the children's understanding of invasion and settlement from earlier study.
● List the children's ideas on page 9.

Independent work
● Explain to the children that they are going to create a timeline of the events of Drake's voyage. They will need to order the events chronologically, including an interesting detail about each stage of the journey.
● Give each child a copy of photocopiable page 159 'Drake's voyage'. Ask them to cut out and stick the information in order on a blank sheet of A3 paper to create a timeline of Drake's voyage.
● Suggest that less able learners simply cut out and stick the information in a sequence on a blank sheet of paper. They need not create a timeline.
● Allow more able learners to use the whiteboard. Ask them to select the seven most important parts of the voyage, typing the text onto the timeline on page 10.

Plenary
● Display page 11 and ask the children to detail their chronological sequences. Invite volunteers to plot the route on the map on page 8.
● Ask the children to consider if the crew would take the shortest route between ports or stay close to the coast. Why?
● Which parts of the journey probably took the longest? Do the dates on the timeline support this? If not, can the children suggest reasons why not?
● Explain that the voyage called in at other ports; can the children suggest where some of them might be?
● Tell the children that more details are included in the full narrative account.

Recording artefacts

Learning objectives
QCA Unit 16 'How can we find out about the Indus Valley civilisation?'
● To use pictures of artefacts to find out about a particular aspect of life in Mohenjo-Daro.
● To answer a historical question in an organised and structured way.

Resources P
Photographs of artefacts found at Indus Valley sites (display only): **www.ancientindia.co.uk/indus/explore** and **www.harappa.com/har/har0.html** have excellent images for educational use; photocopiable page 160 'Archaeologists' report' for each child; pencils; prepared flipchart file – page 1: map of the Indus Valley Civilisation (copyright permitting); page 2: a simple timeline with approximate dates and the names of societies and periods studied, as separate text objects; page 3: blank with heading *What we already know*; page 4: copy of the photocopiable sheet, 'Archaeologists' report'.

Links to other subjects
English
NLS Term1 T17: To write a non-chronological report.
● The Independent work provides an opportunity for children to develop their report-writing skills.

Whiteboard tools
Create the timeline with the Lines tool. Use the Spotlight tool to focus on aspects of artefacts.

🅣 Text editor tool

🕐 Spotlight tool

▎ Lines tool

🖊 Pen tool

🖰 Marquee select tool

Starter
Use the first page of your prepared flipchart to remind the children of the location of the sites of the Indus Valley Civilisation. Point out the distances involved.

Ask the children to identify and move the names of societies and periods previously studied to the correct positions on the timeline.

Discuss the timescales involved. Ask questions such as: *How long ago did this civilisation flourish?* Encourage the children to put this into context by comparing distances on the timeline with other historical periods.

Invite the children to tell you what they know about the civilisation and how we know about it. List their ideas on page 3, under the heading *What we already know*.

Whole-class shared work
● Launch a web browser and open the website: **www.ancientindia.co.uk/indus/explore**
● Click on *Look through an archaeologist's notebook*. Display the picture of *HR 4478* (click on the image in the index) and activate the Spotlight tool 🕐. (Make sure you cover the title of the object.) This enables the children to focus on the artefact without distraction.
● Ask the children to tell you what they can observe, including the material it appears to be made from.
● List the facts about the artefact on page 4 of the flipchart, explaining the headings as you model the task.
● Encourage the children to make and justify deductions about the purpose of the artefact.
● Turn off the Spotlight tool and read the notes. Do the children's notes tally with the archaeologist's? Discuss any differences.
● Is there any information that might have helped the children to make a better deduction. (For example, where the artefact was found.)
● Invite the children to suggest two questions that they might like to ask the archaeologist who found the artefact.
● Repeat with other artefacts. (*VS 3646* is a good one to choose, as its purpose is not fully understood.)

Independent work
● Explain to the children that they will work in pairs to examine pictures of two artefacts and record details about them. Provide each child with a copy of photocopiable page 160.
● Suggest that the children focus their report on dimensions, decoration and purpose.
● Select pictures to suit the abilities of the different pairs of children. Provide less confident children with a more structured record sheet.

Plenary
● Invite individuals to come to the whiteboard, select their chosen picture and explain (using the Pen tool to annotate the image) what they have identified about their objects.
● Discuss the children's questions (see Whole-class shared work, above) and ask for other suggestions. List these on a new page, under the heading *Questions for archaeologists*.
● Ensure that the children appreciate that some of the objects may have been reconstructed. Use this as an opportunity to discuss which materials survive and which do not. How does this affect our knowledge and understanding of the way of life of these people?

It's Greek to me

Starter

Explain to the children that they are going to learn one way in which we still use ancient Greek ideas today. Using the Lines tool ◫, create a simple timeline on page 1 of your flipchart and entitle it *What we already know about the ancient Greeks.*

Invite the children to identify the relative positions of historical periods they have studied. Add dates to the timeline where possible. List what the children already know about ancient Greece. Prompt them to say that the Greeks spoke a different language and used a different alphabet from us.

Whole-class shared work

● Explain to the children that the English language is very rich in vocabulary absorbed from other civilisations and cultures.
● Challenge the children to suggest where some of our vocabulary has come from. Can they give any examples? Prompt them to think about possible reasons for this, such as invasion and travel. List the possible reasons on page 2, under the heading *Origins of English words.*
● On page 3 write the word *History.* Ask the children to define it and write their suggestions below.
● Distribute the dictionaries and ask the children to find the origin and meaning of *history.* Explain the meaning of *etymology* and demonstrate how to find the etymology of the word.
● Ask the children to suggest other school subjects. List these on page 4 with their meanings (as found in dictionaries). Encourage the children to look carefully at the etymology.
● Look at some mathematical words and identify the Greek roots.
● Explain to the children that parts or all of many words we use today have Greek origins.
● Next, focus on some of the more familiar roots, for example *geo-* or *-ology* and ask the children to suggest other examples. List these on page 5, entitled *Common roots.*
● Ask the children to deduce the meanings of the roots. Check these in the dictionaries.

Independent work

● Provide each child with a copy of photocopiable page 161. Explain that they will create their own etymological dictionary by working out and writing the familiar English words using the Greek roots.
● Provide less able learners with a list of English words to match with the Greek roots.
● Challenge more able learners to create neologisms using Greek roots.

Plenary

● Review the children's work on page 5. Invite individuals to come to the whiteboard and combine Greek roots to match the English words.
● Encourage the children to understand that although the words have been formed from Greek roots, many of the concepts would not have been familiar to the ancient Greeks. Highlight these words.
● Explain that some words, such as *television*, are combinations of Greek and Latin roots.

Make a map

Learning objectives
● To use and draw maps.
● To identify physical and human features.

Resources P
Photocopiable page 162 'Make a map'; mapping software (optional). Prepare a flipchart file – page 1: add a range of map words and symbols, from the Resource library and/or drawn with the Pen tool; page 2: repeat the symbols and also add a box with the text label *Key*; page 3: prepare or insert a detailed map to use in the Plenary session (copyright permitting), or display a detailed map on a web browser.

Links to other subjects
History
QCA Units 6A-C 'Why have people invaded and settled in Britain in the past?'
● Adapt this activity for work on invaders and settlers and for local history work.
ICT
QCA Unit 5A 'Graphical modelling'
● Copying, pasting and rearranging map symbols to create a map related to work on graphical modelling.

Whiteboard tools
Drag map symbols from the Resource library. These can be copied and duplicated. Use the Reveal or Spotlight tool to conceal and reveal parts of the screen.

⬛ Resource library

🔺 Marquee select tool

🖊 Pen tool

▦ Duplicate function

◔ Spotlight tool

🖵 Reveal tool

Starter
Display page 1 of your prepared flipchart, which contains a mixture of map symbols and words. Invite the children to match the correct symbols and words. Encourage them to think of examples of those features that they have seen.

When the pairings are complete, sort each matched pair into two categories: *human* and *physical*. As they are sorted, discuss the differences between human and physical features. If the activity is to be linked to a theme such as mountains, coasts or rivers, circle those which would be more likely to be seen on maps linked to this theme. Are there any other symbols which should be included?

Whole-class shared work
● Display page 2 of the flipchart, which shows map symbols and a box labelled *Key*. Explain to the children that they are going to work together to build a map of an area using map symbols and the Pen tool. If required, draw one or two items to set the scene.
● Invite individuals to come up and add a feature to the map. Ask them to explain why they have put it where they have and to enter a symbol in the key if necessary. They may wish to duplicate a symbol ▦.
● Remind the rest of the class to keep an eye on what is being put where. Are there any rules they should follow when creating a map? Give an obvious example such as, when a river and road cross each other, a bridge or ford is most likely needed.
● When the map is finished save it for use later.

Independent work
● Invite the children to work in pairs to make their own map. They may use photocopiable page 162 'Make a map' or use mapping software which provides map symbols and an area for drawing maps.
● Encourage the children to think carefully about the relationship between different features as they place them on the map. Ask them to build up a key as they go along.
● Support less able learners with an adapted worksheet which contains the relevant symbols ready drawn into the key.
● Provide more able learners with a key from an Ordnance Survey map so that they can select from a more detailed list of features to include on their map.

Plenary
● Cover a detailed map with the Reveal 🖵 or Spotlight tool ◔ and reveal it gradually. Focus on one feature at a time, revealing it little by little. Ask the children to predict what could be revealed next. If a river is being revealed, they could suggest a bridge, a weir, or a tributary.
● Use the maps created in this lesson for a locality study, using map symbols shown on a map of the area.

Features of a river

Starter
Open the 'Features of a river' flipchart. Display a map of the local area or click on the web link to view a map of the local area on the Ordnance Survey's *Get-a-map* website. What water features can the children see? What do they know about water features? Do they know any special names? List any vocabulary on page 2.

Look at map symbols for water features, either using images from the geography folder in the Resource library 📖 or via the internet (the Ordnance Survey website *Understanding Mapping* pages are very useful). Add any new terms to the list of river feature vocabulary.

Whole-class shared work
● Go to page 3 and click on the button to open the *Features of a river* presentation. Explain the objectives of the lesson.
● Ask the children to take notes to help them in producing an illustration of the features of a river. Remind them to jot down key words only. Explain that they will be producing their own interpretation of a river from source to mouth.
● Use the interactive map to research the key features of rivers. Encourage the children to look closely at the map and try to predict what is going to be in the related photograph. Encourage discussion of what can be seen and what cannot. What is the feature called and what does it look like?
● Use the Pen tool to annotate pictures and to add text. Use the Camera tool 📷 to save this as a snapshot.
● Work through the various features in any order, going from map to feature and back again.
● Discuss which features have to be in particular places and which could be anywhere.

Independent work
● Work with the children to draw a picture of a river from source to mouth. Include as many features of a river as possible. Use a sheet of A4 paper folded in half lengthways. At one end, fold over two five-centimetre lengths as in the photograph on the last page of the *Features of a river* presentation. Use the peak of the fold to be the highest point of the river, and the lowest end to be where the river flows into the sea. This will give a 3D effect to the finished picture. Label the different features illustrated in the picture.
● Provide a list of basic vocabulary for any children whose notes may not provide them with enough support.
● Invite some children to give a description to the rest of the class explaining the journey of their river.

Plenary
● Use the Ordnance Survey *Get-a-map* site to follow the route of a river looking for various features. Zoom in and out, re-centre and use the hyperlinked compass points to follow the river. If there is a local river of interest follow it to its source and mouth, observing the route it takes and the places it passes through.

Looking at mountains

Learning objectives
QCA Unit 15 'The mountain environment'
● To identify physical and human features of mountains.
● To identify land use.

Resources
'Mountains' flipchart file; atlases.

Links to other subjects
English
NLS Term 3 T13: To write a sequence of poems linked by theme or form.
● Encourage the children to imagine and explore feelings and ideas, focusing on creative uses of language.

Starter
Open the 'Mountains' flipchart and look at the world map on page 2. Read the labels of the main mountain ranges of the world. Can the children tell you where each range is located? Which continents are they in? Which contains the highest mountain?

Drag the name of each range of mountains to its approximate position on the world map. Pull the tab down from the top of the screen to reveal the answers.

Whole-class shared work
● Go to page 3 and enable the Reveal tool 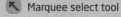.
● Move on to page 4 and gradually reveal the image, discovering that a person is paragliding. Eventually the mountains are revealed.
● Explain that the photographs on pages 5 to 8 are taken in the Austrian Tyrol in the Alps. The pages contain images of human and physical features in the Austrian Tyrol. Allow the children time to complete parts of each activity and to discuss the images.
● Page 9 deals with one aspect of land use: tourism. Try to predict what words are hidden. Ask: *How would it be different here in the winter?*
● Use page 10 to encourage the children to think about what the weather would be like, the steep drop in the land and the effect of the mountains and valleys on water.
● Look at a map of the Austrian Tyrol on the internet. This will put it in its geographical context. Searching for *Mittersill* and then zooming out will show where the Austrian Tyrol is. (Ensure that you choose Mittersill in Austria, not in the USA.)

Independent work
● Use the contrasts evident from the photographs to write a poem called 'Mountains and valleys'. Use the vocabulary to help describe the differences between the two types of land. Display the vocabulary on page 11 for the children to use. Add suitable verbs, adverbs and adjectives to the list of words.
● Decide whether to write a verse on each environment or to use connectives to contrast the two environments.
● If time permits, invite children to type their poems on page 12, and illustrate them with images from the Resource library.
● Work with less confident children to put together descriptive phrases which they can use in their work.

Plenary
● Return to one of the pages containing a suitable picture of a mountain scene. Invite volunteers to stand to one side of the screen and read their poems whilst the children look at the scene.
● Use page 13 to check that the correct features have been allocated to mountain and valley.
● Are the descriptions typical of this mountain region?
● Explain to the children that the next challenge will be to compare other mountain areas they research with this region of the Alps.

Whiteboard tools
Use the Reveal tool to hide and gradually uncover the flipchart pages.

 Marquee select tool

Reveal tool

Delete button

Resource library

Floating keyboard

What time is it?

Learning objectives
● To identify time differences around the world.
● To use maps at different scales.
● To use secondary sources.

Resources P
Atlases; photocopiable page 163 'What time is it?'; prepared flipchart file with hyperlinks on one page and a world time zone map on the next page (copyright permitting). Prepare suitable hyperlinks for: webcam links to view several parts of the world (search for webcam links on the Teacher Resource Exchange at **www.tre.ngfl. gov.uk**); a map to show areas of the world that are in day and night at the current time (try **www.fourmilab.ch** – click on *Earth and Moon Viewer* and *map of the Earth*); an interactive globe that shows day and night, for example at **www.worldtime.com**; a world time zone map, such as the one produced by the HM Nautical Almanac Office.

Links to other subjects
Science
PoS Sc4 (4a) To know that the Sun, Earth and Moon are approximately spherical.
● Adapt this activity to support the work on the rotation of the Earth.

Whiteboard tools
In Design mode, right-/ barrel-click and select Insert Link Object from the pop-up menu. Enter the URL address and click OK to insert a hyperlink. Return to Presentation mode; click on the hyperlink to launch the website.

 Design mode

 Pen tool

 Marquee select tool

Starter
Look at a view of several parts of the world using your webcam links on the internet. Discuss the time of day in the different places. Next, look at a map of the areas of the world that are in day and night at the current time. Discuss how the rotation of the earth gives one half of the world day and the other half of the world night. Illustrate this with an interactive globe that shows the world in light and dark.

Whole-class shared work
● Display a map of the world with the Greenwich Mean Time (or meridian) line marked on it. Explain that for many years this has been the place where time round the world is measured from. Explain how other points around the globe may be the same, ahead of, or behind this time.
● Next show an official world time zone map. Ask: *Why are the lines dividing the zones not always straight? Why do the lines run north to south? What happens when people go on long journeys?*
● Use an online time zone calculator such as **www.timeanddate.com/ worldclock** to investigate times around the world. Start with local time.
● Choose a place further east. Ask the children what happens to the time.
● Choose a place to the west of the local area. What, do the children think, happens to the time now?
● Look at a map of the world on a new flipchart page. Mark the current locality and its time and the two previously researched places and times on the map with the Pen tool.

Independent work
● Remind the children how to locate places round the world using the coordinates given in the index of an atlas.
● Allow the children to copy the three items labelled on the whiteboard so far onto their copies of the map on photocopiable page 163.
● Challenge them to label a further six places around the world. Use a letter for each place. Include the time at the moment. This will only be a valid comparison for a while, but will have more meaning than standard time zone recording.
● Challenge the children to label more places with the correct times. Leave the time and date website on the whiteboard as a source of times. Do not refresh the page and the times will remain applicable.
● Allow the children to use atlases to locate the places on the world map.

Plenary
● Return to the official world time zone map. Show how this map can be used at any time of day. Demonstrate how places in one direction add time on, and the other direction subtracts time, from GMT. Use the Pen tool to mark three of the places and their times on the time zone maps.
● Ask the children if they have heard of any times when people have suffered from jet lag. Can they tell you what caused it?

Sketching action figures

Learning objectives
QCA Unit 6A 'People in action'
● To develop accuracy in selecting and recording from first hand observation.
● To compare methods and approaches used by others to show figures and forms in movement.

Resources
'Harvesters' Lunch' flipchart file; digital camera; individual whiteboards and pens.

Links to other subjects
Science
PoS Sc2 (2e) To know that humans have skeletons and muscles to support and protect their bodies and to help them to move.
● Reinforce knowledge of skeleton and body parts when describing the body shapes of models in the action poses. Discuss which muscles are being used.
PE
QCA Unit 28 'Gymnastic activities (6)'
● Encourage the children to explore and describe a range of actions, shapes and balances they use for a particular gymnastics theme.

Whiteboard tools
Reduce the page scale by clicking on the Teacher tools menu icon, then Menu, and selecting Page scale from the pop-up menu. Upload images via the Resource library (choose Categories in the Resource library tool tray, then Other location and Browse to another location).

 Reveal tool

 Pen tool

 Highlighter tool

📖 Resource library

Teacher tools menu

... Menu

Marquee select tool

Starter
Open the 'Harvesters' Lunch' flipchart. Enable the Reveal tool 🖥 before displaying page 2. During the lesson, slowly reveal the painting, stopping at key points to ask the children what they think the subject, mood and setting of the painting is. When the whole painting is revealed, examine the scene, setting it in the context of the title: *Harvesters' Lunch*. Using the Highlighter tool, circle a *moving* figure, asking the children to explain what they think the character is doing. Discuss the body shapes of the different people.

Annotate the children's responses around the picture. If necessary reduce the page scale to write notes in the area around the page (see Whiteboard tools, below).

Whole-class shared work
● Explain to the children that they are going to work on showing movement in line drawings. Ask for three volunteer models and three photographers to come to the front. Remember to obtain parental permission before photographing children.
● Give the photographers a digital camera. Ask the models to think of an action (associated with a sport or dance perhaps) and then to perform the action.
● Let the photographers take turns to take a digital picture of an action. Load the pictures onto the computer and insert them in pages 3 to 5 of the flipchart (one picture per page).
● Look at the poses on the whiteboard. Using the Pen tool, draw around the outline of the figure in each photo, explicitly describing how the position of each limb, the pose of each hand and foot, the tilt of the head and the shape of the clothes all work together to create an image of movement in the viewers perception.
● Now ask the children to make a sketch on their whiteboards of, for example, an outstretched hand reaching for a football, or a pair of sprinting legs. Comment on their successes.

Independent work
● In small groups, ask the children to take turns to pose in familiar action poses, whilst their peers observe and sketch them.
● Encourage the children to verbalise their thoughts and techniques, describing how they are bringing their sketches to life.

Plenary
● Choose some examples of the children's and other artists' work (copyright permitting) and scan them into the computer, inserting them into page 6. Click on the arrows to go to pages 7 and 8 if more pages are required.
● Display these images on the interactive whiteboard, discussing the positions of the subjects and the techniques artists have used to show movement, such as: body shape, creases in clothing, blurred edges, or hair/clothes blowing in the wind.
● Compare the images to Breughal's picture in the Starter activity. Ask: *If you were going to draw a scene of the* Pupils' lunch *what would you include in the picture? What actions would people be performing?*

Creating a hat

Learning objectives
QCA Unit 6B 'What a performance'
● To evaluate a product, its design and construction.
● To analyse products to generate ideas for their own design.

Resources
'Creating a hat' flipchart file; a range of headwear, both formal and informal (brought in by the children); large paper; photocopiable page 164 'Designing hats'; digital camera; coloured pens and pencils.

Links to other subjects
English
NLS Term 1 T9: To prepare a short section of story as a script.
● Ask the children to work in groups to write a short script for their characters. Remind them to consider the characteristics that they have identified in the designing hats activity.

Starter

Talk to the children about the hats that they have worn or seen. Discuss the purposes of hats: to keep the head warm; to show rank or authority; to protect from injury or simply to look fashionable. Write notes on page 2 of the flipchart.

Tell the children that they are going to investigate a range of hats in order to understand their purpose, construction and something about the wearers. They will then use this knowledge to help them to design a hat of their own.

Whole-class shared work

● Organise the class into mixed-ability groups and provide each group with a hat to investigate.
● Display page 3 of the flipchart and ask the groups to produce a concept map (on large paper) with notes on the following:
  ● Audience: who was the hat designed for?
  ● Materials: list all the materials used.
  ● Construction: how are the individual pieces attached? What techniques have been used?
  ● Style and decoration: how is the hat embellished, and what effect does this have?
  ● Comfort: how has the hat been adapted to make it comfortable to wear?
● Ask the children to take digital pictures of the hat from different angles to illustrate their recorded observations.
● Upload the pictures into a folder on the computer, import them, and display on pages 4 and 5 of the flipchart.
● Invite each group to feed back to the class, describing their hat and referring to the pictures, using the Pen and Highlighter tools to highlight, annotate and label the hat.

Independent work

● Give each child a copy of photocopiable page 164 'Designing hats'.
● Tell the children that it is now their turn to design and make a piece of headgear of their own. The hat will be designed for a particular character from a book or play and must be decorated with things linked to that character.
● Ask them to consider the shape, construction and materials for their hats and try to link these to the character they've chosen. For example, a hat for a wizard may be conical, decorated with dragons, spell books, wands and lightning flashes.
● Allow the children time to complete the activity sheet.

Plenary

● Invite the children to share their designs. Choose some notable examples and scan them into the computer, inserting them into page 5 (click on the arrows to go to pages 6 to 7 if more pages are required).
● Challenge the children to guess which character the hats have been designed for.

Whiteboard tools
Upload images via the Resource library (choose Categories in the Resource library tool tray, then Other location and Browse to another location).

 Resource library

 Marquee select tool

 Pen tool

 Highlighter tool

Drawing a detailed landscape

Learning objectives
QCA Unit 6C 'A sense of place'
● To record a variety of features in a landscape showing understanding of relative size, distance and shape.

Resources
'Harvesters' Lunch' flipchart file; landscape pictures (prints or viewed on a website such as **www.tate.org.uk**); viewfinders cut from card; digital camera; sketchbooks.

Links to other subjects
ICT
QCA Unit 6A 'Multimedia presentation'
● Incorporate the digital photographs and artwork into a multimedia presentation on the local area.
History
QCA Unit 18 'What was it like to live here in the past?'
● When selecting places to visit for the sketching field trip, consider sites with a historical significance such as old mills, docks, Victorian terraces, cobbled streets or monuments.
Geography
QCA Unit 15 'The mountain environment'
● Look at mountain environments that are holiday destinations. Discuss the natural or man-made elements of the landscape, and consider the impact of human activity on the area.

Whiteboard tools
Upload images via the Resource library (choose Categories in the Resource library tool tray, then Other location and Browse to another location).

 Pen tool

 Marquee select tool

 Resource library

Lines tool

Starter
Open the 'Harvesters' Lunch' flipchart on page 9. Click on the arrow to display the picture of Breughal's *Harvesters' Lunch*. Ask the children to describe the work, prompting them to articulate what they see. Help them to analyse the space in the painting using terms like *foreground, mid-ground* and *background*. Draw lines with the Lines tool to show how the road recedes into the background. Ask them to identify natural and man-made elements in the picture. Make sure that they use the language of landscapes in their discussions.

Whole-class shared work
● Take the children on a walk to look at the local landscape. Ask them whether these are natural or man-made environments and identify aspects of the locality: hills, roads, trees, buildings and so on.
● Find a vantage point where the view extends into the distance (this is best identified before the walk). Encourage the children to observe the panorama for a few moments and then to describe what they can see to a talk partner, using the vocabulary introduced earlier.
● Ask the children to choose a view from this location. Using the viewfinders, they should frame the view and sketch it into their sketchbooks.
● Invite the children to take digital pictures of their view.
● Return to class and load the pictures onto the computer.
● Display them on the whiteboard and analyse the landscapes, identifying the foreground, mid-ground and background. Pages 10 to 12 are available if you wish to insert the digital photographs in the flipchart.
● Identify elements within the view and classify them as natural or man-made.
● Highlight elements that help to give the view depth: roads, trees, lamp-posts, buildings, people and so on. Explain how these recede, drawing the eye into the distance.

Independent work
● Challenge the children to use the printouts of their digital photographs, and their field sketches, to produce a more detailed study of a landscape. Their objective is to produce a picture with depth.

Plenary
● Invite confident individuals to show their landscape study to the rest of the class.
● For maximum effect, scan and import the children's work as links or images in the flipchart (using pages 13 to 15).
● Ask them to describe which elements they have included to recede into the distance.
● Invite positive comments from the class on the success of their attempts to create depth.

Shelters

Learning objectives
QCA Unit 6A 'Shelters'
● To relate the way things work to their intended purpose.
● To produce a detailed design for a structure.

Resources 🅿

Photocopiable page 165 'Design a shelter'; digital photographs of shelters (such as: bus-stops; sheds; gazebos; metal industrial units) inserted in individual pages of a flipchart file – choose buildings that the children are familiar with from the locality (copyright permitting) or organise a field trip for them to take their own pictures; individual whiteboards and pens.

Links to other subjects
Geography
QCA Unit 15 'The mountain environment'
● Investigate buildings in a mountain environment. How do they compare with buildings in the local environment or a tropical environment?
Mathematics
NNS: To use read and write standard metric units.
● Encourage the children to consider the dimensions of their finished shelter and the amount of material that they will need.

Whiteboard tools
Upload digital images via the Resource library. Select Categories in the Resource library tool tray, then Other location and Browse to another location. Browse to locate the images and click OK. The images will appear in the Resource library tool tray.

📖 Resource library

🖊 Pen tool

🔺 Highlighter tool

Starter

Ask the children to generate, with their talking partners, as many types of shelter as they can, recording their ideas on individual whiteboards. Discuss their responses, questioning them on the intended user and purpose of the shelters they have identified.

Whole-class shared work

● Explain to the children that they will be designing a model structure.
● Look at the pictures of shelters on your prepared flipchart to generate ideas. Annotate these to draw attention to features of the structures:
  ● frameworks connected at vertices
  ● external cladding to provide weatherproofing
  ● sloped roof for water runoff
  ● materials for cladding and frame
  ● parts of the structures which can support weight
  ● methods of construction and fastening
  ● how corner joints can be strengthened with triangular panels
  ● purposes of different buildings
  ● how local materials have been used because they are accessible (teepees, igloos and Touareg tents are good examples)
  ● whether the structures are meant to be transportable.
● Encourage the children to explain their observations using the vocabulary you have modelled. Discuss how the features of the shelters all relate to their purpose.
● Tell the children that you would like them to design a shelter for a mountain environment. Discuss what this type of environment is like and decide upon a shelter that would be useful. For example, a shelter for hikers on a tourist trail, or a shelter for a school playground in a mountain village.
● Write the purpose of the shelter on a blank flipchart page. Brainstorm the type of materials that would be needed and the properties of these materials.
● On a new page, list the features that would be important for this type of shelter.

Independent work

● Using the ideas that the children have generated from the pictures, discussion and evaluation of the materials, ask them to produce a design for their shelter. Give out copies of the photocopiable sheet.
● Tell the children that they must draw accurately a number of aspects: frontal view, side elevations and rear view, labelling how joints will be secured and including dimensions.
● As the children are working, choose a few designs which demonstrate elements such as accurate drawing, useful annotations, innovative use of materials or inventive ideas. Scan these and save them onto the computer for the Plenary.

Plenary

● Gather the children at the interactive whiteboard and show them the scanned designs, using the Pen tool to highlight points of interest. Encourage supportive feedback from the others and invite pertinent questions on construction and finishes.
● Give the children time to build models of their shelters in subsequent lessons. Take digital pictures of them and insert them into a flipchart for further discussion.

 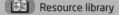

Fantastic footwear

Learning objectives
QCA Unit 6B 'Slippers'
● To understand that products are designed for a particular purpose and are suitable for different users.
● To evaluate products, relating their materials and construction to their intended use.

Resources
'Fantastic footwear' flipchart file; a range of contrasting footwear such as trainers, fins, football boots, ballet shoes, builder's boots and slippers; digital cameras or digital movie makers; photocopiable page 166 'Evaluating footwear'. (Microsoft PowerPoint is required to view the embedded slideshow in the flipchart.)

Links to other subjects
Science
PoS Sc3 (1a) To compare everyday materials on the basis of their material properties.
● Encourage the children to investigate the properties of the materials used. Which group's shoe is more suitable for a particular purpose?
English
NLS Term 1 T6: To produce a modern retelling.
● Recap the story of *Cinderella* and ask the children to write a parody using a different kind of shoe!

Whiteboard tools
View the slideshows in Desktop mode. Upload presentations via the Resource library.

🖥 Desktop mode

🖊 Pen tool

❘ Lines tool

Return to main screen

Resource library

Starter
Tell the children that they will be designing and making an item of footwear of their own, but before they do, they will become experts by looking at a number of items people wear on their feet!

Display page 2 of the flipchart. Ask the children why we wear shoes. Annotate their responses on the board. Guide them to think about the different purposes of shoes.

Whole-class shared work
● Explain to the children that they are going to investigate, describe and evaluate a range of footwear.
● Show each item of footwear and ask the children to identify who might wear each kind.
● Read the shoe-related vocabulary on page 3: *sole; heel; instep; tongue; laces; sock; lining; fabric; stitching.*
● Invite the children to suggest other useful words that could be used to describe shoes. Add these to the word bank.
● Go to page 4. Explain to the children that they will be evaluating a piece of footwear and that you would like them to use their information to create a slideshow presentation.
● Click on the button to launch the 'Fantastic footwear' PowerPoint slideshow template. Talk the children through the template and explain how they can adapt and add to it.

Independent work
● Put the children into mixed-ability groups and give each group a piece of footwear to evaluate. Ask them to consider the following questions:
  ● Who is the footwear intended for?
  ● What materials is it made from?
  ● How are the materials attached?
  ● Why were the materials selected – for decoration, for protection, for waterproofing, for comfort, for grip or for warmth?
  ● How are they fastened?
  ● What is their intended purpose?
● Ask the children to record their observations on photocopiable page 166 'Evaluating footware'. Suggest that they use this information to plan their presentation.
● Provide a digital camera for the children to photograph their piece of footwear. Tell them that they can use these images in their presentation.
● Provide less able learners with more guidance in how to assess their footwear.
● Challenge the more able learners to take pictures of the footwear from different angles to illustrate features such as the sole, lining or any materials used. Encourage them to annotate these in the presentation software.

Plenary
● Return to the flipchart and ask children from each group to present their analysis of footwear.
● Invite questions and comments from the class, encouraging them to ask pertinent questions, using the correct vocabulary.

How do people of different faiths worship?

Starter
Ask the children what they understand by the term *religion*. Invite them to name the religions they have heard of. List these on page 2 of the 'World religions' flipchart. Explain to the children that by the end of the lesson, they should know some key facts about the world's major religions.

Whole-class shared work
● Divide the class into five groups. Explain to the children that each group will be finding out about a major world faith: Christianity; Hinduism; Islam; Judaism; Sikhism. They will then return to the class and teach their peers about their findings.
● Allocate the religions (giving less confident children the faith they are most familiar with, as well as the most easily accessible resources).
● Explain to the children that before they start researching their allocated religion, there will be a short activity to revise what they know already.
● Display page 3 and ask the group that has been allocated Christianity to place the words that relate to Christianity in the circle, using the Marquee select tool. Repeat this with the other groups for the religions on pages 4 to 7.
● Display the questions on page 8 to guide the groups in finding out about the key aspects of a religion.
● Give each group a printout of their completed circle and give each child a copy of photocopiable page 167 'World religions research'. Explain that you would like them to find out more about their allocated religion.
● Discuss where you might you find out the information required. Exercise caution if the internet is used as a research tool. Consult the Culham Institute website (**www.culham.ac.uk**) or REonline (**www.reonline.org.uk**) for suitable online resources.

Independent work
● Monitor the children to ensure that they are focussing on relevant information. Suggest that they scan through the information quickly to locate the necessary information, recording it on their worksheets.

Plenary
● Invite the children to feedback to their peers.
● Reset page 3 and repeat the sorting activity. Activate the Clock tool's Count up option 🔲. One person from the appropriate group must come to the board and drag a word into the circle, before returning to their place. When they have sat down the next person may go. They say *finished* when the last word is placed and they are all seated. Stop the timer and record the group's time on the flipchart page.
● Repeat this for the religions on pages 4 to 7.
● Conclude by identifying points of similarities between the religions. Go to page 9 and drag the religions and common shared aspects into the circle to discuss similarities. For example, Jerusalem is a special place for Christianity, Judaism and Islam because of Jesus' tomb in the Garden of Gethsemane, the Wailing Wall and the Dome of the Rock.

What is a mosque and what is it used for?

Starter
Open the 'Mosques' flipchart on page 2. Tell the children that today they are going to be architectural detectives. Ask if they know what architecture is, but don't confirm what they say at this point. Explain that they will be shown a special place and they have to try to use its features as clues to its purpose. Before the picture is revealed, ask the children to generate some questions that could be asked about the mystery place, for example: *Where is it? What is it like?*
Activate the Spotlight tool ◔ to hide the flipchart, and go to page 3.

Whole-class shared work
● Drag the spotlight over the roofline of the mosque, asking the children to comment.
● Work your way up to the top of the minaret with the spotlight and invite the children to speculate what it might be. Rest the spotlight on the balcony and invite further discussion.
● Continue to reveal features of the mosque and encourage the children to use each piece of evidence to speculate on the type of building and its purpose.
● Finally, turn the spotlight off and reveal the building in its entirety. Discuss what type of building this is and its purpose. (A mosque; a place of worship for Muslims.) There are further images of mosques on pages 4 and 5.
● Guess what the key words could be. Remove the rectangles to reveal the labels. Ask the children to have a go at reading each of the unfamiliar terms and then explain that each of the terms is related to the mosque.
● The children's task is to find out what each one means.

Independent work
● Tell the children that they will be producing a guide to a mosque to help non-Muslims. Explain that the audience is, for example, the Year 5 class. What do the children think that audience would need? (An annotated picture or photograph.)
● Ask the children to use their 'Mosque glossary' sheet (photocopiable page 168) to guide their research. They should use a variety of resources to find the information (exercise caution when using the internet) and write a detailed explanation for each one.

Plenary
● Go to page 6 of the flipchart. Invite volunteers to share their glossary descriptions. Ask the rest of the class to evaluate whether this provides enough information. Choose the best glossary entries to add to the page.
● Invite volunteers to label and annotate the picture of the mosque on page 7.
● Use the stack of blank labels in the corner and invite the children to use the Floating keyboard to type their information in the boxes.
● Evaluate the annotated page and ask how effective this would be at helping someone learn about the mosque. Use voting methods, for example (a) for extremely effective to (f) not effective at all.

Learning objectives
QCA Unit 6F 'How do people express their faith through the arts?'
● To appreciate that art can be very sacred and spiritual for believers.

Resources
Access to the internet; website **www.national gallery.org.uk** saved in favourites in web browser; A4 (or smaller) sugar paper; sketching pencils; paints and brushes of various thicknesses; digital camera; soothing classical music.

Links to other subjects
Art and design
PoS (4c) To learn about the roles and purposes of artists working in different times and cultures.
● Relate this lesson to artists such as Michelangelo, who is famed for painting the ceiling of the Sistine Chapel.
English
NLS Term 1 T17: To write non-chronological reports.
● Ask the children to write commentaries for their tableau, succinctly describing the events they depict.

How do people express their religious beliefs through art?

Starter
Ask the children what kind of subjects artists choose for their work. Discuss their responses. Explain that there are many inspirations for art. One of them is religion, which has inspired people from different faiths to express their beliefs in many ways; sculpture, painting, architecture and stained glass windows among them.

Whole-class shared work
● Open the website for the National Gallery. Tell the children that the National Gallery contains one of the most extensive art collections in the world. The collection is made up of artworks of many kinds and religious art comprises a substantial part of the collection.
● Ask the children to name some events in the life of Jesus that they think an artist may have depicted. List some of these on a blank flipchart page.
● Show the children the search tool at the top of the page and type in *Jesus Christ*, using the Floating keyboard. Thumbnails of the paintings of Jesus will appear. Searching with more specific keywords can narrow results.
● Choose some of the thumbnails to enlarge and discuss their subject. What is the children's emotional response? Ask questions such as: *Does the work give any clues about the beliefs of the artist? How did the artist paint these events when none of them were witnessed? How do you think these paintings were used? How does the artist use colour to influence mood? What do the expressions and gestures of the subjects demonstrate to us?*
● Compare the use of art in Christian worship to Islamic art. Explain that pictures or statues are not acceptable to many Muslims. Instead Islamic art concentrates on shape, pattern and calligraphy; it incorporates natural elements such as flowers and leaves, which are all God's creation.

Independent work
● Explain to the children that they are going to work in groups to create tableaux based on iconographic paintings of a scene from the life of Jesus Christ.
● Choose a subject for the paintings related to the church calendar. Allow children time to read about the event in a Children's Bible.
● Ask the children to recreate this tableau in front of the rest of the class. When you tap them on the shoulder, their character must come to life and explain their viewpoint of the scene.

Plenary
● Play some soothing classical music. Invite the groups, one at a time, to create their tableau at the front of the class. Give each character a turn to comment on the scene which they are depicting.
● Take photographs of the work, importing each tableau into a separate flipchart page. (Remember to obtain parental permission before photographing children.) The children can then annotate the photographed tableau in a subsequent session to reflect on the scene that they portrayed.
● Invite the children to comment on the work and the success of the tableau artists in evoking a response from the viewer.

Whiteboard tools
View websites through the Activprimary Web browser if available.

 Pen tool

 Floating keyboard

Evaluating and refining gymnastic actions

Learning objectives
QCA Unit 28 'Gymnastic activities (6)'
● To combine and perform gymnastic actions, shapes and balances.
● To evaluate their own work and suggest ways of making improvements.

Resources
Gymnastic apparatus; digital cameras.

Links to other subjects
ICT
QCA Unit 6A 'Multimedia presentation'
● Use a multimedia authoring program to organise, refine and present information in different forms for a specific audience.
English
NLS Term 1 T17: To write non-chronological reports.
● Ask the children to write and prepare a gymnastics manual for a multimedia presentation for the Year 5 children, including photos and captions. Suggest that they also use a digital camera to record different apparatus layouts and how they can be used.

Whiteboard tools
Insert photographs into a blank flipchart via the Resource library. Use the Shapes tool and the Floating keyboard to create labels to annotate the photographs.

Shapes tool

Floating keyboard

Text editor tool

Resource library

Marquee select tool

Starter
Explain to the children that they will be working with a partner to devise, practise and perform a gymnastic routine involving a variety of actions, balances and methods of movement. In this lesson they will be practising and recalling their learning in gymnastics from their time in Key Stage 2 in preparation for the gymnastic routine.

Remind the children that it is important to begin the lesson with a warm-up activity. Talk about how breathing rate increases because muscles need more oxygen to work effectively. Go on to explain that heart rate also increases to move the required oxygen from lungs to muscle groups.

Whole-class shared work
● Ask the children to crouch, still and silent. Then slowly, without wobbles, *grow* very gradually, extending their body, limbs and head to their full height. Count down from five as the children hold the stretch.
● Increase heart rate by jogging on the spot, increasing and decreasing pace at your command. Insist on quiet, controlled footsteps to develop increased body awareness.
● Ask the children to practise the basic jumps, travelling around the hall in a clockwise direction, maintaining adequate space. Vary the jumps from one foot to two feet, two feet to two feet, left foot to left foot and so on.
● Emphasise the effect of bending knees to give more spring on take off, and also the importance of *giving* on landing, both for safety and professionalism!
● Ask a small number of photographers to capture good examples on the digital camera. (Remember to obtain parental permission before photographing children.)

Independent work
● Ask the children, in groups, to set up apparatus in a way that will encourage them to experiment.
● Invite the children to practise finding as many ways of traversing the apparatus as possible: sliding (on various body parts), hopping, rolling, on hands, on knees and so on. Ask photographers to take photos of as many interesting examples as possible.
● Invite the children to experiment with balances, making sure that they hold the balance for three to five seconds. Challenge them to find as many positions to balance in as possible (both with and without a partner). Photographers should look out for interesting body shapes.
● Now experiment with jumping for height, to cover distance, and low level. Make sure the children land correctly.
● Ask photographers to look for controlled take-offs and landings and capture them.
● Return the apparatus and cool down.

Plenary
● Transfer the pictures to the computer. Upload good examples of moving, balancing and jumping, with headings, onto separate flipchart pages.
● Arrange the photographs on each page and label them. Create labels by inserting a rectangle using the Shapes tool and typing a short caption.
● Give the children specific feedback on their ideas, compositions and how to improve the quality of their movement. Invite constructive criticism from the class.

Peer-group coaching in games

Learning objectives
QCA Unit 24 'Invasion games (4)' QCA Unit 25 'Striking and fielding games (2)' QCA Unit 26 'Net/wall games (2)'
● To evaluate strengths and weaknesses in performances and to suggest areas for improvement.

Resources
Games equipment; a large space (such as the school field) to accommodate small groups working independently; examples of sports-coaching books written for children; digital cameras; multimedia presentation package, such as Microsoft PowerPoint.

Links to other subjects
ICT
QCA Unit 6A 'Multimedia presentation'
● To use a multimedia authoring program to organise, refine and present information in different forms for a specific audience.
Speaking and listening
Objective 60: To understand and use a variety of ways to criticise constructively and respond to criticism.
● Encourage the children to listen carefully to each other's presentations, and to offer constructive feedback.
PSHE
PoS (3a) To understand the benefits of exercise; (5b) To feel positive about themselves.
● Help the children to respond positively to the feedback to their presentation. Encourage them in their contributions to improve their own and others' performances.

Whiteboard tools

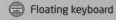 Floating keyboard

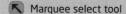 Marquee select tool

 Pen tool

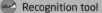 Recognition tool

Starter
This lesson may take place over a number of sessions, depending on the amount of time allowed for investigation and the complexity of the multimedia presentation required.

Ask the children to reflect on the games they have played in Key Stage 2. Discuss their favourites, encouraging them to express opinions clearly.

Open a new flipchart page. Ask individuals to write on the board, using the Floating keyboard or the Recognition tool ●, the name of their favourite game (for instance, tennis).

Next, ask the children to sort all of their games into one of the following categories: *invasion, net/wall, striking* and *fielding*.

Whole-class shared work
● Explain to the children that they will produce a multimedia presentation on a sport of their choice. Their task will be to evaluate their performance in this context and then identify a small number of common weaknesses which may be responsible for affecting the success of the game. Finally, they will share the completed coaching session with a real audience.
● Analyse the games that the children have identified on the whiteboard asking whether there is an even spread across the different categories, or if some types of games preferred more than others. Discuss the children's reasons for choosing a particular sport.
● Focus on each category in turn. Encourage the children to talk about common weaknesses and areas in which performances can be improved.
● Divide the children into mixed-ability groups, according to the game that they would like to work on.
● Allow the children to play their chosen game and focus their attention on aspects of their performance that could benefit from development (stamina, accuracy in passing, breaking into adequate space, dodging opponents and so on).

Independent work
● Challenge each group to devise an exercise, strategy or tip that will improve performance in the area that they have chosen to work on.
● When they are satisfied that their coaching tips are effective, ask the children to take carefully framed digital pictures which will illustrate their presentation. Demonstrate how to use zoom and the viewfinder to take satisfying pictures. (Remember to obtain parental permission before photographing children.)
● If a digital video camera is available, encourage the children to film short videos, with adult support, to demonstrate good techniques.
● Using the interactive whiteboard, show the children how to plan, prepare and create a page in a multimedia presentation package. Model how to insert, resize and annotate photographs on the interactive whiteboard.

Plenary
● Allow time for the children to practise their presentation techniques, including the roles of the children within the group, speaking audibly and addressing the audience.
● Encourage peers to offer constructive criticism in order to improve their presentation.
● When their performances are polished, invite Year 5 children or parents to come in and watch the presentations.

What's in the news?

Learning objectives
QCA Unit 11 'In the media –
what's the news?'
● To research, discuss and
debate topical issues,
problems and events.
● To evaluate how the media
present information.

Resources
'Newspaper reporting'
flipchart file; BBC Newsround
website **http://
news.bbc.co.uk/cbbcnews**
photocopiable page 169
'Newspaper reporting'; a
collection of appropriate
newspapers (broadsheet and
tabloid) with coverage of the
same event or subject.

Links to other subjects
English
NLS Term 1 T15: To develop a
journalistic style;
T16: To use the styles and
conventions of journalism to
report on, for example, real or
imagined events.
● Challenge the children to
write a newspaper article on a
topical local subject, making
sure they produce a balanced
report. Alternatively, ask more
able writers to identify a
biased perspective to write
from and ask others if they
can recognise the point of
view that has influenced it.

Starter
Display page 2 of the flipchart. Ask the children to consider how we find out about events in our school or locality. Make a note of the different ways on the whiteboard. Talk together about an event at school: a fictitious fight perhaps. Explain that when the children retell the story, it may be told with some bias depending on the point of view of the person describing it and the audience.

Now ask about events on a wider scale, nationally and internationally. Ask: *How do we find out about events far away?* Scribe the children's answers (such as news reports from newspapers, magazines, TV news and the internet). Encourage the children to consider whether these are ever biased.

Whole-class shared work
● Explain that today the children will be analysing newspaper articles to find out how they share information with the reader and whether there is any bias involved.
● Go to page 3 and discuss the elements of a newspaper report: *Who? When? What? Why? Where?*
● Next, open the Newsround site (you could save this in Favourites for ease). Explain the audience and purpose of this site.
● Search for an article that may be of interest to the children and read it together, discussing any points that arise.
● Ask the children to identify a sentence in the text that says succinctly what happened.
● Return to the flipchart and make a note of what happened in the *What?* circle.
● Repeat for *Who? When? Why?* and *Where?* asking the children to scan through the text to locate the specific information needed.

Independent work
● Organise the children the children into groups and provide each group with a newspaper. Ask them to search for information regarding an event, person or story you have identified. Invite them to record their findings on photocopiable page 169 'Newspaper reporting'.
● Ask the children to look for clues as to the audience for the different newspapers, and any bias that may exist.
● Support less able learners in understanding the difference between fact and opinion in the way that the stories are presented.
● Extend more able learners by asking them to compare how the same news story is presented in two different newspapers or news sources. Suggest that they complete the photocopiable sheet in different colours for each news source.

Plenary
● Invite the children to feed back their findings. Compare and contrast the way in which the articles have been written. Are there any differences in the information given; the style of the text; the language used; the amount of detail.
● Ask the children to identify some facts and opinions given. Write their responses on page 4.
● If possible, show the children a news programme from the day in question. Are there any differences in the details of the report?

Whiteboard tools
Either use Activprimary's Web
browser or the computer's
browser to look at the
website. Use the Highlighter
tool to identify key facts and
opinions in online news
articles.

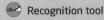 Recognition tool

 Pen tool

Floating keyboard

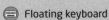 Highlighter tool

Moving on

Learning objective
QCA Unit 12 'Moving on'
● To understand that transition and change are a natural part of everyone's life.

Resources
Photographs of the class starting school, scanned and saved to the computer; individual whiteboards and pens; large sheets of paper.

Links to other subjects
Speaking and listening
Objective 64: To improvise using a range of drama strategies and conventions to explore themes such as hopes, fears, desires.
● Challenge talented actors to develop some of the freeze frames into a short play about a first day at high school which can be performed for the class.

Starter

Start the session by looking at large photos, on the whiteboard, of the class when they were in Reception. Ask the children to recall how they felt on those first few days. Talk to them about transition, explaining what the word means.

Explain that this lesson will be about sharing feelings on their forthcoming move to high school. Establish that although this is a very exciting time, it can also make us feel understandably nervous. Ask the children to work in pairs to list, on their individual whiteboards, times in their lives when they have experienced transition. Invite them to share these with the group. Be sensitive to individual circumstances, as some of these transitions may have been traumatic.

Whole-class shared work

● Explain that we all have fears about transitions because we don't know what to expect.
● Organise the children into mixed-ability groups. Give each group a large sheet of paper and ask them to write down their fears and worries about high school. These may include worries that they perceive others may feel.
● Share the children's ideas and ask them to explain any that are unclear. List common concerns on one half of a blank flipchart page.
● Balance the list of fears by asking the children to make a list of the things that they are looking forward to. List these positive thoughts on the other half of the page.

Independent work

● Invite each group to consider one of their identified concerns in turn. Their role is to compose a scene that depicts their worry through facial expression, body shape and gesture.
● Give the children time to practise and perfect their poses. Appoint a child from each group to photograph the scene. (Remember to obtain parental permission before photographing children.)
● Transfer these images into the flipchart and put each one on a different page.
● Show the children how to insert a speech bubble onto each scene from the Resource library 📖. (Select Literacy, Stories, Props for stories, then Speech bubbles.) Drag the speech bubbles onto the appropriate place on the page, resizing as necessary.
● Together, discuss what the freeze frames demonstrate about the characters within. Work together to think of imaginative and purposeful dialogue to type into the speech bubbles to further develop the situation.
● In a circle-time session, look at the freeze frames in turn, discuss the implications of their messages and talk about strategies to allay their fears.

Plenary

● Introduce a worry box to the class, into which children can post their concerns about the pending move. These can be done anonymously if the children feel self-conscious.
● Make time in the late summer term every week to air the children's concerns and hopefully assuage any fears they may have.
● Regularly update the flipchart page containing the fears and positive thoughts to monitor whether fears are being allayed. In some cases, the fears may become overwritten by positive thoughts, which can then be transferred to the other side of the page.

Whiteboard tools
Upload images via the Resource library (choose Categories in the Resource library tool tray, then Other location and Browse to another location). Drag photographs and speech bubbles from the Resource library. Use the Floating keyboard to add text to the speech bubbles.

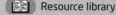 Resource library

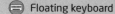 Floating keyboard

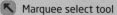 Marquee select tool

Drake's voyage

◾ Here is some information about Drake's circumnavigation of the world.
Cut out the strips and place them in chronological order.
Use this information to complete a timeline of Drake's voyage.

Date	Location	Notes
18 June 1580	Cape of Good Hope	Drake and his men didn't land.
27 Jan 1578 – 10 Feb 1578	Cape Verde Islands	One of the islands is volcanic.
13 Oct 1579	Caroline Islands	The *Golden Hind* is met by men in canoes.
9 Jan 1580	Celebes	The *Golden Hind* ran onto a rock. Cargo was jettisoned.
5 April 1578	Coast of Brazil	They hadn't seen land for 54 days.
29 Nov 1578	La Mocha	The people living here brought potatoes to Drake's crew.
13 Feb 1579	Lima	Drake took silks and linen cloth from a Spanish vessel in Lima.
14 Nov 1579	Moluccas	Spice islands where Drake and his crew took many spices on board ship.
8 Feb 1580	Moluccas	Drake set sail for Java then England.
June 1579	Nova Albion	Drake put up a monument.
15 Nov 1577	Plymouth	*Pelican* and four other ships sailed from Plymouth. There were 164 men on board the ships.
3 Nov 1580	Plymouth	Before landing Drake found out whether the queen was still alive.
20 June 1578	Port St Julian	They found a gallows used by Magellan.
27 April 1578	River Plate	There was deep fresh water.
22 July 1580	Sierra Leone	They took on provisions.
7 Sept 1578	Southern Ocean	A great storm blew the ship 600 miles south.
8 Oct 1578	Strait of Magellan	Captain Winter sailed the *Elizabeth* back to England.
August 1578	Strait of Magellan	Drake changed *Pelican's* name to the *Golden Hind*.
5 June 1579	West coast of America	Perhaps Drake was looking for the North West Passage?

An archaeologist's report

Written by _____ and _____ on _____

Write a report about your artefact. You should include information about its size, the material it is made from (if you know), how it is decorated, and what you think it might have been used for. Finally you should write one or two sentences to explain what this artefact tells you about the people who lived close to the Indus Valley when it was made.

My artefact is ...

Make a careful, detailed drawing of your artefact here.

This artefact tells me that...

Writing Greek

■ Use the Greek prefixes and suffixes to make English words. You may have to change some of the Greek roots to make the English spelling correct.

Greek root	Meaning of the Greek prefix and suffix		English word
astro (star)	distant writing		
bios (life)			
dia (across)	many corners		
geo (earth)			
gon (corner)	distant sound		
graphy (writing)			
hydro (water)	science of the stars		
ology (science)			
meter (measure)	measure across		
phono (sound)			
poly (many)	distant watching		
scope (watch)			
tele (distant)	science of water		
	science of life		

Make a map

◀ Draw your map using map symbols. Add to the Key each new symbol you use.

◀ When you add a new feature, think carefully where to put it.
Are there things it should be near? Are there things it should not go near?

◀ What features are essential to the type of area you are drawing?

Title

Key

Symbol	Meaning	Symbol	Meaning

What time is it?

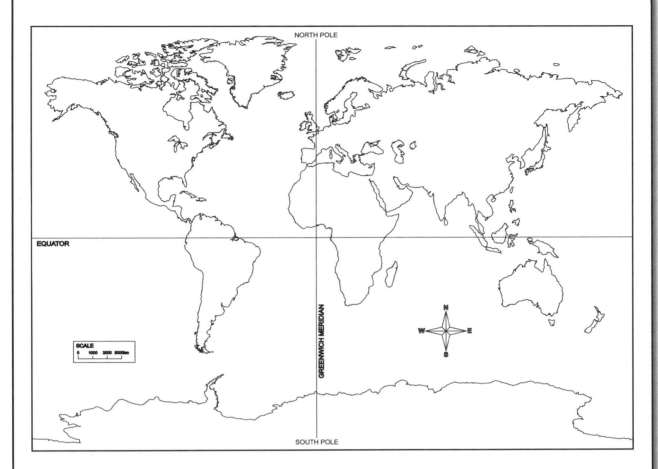

Key

Letter	Place	Time

Designing hats

Who is your character?	What characteristics could your hat show about your character?
Which book is your character from?	
Who is the author of your chosen book?	

Design your hat below, adding labels to any decorations you add.

◣SCHOLASTIC
www.scholastic.co.uk

Design a shelter

Shelter design

Materials required

Tools required

Design the front elevation here

Rear elevation

Side elevations

Evaluating footwear

◢ Use this writing frame to help you to prepare your presentation:

Who is the footwear intended for? _____

_____

What is the intended purpose of the footwear? _____

_____

What materials are the shoes made from? _____

_____

How are the materials attached to the shoes? _____

_____

How are the shoes fastened? _____

_____

Why were the materials selected? _____

_____

Decoration ☐

Protection ☐

Waterproof ☐

Comfort ☐

Grip ☐

Warmth ☐

Other

◗ S C H O L A S T I C
w w w . s c h o l a s t i c . c o . u k

World religions research

What is the religion called? What are the followers called?	Are there any special stories told by followers?
Does this religion have a symbol?	Do followers gather in a special building?
Which figures are important to followers of this religion?	Who are the religion's leaders?
Does the religion have special scriptures (special books)?	Does this religion have any special places?
Do followers wear special clothes or take part in rituals?	Are there any special objects or artefacts used by followers of this religion?

Mosque glossary

Introduction

Mosque Keyword	Definition
Minaret	
Muezzin	
Imam	
Mihrab	
Minbar	
Mecca	

Interesting facts

Newspaper reporting

Read your newspaper article then scan through it to find out each of the things below. Make notes in the circles.

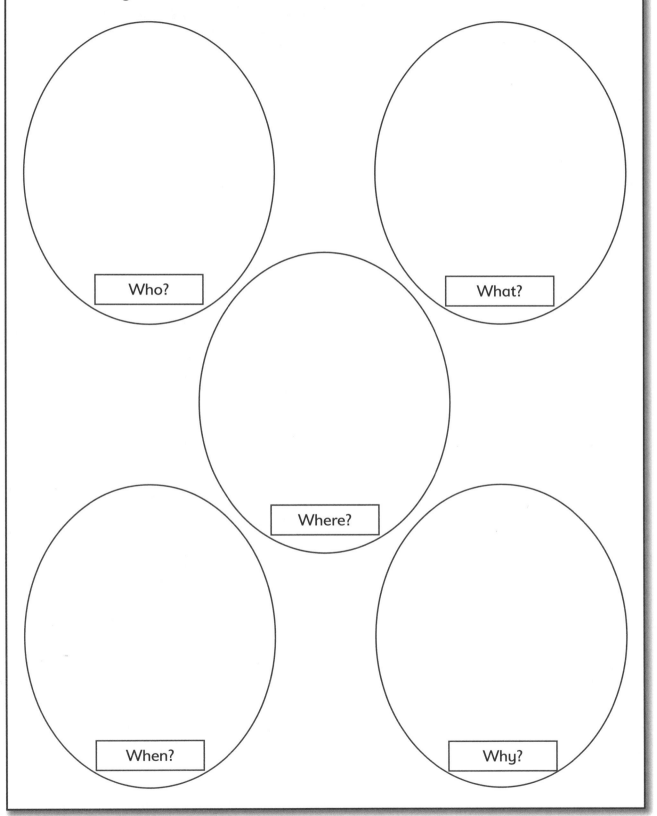

Who?

What?

Where?

When?

Why?

Whiteboard diary

Teacher's name: _____

Date	Subject/ Objective	How was the whiteboard used?	Evaluation

100 Activprimary™ WHITEBOARD LESSONS • YEAR 6

SCHOLASTIC
www.scholastic.co.uk

Whiteboard resources library

Teacher's name: _____

Name of resource and file location	Description of resource	How resource was used	Date resource was used

Using Activprimary

This brief guide to Activprimary offers a few tips on using the application. It is based on the training manual *An introduction to Activprimary (Version 2 for Windows)*. The PDF of the manual is distributed as part of the Activprimary software package, but it is also available online and on the CD-ROM that accompanies this book (under the Help section). To learn more about how to use Activprimary, try the online tutorials at **www.prometheanworld.com/uk/html/training/tutorials.shtml** (the hyperlink is provided on the CD-ROM in the Web links section).

Flipchart mode and Desktop mode

Desktop mode

Return to main screen

When Activprimary is launched, it automatically takes you away from your desktop screen to Flipchart mode. A flipchart will be open and ready for use. Click on the **Desktop mode** button to access your desktop and any other applications, without closing Activprimary. The Desktop toolbox means that you can still use a selection of Activprimary tools with other applications. To get back to Flipchart mode, click on the **Return to main screen** button in the Desktop toolbox.

Design mode and Presentation mode

Design mode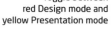
Toggle between
red Design mode and
yellow Presentation mode

Teacher tools menu

Switch between Design mode and Presentation mode by clicking on **Teacher tools menu** and then **Design mode**. When you are in Design mode, the Teacher tools icon border is red; it is yellow in Presentation mode.
Use Presentation mode when giving classes. Design mode allows access to all the design features of Activprimary to create or change a flipchart. Some features are only available in Design mode, including:

- The Properties button is available in the Object edit toolbox. The options available will depend on the object selected.
- Right-clicking (or barrel-clicking) shows a menu for any selected object or background.
- New folders can be created in the Resource library.
- Page organiser button is available via the Page number button.

Navigating your flipchart

Next and Previous page buttons

Page organiser

Use the **Next page** and **Previous page** buttons to move through the pages in the flipchart file. If you are on the last page of the flipchart, clicking the Next page button will add a new page. You can view the pages in the flipchart by clicking the Page number button. The Tool tray will display thumbnails of the pages; access a desired page by clicking on its thumbnail. In Design mode, you can move or copy objects from one page to another by dragging it to the thumbnail in the Tool tray. The **Page organiser** button will appear in the Tool tray; this allows you to move, copy and delete pages.

Selecting and manipulating objects

Marquee select tool

Use the **Marquee select tool** to move objects on the screen and to drag resources from the Tool tray (such as shapes, lines, backgrounds, grids or images). Click on an object to select it. Select multiple objects by clicking on

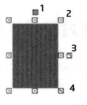

3. Rotation

the background and dragging a selection box around the objects. The selected object(s) will be surrounded by a number of squares called Pick-up boxes (see the numbered diagam on the left).
Click and drag these boxes:
1. to move the object around the page
2. to resize the object
3. to rotate the object
4. to change the size of a shape without changing its proportions.

Adding text to a flipchart page

Text editor tool

Floating keyboard

Pen tool

Recognition tool

Handwriting tool

Text editor tool: Use this to enter a block of editable text. Click on the page, where you would like to insert the text. You can then input text using your computer's keyboard or use the **Floating keyboard** in the Text tool tray.
Pen tool: This allows you to add free-hand writing to the screen, in the same way that you would use a conventional whiteboard.
Recognition tool (in Special tools): This tool recognises free-hand writing and converts it to editable text. A **Floating keyboard** is also available in the Recognition tool tray. The **Handwriting tool** in the Desktop toolbox also allows you to convert free-hand writing to text in a word-processing document or in a spreadsheet.

Use the Dice tool as a random number generator

Dice tool

The **Dice tool** (in the Special tools menu) is a useful and fun way to generate random numbers. You can select and roll up to five dice; click on the equal-sign button to add the sum of the dice roll to the flipchart page. However, you can also use the dice to test the children's understanding of place value, for example, by using three dice to create a three-digit number. So *643* would be written as shown left.

would be written as *643*.

Using the Camera tool

Camera tool

The **Camera tool** is useful for taking snapshots of annotated screens. Use it, for example, to take a snapshot of a completed sequence from one of the activities on the CD-ROM, which can then be saved to a flipchart page and annotated. You can also take screenshots of annotated documents to show, for instance, highlighted headings and sub-headings. It is advisable to exercise caution if taking screenshots of published material or anything on the internet and to check for copyright permission first.

Using the Eraser tool

Eraser tool

Activprimary's **Eraser tool** does not technically remove images from the page; it creates a colourless object over the top, which displays anything on the middle or bottom layer of the flipchart. This eraser object can be moved around to cover other elements on the flipchart page. It can be moved and manipulated like any other object. The spyglass, which is provided in some of the flipcharts on the CD-ROM, incorporates an eraser object that allows the user to see through objects to *hidden* answers.

173

The Activprimary toolboxes

The information is taken from the training manual *An introduction to Activprimary (Version 2 for Windows)*. The PDF of the manual is distributed as part of the Activprimary software package, but it is also available online and on the CD-ROM that accompanies this book (under the Help section). Try the online tutorials at **www.prometheanworld.com/uk/html/training/ tutorials.shtml** (the hyperlink is provided on the CD-ROM in the Web links section).

The Main screen and toolbox

Across the bottom of the screen is the Tool tray. When certain tools are selected, additional options for them will appear in here. You can reposition the Tool tray and the Main toolbox through settings (Teacher tools menu button>Menu>Settings> Toolboxes).

In the corner of the flipchart page, you will see the Flipchart Bin. Use the Marquee select tool to drag objects into the Bin to delete them.

At the side of the screen is the Main toolbox. It is divided into two main areas: the Teacher Area (the upper section) and the Pupil Area (the lower section). The Teacher Area contains administrative tools aimed solely at the teacher.

Teacher tools menu

New flipchart

Open a flipchart

Save a flipchart

Print

Page reset

Page notes

Web browser (AP2.5 only)

Notes and pointer (AP2.5 only)

Tickertape (AP2.5 only)

Design mode Switch between Design mode and Presentation mode.

Menu Customise preferences for Activprimary.

Exit

Activities explorer Access pre-made activities, including the NNS Interactive Teaching Programs.

Sound controller/recorder

Special tools (See page 175 for details.)

Clear tool With this tool you have three options: Clear Screen, Clear Objects and Clear Annotations.

Desktop mode Access your desktop without closing the program.

Activote Take an interactive vote (with voting devices only).

Page number button. Click on the Page number button to open the Page Organiser in the Tool Tray.

Next/Previous page buttons If you are on the last page, clicking the Next page button will add a new page to the end of the flipchart.

Marquee select tool

Pen tool Select this to access the Highlighter and Eraser tools.

Lines tool

Shapes tool

Text editor tool

Fill/Colour picker tool Select a colour using the Colour picker tool and add it to the Colour palette.

Grids

Backgrounds

Resource library

Undo/Redo buttons

The Resource library

The Resource library is a series of folders whose contents can include images, word banks and sounds. You can also create your own folders and store your own flipchart items in the Resource library.

Rubber stamp tool Place multiple copies of an image.

Previous / More images

Categories Access the Resource library directory and browse the categories.

Shared collections

Personal collections

Other location Access other resources on your computer using the Browse to Another Location button .

Create new folder Create a new directory to store your own resources in. (This option is only available in Design mode.)

ACTIVPRIMARY

The Special tools toolbox

These options will appear in the Tool tray when the Special tools button is clicked.

Spotlight tool Cover the screen apart from a re-scalable area that follows the cursor, revealing parts of the flipchart beneath. There are options for rectangular or circular spotlights.

Reveal tool Cover up the desktop and then reveal the flipchart from the top, bottom, left or right.

Dice tool Roll up to five dice and add the totalled number to the flipchart.

Protractor tool

Ruler tool

Compass tool (AP2.5 only)

Fraction creator toolbox Handwrite a fraction and add it to the page as text.

Recognition tool Convert handwriting to editable text.

Floating calculator Add the entire calculations to the flipchart as editable text. The Floating calculator remains on-screen in Desktop mode.

Camera tool Capture part of the flipchart as a picture.

Screen recorder (AP2.5 only) Record actions performed on screen as a video file.

XY Origin Place a rotation point on the page and rotate objects around this point.

Clock tool You can also set a timer to perform an action after a specified amount of time.

The Object edit toolbox

When you double-click on any object the Object edit toolbox will open. This toolbox contains appropriate tools for editing the selected object.

Increase object size Increase the size of a selected object in 10% increments.

Decrease object size Decrease the size of a selected object.

Delete Click this button to remove the selected object.

Duplicate Make an identical copy of the selected object.

Edit text Enables you to change the text on your flipchart. Available options appear in the Tool tray.

Properties This is only available in Design mode and lets you change an object's attributes.

- **Identification** Set the name of the object or group a collection of objects.
- **Position** Manually alter the object's position on the screen, or lock it in position.
- **Appearance** Change aspects of an object appearance, such as its layer, translucency, outline and fill colour.
- **Container** Allows an object to carry with it a smaller object placed on top.
- **Actions** Set an action that an object will perform when clicked in Presentation mode.

The Desktop toolbox

The Desktop toolbox appears when you click on the Desktop mode button. The tools work in the same way as they do with an Activprimary flipchart.

Return to main screen Return to the main flipchart.

Marquee select tool Operate your desktop as you would if Activprimary wasn't running.

Pen tool

Highlighter tool

Clear Screen

Spotlight tool

Reveal tool

Undo button

Redo button

Activote

Colour palette **Line thickness**

Handwriting tool Convert free-hand writing to text.

Camera selector

Camera tool

Floating keyboard (AP2.5 only)